81 DAYS BELOW ZERO

81 DAYS BELOW ZERO

THE INCREDIBLE SURVIVAL STORY OF A WORLD WAR II PILOT IN ALASKA'S FROZEN WILDERNESS

BRIAN MURPHY

WITH TOULA VLAHOU

Da Capo Press
A Member of the Perseus Books Group

Designed by Jack Lenzo

Set in 11 point Fairfield by The Perseus Books Group

Cataloging-in-Publication data for this book is available from the Library of Congress.

First Da Capo Press edition 2015
First Da Capo Press paperback edition 2016

ISBN: 978-0-306-82328-2 (hardcover)
ISBN: 978-0-306-82452-4 (paperback)
ISBN: 978-0-306-82329-9 (e-book)

Published by Da Capo Press
A Member of the Perseus Books Group
www.dacapopress.com

Da Capo Press books are available at special discounts for bulk purchases in the U.S. by corporations, institutions, and other organizations. For more information, please contact the Special Markets Department at the Perseus Books Group, 2300 Chestnut Street, Suite 200, Philadelphia, PA 19103, or call (800) 810-4145, ext. 5000, or e-mail special.markets@perseusbooks.com.

LSC-C

10 9 8 7 6 5

To my daughter Zoe,
who will always be my Princess Zozo

CONTENTS

Preface .... *ix*

INTRODUCTION–Mount Athos, Greece 1
CHAPTER ONE–December 21, 1943 5
CHAPTER TWO–December 22, 1943 27
CHAPTER THREE–December 23, 1943 37
CHAPTER FOUR–June 23, 1994 53
CHAPTER FIVE–December 25, 1943 61
CHAPTER SIX–December 29, 1943 73
CHAPTER SEVEN–December 29, 1943 87
CHAPTER EIGHT–December 30, 1943 97
CHAPTER NINE–August 31, 2006 109
CHAPTER TEN–January 10, 1944 115
CHAPTER ELEVEN–January 19, 1944 129
CHAPTER TWELVE–February 10, 1944 139
CHAPTER THIRTEEN–September 15, 2006 153
CHAPTER FOURTEEN–March 3, 1944 165
CHAPTER FIFTEEN–March 9, 1944 171
CHAPTER SIXTEEN–March 10, 1944 177
CHAPTER SEVENTEEN–March 13, 1944 185
CHAPTER EIGHTEEN–March 14, 1944 193
CHAPTER NINETEEN–March 7, 2007 199
CHAPTER TWENTY–September 7, 2007 207
Epilogue 213

Acknowledgments 219
Selected Bibliography and Sources 221
Index 227
Photos following page 114.

PREFACE

These are true stories. This book chronicles, to the best of my abilities and available resources, the solo trek of First Lieutenant Leon Crane through the Alaskan wilderness in the winter of 1943–1944. It also recounts the efforts, decades later, to recover the remains of the pilot who sat beside Crane in the cockpit of their B-24D bomber, Second Lieutenant Harold E. Hoskin.

Obviously, there are gaps in retelling a solitary ordeal when the central figure is no longer with us. Crane died before I began this project. Among the challenges: seeking to convey Crane's emotions and inner dialogue. Such passages are based, as much as possible, on extrapolations from his own words as well as insights into his personality from his family and acquaintances. I have endeavored to remain as true to Crane's character as within my powers.

All names and places in the book are real. Some of the military facilities mentioned have been renamed since the period covered by the book. Ladd Field is now Fort Wainwright, and Hickam Air Force Base became part of Joint Base Pearl Harbor–Hickam. Also, for consistency, I referred to the Army's military aviation command during World War II as the U.S. Army Air Forces, its official designation after 1942. It was previously known as the U.S. Army Air Corps. The Air Corps remained active as a part of the Air Forces throughout the war, and many airmen used the two names interchangeably. The Army Air Forces was the forerunner for the U.S. Air Force.

In a few instances, I made decisions on the spellings of names from Native Alaskan languages and the Cyrillic script. I used the form I believe best represents the name. In references to the indigenous tribes, I use the term *Athabascan*. This reflects the general culture that binds various Native clans and dialects across interior Alaska.

On very rare occasions, the sequence of events was slightly reordered for narrative flow. In no case does it alter the scope of the story.

It's also important to call attention to some place-names to avoid confusion. There are sites that share similar or identical names to places in the book, notably the Charley River, Coal Creek, and Woodchopper. Alaska's Kandik River was once called Charley (or Charlie) Creek. It flows into the Yukon River, but not in the area walked by Crane. There is a Coal Creek in the Canadian Yukon. It, too, has no connection to this story. An abandoned mining camp called Woodchopper is located northwest of Fairbanks, far from the crash site.

All temperatures are expressed in Fahrenheit.

I close with a personal note. I am neither a military historian nor an expert on the Alaskan wilderness. In fact, I had never stepped foot in Alaska before beginning this project. Many caretakers of military history and Alaskan lore often consider laymen or generalists, such as me, clumsy intruders. In reply, I can only say that I did my best to tell this one story. I leave it to others to further analyze the fascinating role of Alaska during World War II or bring deeper personal insights into survival in the Far North.

See how my feet are moving—awfully funny they look—
Moving as if they belonged to a someone that wasn't me.
The wind down the night's long alley bowls me down like a pin;
I stagger and fall and stagger, crawl arm-deep in the snow.
Beaten back to my corner, how can I hope to win?
And there is the blizzard waiting to give me the knockout blow.

—"*Lost,*" by Robert W. Service (1874–1958)

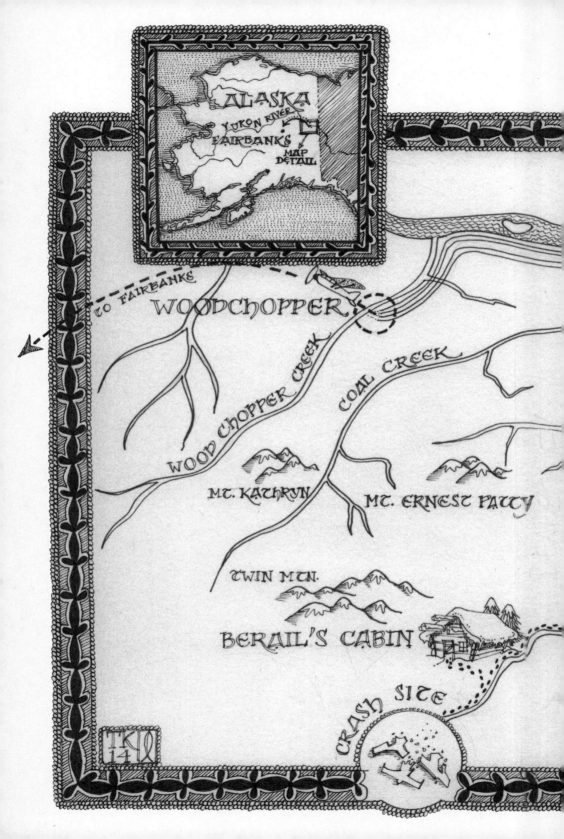

ALASKA

YUKON RIVER

FAIRBANKS

MAP DETAIL

TO FAIRBANKS

WOODCHOPPER

WOOD CHOPPER CREEK

COAL CREEK

MT. KATHRYN

MT. ERNEST PATTY

TWIN MTN.

BERAIL'S CABIN

CRASH SITE

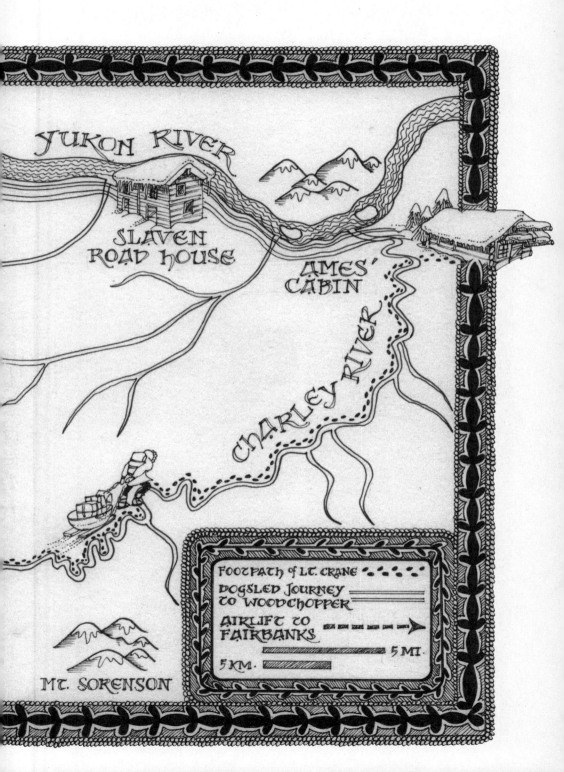

YUKON RIVER

SLAVEN ROAD HOUSE

AMES' CABIN

CHARLEY RIVER

MT. SORENSON

FOOTPATH of LT. CRANE ••••••••

DOGSLED JOURNEY TO WOODCHOPPER ————

AIRLIFT TO FAIRBANKS ◄━ ━ ━ ━ ━►

5 MI.

5 KM.

INTRODUCTION

Mount Athos, Greece

I chose a path that twisted toward the sea.

Early spring wildflowers—delicate crimson poppies and sturdy yellow crocuses—flapped like small flags in the squalls off the northern Aegean. The air carried a salty sharpness from cold rains that washed over the land in waves. I pressed on. Alone, downhill, around one hairpin turn after another. I walked until the path was overtaken by green brambles. The thorns soon gave way to rocks. Then they dropped off into a wind-sculpted sea.

Here, on this outcrop in Greece, I thought about solitude.

No, let's be more precise. I wasn't imagining the pleasant isolation of a solo hike or some other private sojourn, such as my visit to the centuries-old monasteries of Greece's Mount Athos peninsula and this walk on a raw March afternoon to the edge of nowhere. Instead, I wondered about detachment in a crueler, more primitive form. A kind that's vanishing—and increasingly difficult to even imagine—in a world crowded and connected.

In these rare castaway places, the separation is absolute. There is no way to reach out and declare four powerful words.

I am still here.

The only way is to somehow claw back to a world that now refers to you in the past tense. Call it an earthly purgatory. Only a few have experienced it. Fewer still have faced it alone.

This, perhaps above all things, is what pulled me so strongly to the story of a lost World War II pilot and his improbable passage through the Alaskan wilderness after bailing from a crippled plane.

1

First Lieutenant Leon Crane, in a palpable sense, returned from the dead.

Search parties had given up. A military letter addressed to Crane's father, written seven weeks after his son's plane went down, promised "additional information" if it became available. But the letter really amounted to an advisory to abandon hope. It included an attempt to connect Crane's family to a wider grief by listing the next of kin of the other four airmen on their missing B-24D bomber. The Arctic survival manual they were issued had already provided obituary material for those lost without supplies or weapons for any length of time. "Freezing to death may come after prolonged exposure," it read, "coupled with lack of food, extreme fatigue or exhaustion."

I often imagined myself in such a shadow walkabout: alive, but dead to everyone else. I think of my wife and daughter accepting condolences. Word spreading among friends. My family arranging a headstone for an unoccupied grave. And I am powerless to call it off.

Tens of thousands of servicemen on all sides were declared missing in action (MIA) in World War II, and their families, too, undoubtedly felt this same unclosed sorrow. The Pentagon says more than seventy-three thousand U.S. military personnel are still listed as unaccounted for from World War II and about ten thousand more from later conflicts. Just a tiny fraction—a number so small there isn't even a subcategory in the military's granular record keeping—turned up safely on their own like Crane.

As a journalist for more than three decades, my tally of assignments, big and small, has covered six continents. There is, of course, the fair share of sitting through tiresome conferences or scribbling down predictable political grandstanding. Yet there are those other moments—wonderful moments—of chasing a story. It could be anything, really. All it needs is some of the elements we all recognize: maybe valor, or betrayal, or suffering, or, perhaps best of all, resilience and endurance. I'm proud, in this way, to call myself a storyteller. Stories have always been, at their heart, affirmations of humanity in all its forms. In the case of a lost man who had no business surviving in a frozen land, there is much to say.

I am not, however, the first to recount Crane's remarkable return. Crane's story received attention in magazines and newspapers at the time. One nice headline called him "The Man Who Came Back." Crane was later mentioned, from time to time, in books on Alaska. A hero of this book, historian Douglas Beckstead, published some articles on his research into the crash.

But the full arc of Crane's deliverance has never been told. This book is overdue. For a storyteller, there is no greater reward.

In later years, Crane very rarely spoke of his time in the Alaskan wilds and, when pressed, gave only the vaguest replies. He viewed his struggle as nothing more than an uninteresting footnote in the greater context of the war. It's likely he would have disapproved of this retelling or, at best, dismissed it as pointless. I disagree. It is, to me, a measure of the human spirit. Such things should not be forgotten or locked away.

Mount Athos is known in Greek as Agion Oros, or the Holy Mountain. From where I sat that March day, I could see the outlines of two other peninsulas that jut out to the west before the sea opens again. On the far shore, after the two rocky fingers, the land begins to swell toward another sacred peak, Mount Olympus, the home of the gods of antiquity. The allegories and fables built around their reign, and passed on to us, are as expansive as the human imagination. All great and enduring stories are so. Some of the sharpest lessons from Olympus spoke directly to overwhelmed travelers struggling to reach home. The gods, we are told, smile on resourcefulness and humility. They punish hubris.

A young pilot from Philadelphia, who fell from the sky in December 1943, would come to learn that well.

ONE

DECEMBER 21, 1943

Ladd Field

On a morning just above zero, a pilot with bed-rumpled hair hurried through tunnels under the Alaskan snow. The rubber soles of his shin-high Arctic boots slapped on the red concrete floor. With his sleeve, he wiped away crumbs from toast eaten on the run. He made sure to stay to the smooth outside wall of the passageways, careful not to snag his flight suit on the networks of pipes, heating ducts, and bolted braces that shared the warrens beneath Ladd Field.

He also paid attention not to rush too fast. He knew that any beads of sweat would turn into icy lesions the moment he stepped outside.

But he had bigger worries. He was late. Embarrassingly late. Damn, grumbled First Lieutenant Leon Crane as he hit a bottleneck of airmen near the busy stairs leading up to Hangar 1. He pushed his way through with a few muttered apologies.

He blamed it on the cards.

Their poker game had run longer than usual. That's what happens when six hard-nosed players get together. Hefty bets were laid down, and the pots swelled to tempting sums. Crane was up as much as seventy-five dollars—a nice chunk of his monthly Army pay—before shedding about half his winnings with some long-shot betting. This most definitely wasn't his style. He considered bluffing for fools and trying to cheat the odds as even more clueless. This night, though, he was having some laughs and didn't want to be on the sidelines, even if it cost him some cash.

Finally, a little after two in the morning, they called last hand. Remember, one of the players said, some of us have to fly in the morning. Right, answered Crane. And I'm one of them. Let's wrap this up.

Crane was scheduled at the hangar about seven thirty. But it wasn't until eight that he squinted over at the alarm clock, which he had forgotten to set when he flopped into his bunk after the card game broke up. He pulled away his blankets and swung onto the carpeted floor in one motion. He rarely overslept. The Alaskan winter, however, still had him off balance. It was that way for many other guys experiencing their first Far North winter. Late afternoon was already so dark that it felt like deep into the evening. What passed as morning was really just an appendage of night.

Crane's roommate was already up, but didn't know Crane's flight schedule and hadn't thought to wake him.

The lights from the airfield made starbursts on the frost-glazed windows, which were Coke-bottle thick to keep out the cold. Crane checked the clock again. Sunrise was still nearly three hours away on the first day of winter.

First day. That was a well-worn joke at Ladd. Only calendars and almanacs called it the beginning of the season. In Fairbanks the subzero bite had set in months earlier. Yet there was still some reason to mark December 21. It was finally the turning point of the darkness. From now on, the sun would linger a bit longer each day. If nothing else, the winter solstice was a chance for a collective sigh of relief. They were passing through the dark season's tightest corridor. On this day, on the stingiest break from the night, there are fewer than four hours of milky daylight in Fairbanks, about 110 miles below the Arctic Circle.

Crane still felt tired. But he figured he'd catch a nap later when he was back at base. After all, there wasn't much else to do in the deep-freeze months when you weren't airborne. There were reports, meals, shut-eye, maybe a prowl around Fairbanks, a couple miles down a dirt and gravel road with ruts and ice heaves. Poker remained the time waster of choice for many. That often included Crane. The shifting odds, the step-by-step betting—it all appealed to Crane's engineering sensibilities and love of problem solving. He became a student of the fifty-two-card deck as a fraternity newbie at the Massachusetts Institute of Technology (MIT), with its rarefied IQs and one future Nobel laureate as a Phi Beta Delta brother. Crane was now developing a reputation at Ladd Field as a player of considerable finesse, knowing when to push his luck and knowing when to pull back. He did nothing to dispel the image of cool and cunning. Crane hated boasting, but he also liked people to recognize he was clever.

He was popular on base since arriving October 10 on one of the transport flights that hopscotched north from Montana. Crane brought none of the silly swagger carried by some of the more insecure guys. He grew up in West Philadelphia watching how braggarts and bullies were eventually cut down to size. It paid to be quick-witted and resourceful on those row-house streets, especially during the scruffy Depression years. And, above all, it was essential to learn to go with the flow. By the time Crane was starting grade school, the Jewish families such as his were well aware that their West Philly enclaves were under pressure. Like thousands of others, Crane's immigrant parents were drawn initially to the neighborhood by the tidy, affordable homes built astride the electric trolley lines running down Baltimore Avenue and other streets. These, too, became attractive spots for African Americans, who began to pour north during World War I. European immigration was at a near standstill, and help-wanted signs were cropping up in factories from the Midwest to New England. The northward migration kept churning during the boom years in the 1920s and the lean times of the Depression that followed. Some of the West Philly old-timers grumbled in Yiddish or Russian or Polish about the "strange element" coming over the Mason-Dixon line, as one amateur Philadelphia historian termed the Deep South exodus. There were also unkind cuts about the newcomers' music and food and unfathomable revival-style churches. Such naysayers, though, got an earful in return from the neighborhood's more accommodating souls. Don't forget your own wandering roots, the critics were told. Remember the intolerance and violence directed at the places you left behind, like the ghettos in Warsaw and Odessa.

Crane and his school buddies didn't dwell much on the broad social forces at play around them. Like all young ones, they just instinctively grasped the basics of getting by. That usually meant keeping eyes open and mouth shut. That last part was maybe the easiest of all for Crane. He had always liked the company of his own thoughts. He could lose himself for hours in articles on aeronautics or the latest experiments with jet propulsion or marvel over designs in *Popular Mechanics,* which he dutifully bought each month and read until the pages were dog-eared and thumb smudged.

The alarm clock clicked to 8:10.

Crane threw on his flight suit and parka over thermal underwear. He suddenly felt uncomfortably warm. The radiators and insulation in the bachelor officers' quarters were so good that— even in the harshest cold—their marathon poker games could be played in shirtsleeves. Such trappings didn't extend to all at Ladd, though. Some of the enlisted men were put in hastily built barracks that earned nicknames like Pneumonia Gulch. In winter, mop streaks on the barracks' floors would freeze before they could dry.

Crane was among the fortunate airmen assigned the latest down-filled gear. It was made for the military under a deal with outdoor clothing pioneer Eddie Bauer, who began exploring new fabrics and fillings after a near-fatal brush with hypothermia while dressed in waterlogged wool. Cold-weather protection for soldiers, sailors, and airmen had taken on added urgency as wartime missions moved into places such as Alaska and Greenland. The down suits had gotten generally high marks from the Ladd pilots. They weren't always so kind toward the design gatekeepers at the War Department. The canvas cockpit seats in the big bombers, for one, could become as cold and hard as marble slabs when the temperature slipped into the single digits. And who was the genius who decided that many of the warplanes didn't need windshield wipers or decent heaters?

As Crane zipped up his parka, he felt paper crinkle inside one of the pockets. He had forgotten about the letter. It arrived a few days earlier from his father, who ran an auction business in Philadelphia. Dad did well, and Crane was quite proud of him. The business was successful enough to keep four children and his wife comfortable during the Depression. Crane had read the single-page letter, but quickly. He figured he would linger over it later with a cup of coffee. He liked hearing about the family and neighborhood, written in his father's precise but slightly overformal English, learned after emigrating from Ukraine. Crane thought about tossing the letter on his bunk.

But why waste even a few seconds to dig it out? He needed to get moving.

Even after more than two months at Ladd, Crane felt he was still a novice in the preparations and precautions to handle winter in interior Alaska. Sometimes he'd forget to pull up his parka hood and not realize his mistake until his ears were iced and aching. It took only a few seconds. The winter in Fairbanks is tricky that way. Winds are usually very light. Add that to the Fairbanks area's typical low winter humidity—sometimes almost at desert levels— and it can, at first, feel less bone-chilling than a wind-whipped December day in Philadelphia. But below zero is serious business. Ignore it at your own peril. Just a few days earlier, a mechanic on the airfield lost most of the skin on his right palm after grabbing a pipe with his bare hands. It was minus twenty-five that day. Crane went through the learning curve like everyone: never forget your mittens or liner gloves; make sure your face is dry before going outside; don't breathe too deeply to avoid what the medics called "lung frosting." In a nutshell: respect the Alaskan winter.

Somehow, Crane seemed to handle the subzero better than many other guys shipped *overseas*. That's what the War Department termed the Alaska territory. It was the same designation for Hawaii and other U.S. possessions. This was the homeland and the stores were American and the currency was the greenback, but they still didn't have a star on the flag.

Leon, what's the rush? asked his roommate, a beefy Mississippi lieutenant known as Stud.

I'm way behind, Crane huffed, as he tossed on the rest of his gear. I forgot to set the alarm. Is that time right? Is it really ten after eight?

That is it, said Stud.

Under his breath, Crane grumbled his trademark curse: Hell's bells. He jammed his feet into his boots and started for the door.

Slow down there, Stud said. I'm not flying today. I'm making a run into Fairbanks. And that means I got the keys to a jeep.

Crane brightened. Great. Can you give me a lift?

Stud grabbed the keys. It was a bit of a surprise. Stud did just about everything he could to avoid being out in the cold. He never stopped grousing about the winter and how he missed the sticky warmth and Spanish moss of Dixie. Crane would remind him to be careful of his wishes. There was more than enough heat and humidity to go around in the horrific South Pacific battles. Alaska wasn't such a bad deal, Crane told him. Crane tried to keep a good attitude about the place. It was a lot better than being shot at. And Crane was also built well for these extremes: a shade under six feet and 170 pounds, with the muscles of a natural athlete—although he usually preferred playing his clarinet to playing ball. He was on the lanky side and wore his trousers high up on his narrow waist. Yet he had just enough heft in his twenty-four-year-old biceps and thighs that no one would call him scrawny. If he had been born a generation earlier, it would have been easy to imagine Crane as a silent-movie star. His dark almond-shaped eyes and thick lashes demanded attention.

Thanks a lot, Crane said to Stud, who was jingling the jeep keys. I really appreciate the ride.

Stud drove Crane the short hop over to the Officers' Club. It gave Crane enough time to gulp half a cup of coffee and snag a piece of buttered toast. Crane then raced down the stairs into one of the tunnels that allowed Ladd personnel to pop from building to building while avoiding the winter blasts. On the way, Crane passed the exchange, the all-in-one store on the base. On a whim, he grabbed two packs of matches—a total of forty sticks. Crane didn't smoke. But the pilot who would sit in control of their B-24D Liberator bomber that day, Second Lieutenant Harold Hoskin, was always nursing a pipe. Maybe he'll need a light, Crane thought. It was a tacit rule that the copilot's job was to make life just a little easier for the guy to his left in the cockpit. They'd probably be up for a least a couple hours on another test mission. Hoskin— pronounced as *Haw-sken* in his northern Maine accent—would definitely want to puff away if they were lucky enough to hit some smooth air.

By the time Crane arrived at Hangar 1, the ground crews were pulling away the cold-stiffened tarps from their Liberator, serial number 42-40910. It was christened the *Iceberg Inez* after arriving at Ladd about a month earlier.

Some mechanics in the hangar were gabbing about the morning radio bulletin. British warplanes had hammered Frankfurt with two thousand tons of bombs in a single day. That type of pounding was hard to grasp, even for those who spent all their time around warplanes. Guys in the hangar were trying to get their heads around 4 million pounds. Let's see, a B-24 weighs about thirty-eight thousand pounds with its bomb bays fully loaded. That would be the equivalent of more than 105 of those four-engine monsters. Buddy, can you imagine that?

From the vantage point of Alaska, there was a strange seesaw relationship with the war. The battles sometimes seemed to be taking place in another world, distant snippets from radio reports and newsreels. Then, at other times, the airfield would kick into round-the-clock operations, with a huge array of aerial firepower coming and going. Suddenly, the war felt much closer. Japan had already taken a swipe at Alaska. That was among the reasons so many airmen were now packed into Ladd. If the Japanese came back for more—doubtful yet not impossible—America would be sufficiently muscled up this time. But Fairbanks had a bigger role than just bolstering defenses. It was a key transit point in one of the most massive movements of fighting machinery in history. Under a deal with the Kremlin, wartime ally Uncle Sam was sending a steady flow of planes and equipment to Alaska as part of a critical back-channel supply line. The planes were handed off to Soviet crews at Ladd, flown over the Bering Sea to Siberia, and, often within days, in the skies on Europe's Eastern Front.

With so much airpower passing through, Alaska also became a convenient proving ground for the broader concerns of waging war in the high latitudes or extreme cold. No one knew where the next front could be. Iceland? Norway? It made sense to be prepared.

This is where the test crews, dubbed the Cold Nose Boys, came in. Their flight reports allowed military designers to make needed tweaks and modifications. America's interest in getting it right was elevated after watching how the Russian winters foiled the often superior German planes and artillery. Yet extreme cold can be a hard puzzle to crack. It did a lot of mischief. The cold gummed up hydraulics, seized oil lines, locked up flaps, made some wire as brittle as straw, and vexed just about every onboard system on the planes. At the beginning of the war, the Ladd commander sent an urgent message to Washington, warning there were no American planes fully reliable at temperatures below minus twenty-five. It could be colder than that just on the Ladd runway in winter. Ladd's Cold Weather Test Detachment was a chance to explore what was needed for an all-weather fighting force. Defense contractors—always eager to cut a new deal—sensed the opportunities, too. Technicians from alpha-dog firms such as Lockheed and Pratt & Whitney became frequent visitors at Ladd to look over the test results. Trouble was that sometimes there was only wreckage to try to deduce what went wrong. More than thirty planes with connections to Ladd Field had crashed or experienced some kind of major failure between April 1941 and the morning Crane and Hoskin were ready to take up the *Iceberg Inez*. That didn't count the hundreds of other crashes and mishaps on other Alaskan bases and among the Soviet pilots heading west with their American-made planes.

Crane wandered through the cavernous Hangar 1, looking for Hoskin. Huge polished steel panels divided the American and Soviet sections. The hangar was the biggest enclosed space north of the forty-eight states, measuring nearly 330 feet long and more than 270 feet wide. Like every airman at Ladd, Crane liked the energy of Hangar 1. It smelled of fuel and coffee and was alive with the sounds of phones ringing, orders being barked, and tools clanging. High-wattage lights, fixed three stories above, gave everything the slightly washed-out tinge of a flashbulb photo. It was nearly nine o'clock, and there was still no hint of dawn. That was almost two hours away.

Crane found Hoskin checking the weather reports. He offered his excuses for being late. Hoskin gave a not-to-worry wave. He was never one to make a scene. Hoskin liked to keep it light, the mark of someone who always had an easy relationship with success. He kept his gaze fixed on the weather forecast.

Well, it's messy, Hoskin told Crane. But what else is new, right?

No one could count on easy flying conditions this time of year. There was deep cloud cover. The winds were just a puff in the Fairbanks valley, but above five thousand feet they were roaring in from the southeast at up to fifty miles per hour. They were expected to increase later in the day.

Crane had missed the morning rundown on the mission. He knew Hoskin as one of the new pilots around base, but hadn't been teamed with him before on a flight. For Crane, it was an interesting change of pace to be aboard the B-24. He normally flew far smaller fighters on cold-weather tests and, in his role with the 6th Depot Repair Squadron, helped prep them for the Soviets.

Hoskin quickly filled him in on the day's run. They'd head east and conduct feathering tests. This required shutting down one of the B-24's four 1,200-horsepower engines and adjusting the props until they offered the least resistance to the airflow. It's similar to the effect of sticking your hand from a car window on the highway and finding the most aerodynamic position. This is vitally important for a plane with a failed engine. A dead prop not properly feathered can cause dangerous drag as the flat blade surface is slammed by the airstream. The need for feathering is far greater in a single-prop plane, which needs to be as trim as possible to successfully glide down without power. But feathering was still important on the multiengine bombers to avoid straining the remaining engines. The onrushing air could also turn the props if not properly feathered, something logically known as windmilling. This can make the plane harder to handle and mess up the inner workings with negative torque, which means the propellers are driving the engine mechanisms rather than the reverse. In other words, it's better to have no engine than one with the props turning on their own. Feathering is a standard test, but nothing in Alaska's supercold is routine.

Crane had heard all the hair-raising stories as soon as he arrived on base: the crashes, near misses, and how systems simply went dead in midflight. For combat crews, such talk would seem foolhardy. Among the many superstitions on the battlefield was keeping gossip to a minimum about missions that ended badly. What's the point in tempting fate? At Ladd, though, there was no antiaircraft flak or enemy fighters to worry about. The common foe was the winter weather. The thinking went: the more the pilots swapped theories about frozen flaps or cold-clogged oil lines, the better the chances of anticipating a problem in flight. Plus, Cold Nose duty was an open-ended proposition. Combat aircrews were usually sent home after a couple dozen missions or so. Each time back at base was one step closer to getting those see-you-later papers. At Ladd, some pilots logged thousands of hours over many months with no finish line in sight.

Among the latest Ladd stories involved two B-24s and a cursed stretch in February 1943, eight months before Crane's arrival. On February 4, a B-24D took off from Anchorage on a mission to photograph a solar eclipse while heading to Ladd. Fourteen people were aboard. Two engines failed, and the pilots were unable to properly feather them. They managed to ditch the aircraft in a snowfield. All survived, although some suffered severe frostbite before rescue. Eight days later, another B-24 mission was staged to mimic the conditions of the previous flight, suspecting that the cold had fouled up the hydraulic and oil lines. Two engines were shut down with instructions to feather them and then allow them to windmill. The plane went into a nosedive. All seven aboard were killed.

Crane's job as copilot included eyeballing the plane, checking the fuel, and loading the parachutes. He needed a bit of extra time with the big bomber. Crane was far more familiar with the P-39 Airacobra fighter, which could fit under the shadow of a B-24 wing.

"How's it going, Leon?" yelled Hoskin over the hangar din. Hoskin's baby-face cheeks seemed perpetually chapped by the weather. But he had a closer relationship with cold than most from "outside," which is what longtime Alaskans call the rest of the world. In the Hoskin family home back in Maine, there was no heat in the upstairs bedrooms. The family oven-baked soapstone to use as bed warmers.

We look good to go? said Hoskin.

Crane gave a thumbs-up with his sheepskin-lined mittens. We're good, Crane shouted back.

Crane and Hoskin left the hangar and climbed aboard the B-24 through the open bomb bay. They first wanted to make sure all was fine with First Lieutenant James B. Sibert, a prop specialist in charge of the equipment to measure the feathering tests and monitor related aspects, such as engine oil pressure. Sibert, a new arrival from Wright Field in Ohio, set up in the rear of the plane. Hoskin and Crane then squeezed along the narrow catwalk through the center of the aircraft. They ducked past the radio operator's post and into the cockpit. On their radio, they rechecked the crew.

"All set," said Sibert.

"Roger," added radio operator Staff Sergeant Ralph Wenz, who was in the nook directly behind the cockpit.

"All good," said the crew chief, Master Sergeant Richard Pompeo, who assisted with takeoff procedures from a hatch behind Hoskin.

Outside, a ground crew engineer manually rotated the propellers on each of the engines to clear any excess fuel or oil in the combustion chambers. A fire extinguisher was always on hand. B-24 engines had been known to flare up when the batteries were switched on. Crane stuck his head out the cockpit to check the flaps and rudders.

Crane jabbed the engine prime pump and made sure the fuel mixture was on auto lean, increasing the air level in the fuel to avoid fouling the spark plugs. Hoskin pulled back the throttle to about one-third open. The first engine to fire up was number three, which was closest to the copilot and powered the hydraulics. Engine four, farther out on the copilot's wing, was next. Then engines two and one on the pilot's side. Crane checked the engine temperature and oil pressure. All fine.

Just before 9:40 a.m., the *Iceberg Inez* taxied out. A salmon-colored smudge of dawn painted the southeast sky. The sun, however, wouldn't poke above the horizon for another hour.

Crane looked over at Hoskin. Not bad, Crane smiled. We got off on time for once.

In winter, crews lobbied hard to be among the first flights of the day. After a dozen or so takeoffs, the runway could be shrouded in superchilled exhaust clouds. It's an effect known well in Alaska as "caribou fog," describing how herds become covered in an icy mist from their own breath.

Crane flicked the fuel mixture to auto rich, cutting down on the air ratio in the fuel lines. External flaps were set at a 20 percent angle. Hoskin pulled down on the four throttle levers. The big plane lumbered down the runway toward takeoff speed, about 110 miles per hour. It was only slightly more than needed to get the P-39 off the ground. But to Crane it felt much slower in the bomber, sitting more than seventeen feet above the tarmac instead of hugging the ground in the fighter. He kept a careful eye on the supercharger pressure, which registers the flow of compressed air into the engine for greater efficiency.

The nose lifted. Hoskin pulled back on the yoke. The *Iceberg Inez* climbed.

Hoskin banked the plane to the southeast, directly into the wind. He wanted to check out a place called Big Delta, site of a smaller air base about sixty miles to the southeast. Hoskin arrived in Alaska in late October—more than two weeks after Crane—and was eager to learn nearby landmarks on the ground.

They flew into the wind, down the Tanana River valley. Rolling hills rise along its banks. From the air, only a few dots of green spruce were seen as the gloss from the coming sunrise touched the high ground. In the Alaskan interior, the early winter storms do not melt until spring. Snow sits heavy on the spruce and glazes the barren birch and other trees in near-postcard perfection.

The cloud ceiling was low and dense. Crane looked for any breaks. They wanted relatively cloud-free air for the prop tests to avoid skewing the equipment readings. They also wanted to give the prop specialist, Sibert, the ability to see the blades. But the concept of clear-air turbulence was not yet fully understood. Many pilots at the time were caught by surprise by rapid downdrafts and other violent winds in skies they believed to be clear and, to their mind, calm.

Hoskin moved the plane higher, to near ten thousand feet.

"Oxygen, guys," Crane said through his throat mike that was pressed tightly just below his jaw line, which was rough with stubble. He'd had no time to shave that morning.

They each slipped on the masks, breathing in the garden-hose smell of the rubber. Putting on the masks at ten thousand feet was a bit early, but Hoskin wanted them to be ready in case he needed to punch the plane higher through a break in the clouds.

At 10:03 a.m., Wenz radioed their position back to Ladd: forty miles southeast of base. Hoskin got on the intercom to check on prop expert Sibert.

Hoskin to Sibert: Do you read?

Sibert replied in his squeaky soprano that was an endless source of ribbing: "Okay, Harold."

It was 10:30. Wenz sent a quick all-good message back to Ladd. Wenz was already an experienced hand in the fickle Alaskan skies. Before the war, he came north from Wyoming and worked mail flights for a few years. He'd seen far more dicey flying conditions than today. He knew, though, that the winter cloud cover can be thick for hundreds of miles in every direction. If they couldn't find a break in the ceiling soon, Wenz figured his next transmission to Ladd would be to say they were coming home.

Just over fifteen thousand feet, the plane bounced through curtains of ragged clouds. The craft began to buck. There was no worry as equipment rattled about. The B-24 had its quirks— including being considered more temperamental in flight than its venerable older cousin, the B-17 Flying Fortress—but it could handle far worse than these castoff clouds known as scud, which are pulled away from bigger formations by wind drafts. The wash from the big propellers twisted the scud like cotton candy.

They were over Big Delta. Wenz got back on the radio at 11:08 a.m. At about sixty-five miles from Ladd, the radio was near the edge of its range.

"Ladd, this is four-zero-niner-one-zero. Over," he said

"Roger that, niner-one-zero. Over," the reply came.

"About ten miles east of Big Delta. Looking for a break in the clouds for prop tests. Over."

"Roger. Good luck. Over."

Hoskin steered the plane east in big sweeps through the clouds, looking for some clear air. It was approaching noon and near the time to call it quits. Sunset came at 2:41 p.m.

Take a look, Hos, Crane said. The clouds were brightening ahead.

As they got closer, the sky opened up. It was a clear column that rose to what looked like twenty-five thousand feet. Maybe higher. Perfect for the three-stage prop tests if the clouds behaved. They had to make observations at fifteen thousand, twenty thousand, and, finally, twenty-five thousand feet. This would be a chance to knock off the higher-altitude tests first.

Hoskin put the plane into a corkscrew climb. He wanted to stay inside the shaft of open air. Crane checked the gauges. The copilot's seat faced most of the diagnostics and dials monitoring the plane, a behemoth more than 67 feet long, a wingspan of 110 feet, and a skin that looked reptilian, with hundreds of thousands of rivet bumps. In front of Hoskin, one of the circular gauges showed the "free air" temperature outside. It was nearly minus seventy. Above that was the altimeter, which was ticking off their ascent.

The weak Arctic sun cast gauzy shadows through the cockpit canopy.

At twenty thousand feet, they ran the feathering tests. All looked good. The gauges acted up for a moment, but they could still see the ground through the section of clear air. The plane felt good, despite the momentary glitches with the dials and diagnostics. They decided to keep climbing.

"Let's give it a try at twenty-five thousand," Hoskin said. Crane nodded.

The starboard wing rose as the plane went back to a spiral climb. It gave the cockpit a blinking effect of bright and dark as the plane swept past the clouds, brightened by the low-hanging sun on each turn. Then the sun's honeyed shimmer started to fade.

Looks likes our hole is closing up, Crane said, as they passed twenty-three thousand feet and the clouds moved in.

Crane opened his notebook. He began logging the altitude and airspeed.

A second later, Crane's notebook was dragged from his hands. G-forces, strong as a roller-coaster plunge, slammed Crane and Hoskin. They lurched at the controls.

The ship was in a spin, ripping through walls of choppy, gray clouds. The only thing that made sense was that somehow the plane had stalled, which happens at speeds somewhere below 135 miles per hour depending on the plane's weight and flap settings. Almost nothing else can cause a sudden spin like this.

Wind screamed over the cockpit glass. The airspeed gauge snapped past the maximum cruising speed of about 300 miles per hour and was redlining. The B-24 was built to go faster in a brief, controlled dive. This was anything but controlled. At least one engine had failed. But why was the rudder fighting back their commands to get the plane level? Hoskin and Crane tore off their oxygen masks and struggled against the spin. The plane wasn't responding.

Keep pulling, Hos yelled.

The flight instruments were blinking out. The electrical system was somehow compromised, too. They broke through the clouds. Below, the horizon was spinning wildly: snow, mountain ridge, trees, more snow. Over and over. Finally, Hoskin and Crane began to gain some control over the plane. The spin slowed.

Hold on, Hos shouted over the whine of the runaway engines and wind. I think we got her. Hold on.

The plane leveled off, still shaking and drifting, but at least out of the spin. There was no way to tell how fast they were moving.

The instruments were dark or locked up in total malfunction. But the airspeed was definitely too high. Hoskin tried to move the nose a bit higher to slow the plane and reclaim control. A second later, the plane fell off in a spin in the opposite direction. They were pointing almost straight down. Crane and Hoskin pulled hard to try to level off.

Then something like a pistol shot came from the tail. Cracking sounds followed, echoing through the plane. The elevator controls were out. The situation just went from dire to disaster. Elevator systems control the pitch of the plane, basically its ability to stay parallel with the ground. Now, the plane bounced wildly. Its nose reared up for a moment and then dropped suddenly like a breaching whale. Without the elevators, the plane was effectively an unguided missile with only a few rudder options to try to bring it level again.

They were going to crash.

"Open bomb bays," Crane shouted over his shoulder to Pompeo, who had moved to a spot in the rear of the cockpit for just this contingency. Pompeo reached onto the center console and pulled the bomb-bay levers. The wide aluminum hatches rolled up into the plane. The temperature inside plunged, as minus seventy-degree air poured in.

Just then, Crane's throat mike ripped away. The ship was back in another spin, dropping fast toward the wilderness of the Alaskan Yukon. There was nothing left to do.

Bail out, Hoskin yelled. Crane slammed down the crash alarm switch. Bells jangled through the craft like a fire drill.

Forget the controls, Crane said, tugging on Hoskin's flight suit. We're going down. Let's go. Now!

Crane didn't think it was worth mentioning Hoskin's pregnant wife as motivation to bail. Who else would be on his mind? It was jump and maybe, just maybe, survive. Or stay and certainly die. They all knew it.

Crane screamed: Hos, now!

Crane yanked off his mittens to secure his chute. It took huge effort just to close off the chest buckles. The pack hung from his backside, flapping against his legs. He struggled out of the cockpit. The forces from the spin made every step feel as if he were draped in lead weights. He ducked under the fittings for the topside turret. The radio operator's space was to his left. Light streamed in from a small window above the metal desk.

Where the devil was the radioman, Wenz? He should be at his dials, but the station was empty. Did he stumble back to the rear of the ship for some reason? Normally, the G-forces would pin the radio operator to his spot.

There was no time to ask. Pompeo was rigged up to jump with a chest chute, but was hesitating. Crane noticed that Pompeo wasn't wearing his down-filled gear and instead had only a light-blue plug-in suit—a multipiece outfit whose inner layers operated like an electric blanket. These were nice and toasty when hooked up to the rheostat, but offered little more than modest protection when disengaged. It was the equivalent of wearing a windbreaker into a hurricane. Frostbite cases were common if a plug-in suit stopped working during a mission. Pompeo had brought a "barracks bag" aboard with his down parka and other clothes, but either didn't have time to fish it out or the bag was flung away in the spin.

"Should I bail?" Pompeo asked Crane.

"Christ almighty, yes! Get out!"

Pompeo crawled ahead onto the metal catwalk, about the width of a legal pad. Crews often complained about the narrow catwalk and the general rattle-box feel in the heart of the plane. The flying boxcar, some called it. Another darker name was the flying coffin, since the only exits—if the bomb bays were sealed or blocked—were out hatches deeper into the fuselage.

Pompeo slipped off the catwalk. Spiky frost was forming on any bit of moisture on the olive-drab walls, showing up like veins inside some kind of leviathan's belly. Pompeo dove through the bomb bay. Crane looked back. Hoskin was near the radio station, still messing with his parachute harness.

Crane took two steps more. He looked back to see Hoskin fumbling.

Damn it, Hos, he yelled. What are you waiting for? Now!

And then Crane was falling.

Crane's lips instantly froze and cracked like old plastic. The wind chill was well below minus 100. He didn't notice. He was too struck by the split-second change from the groaning plane and the breath-sucking G-forces to the near silence of free fall. It felt oddly like floating, he thought. There was no immediate sensation of slicing through the air. Maybe this type of unearthly cold doesn't register right away, he thought. Like how an unexpected slap takes a second to sting.

Crane felt for the rip cord. The chute poured out. He swayed beneath it, rocking like a pendulum. The last moments of the *Iceberg Inez* played out before him.

He watched another chute drift behind a ridge at least a mile away. Was that Pompeo? Or could that be Hoskin? Did he make it out?

The plane was off to his left. It rocked and spun like a sheet of cardboard caught in the wind. Flames spilled off the fuselage. It spiraled a few more times and then slammed into a slope of spruce and loose rock. A fireball rose. No one could survive that, Crane thought in horror. Winds carried the black smoke over the valley. They also pulled Crane.

He thudded into the snow. It was light and powdery. Crane stumbled onto his back. The snow sprinkled over his face, melting on his cheeks. His chute billowed over like a shroud.

The wreckage burned on the slope about two miles away. The gas on board would probably keep the blaze going a while, Crane thought. At least that sad fact might be good for the rescue mission. He knew search teams would be mobilized after they failed to return. But the fire also meant that the weapons and supplies on board were lost. The provisions included sleeping bags, signaling flares, and an ax. A pistol and ammo also hung at the entrance to the bomb compartment. Crane didn't remember seeing them there. Maybe Pompeo grabbed them before he bailed.

But where was he?

Crane shouted out their names.

Pompeo. That carried some hope. He at least got it out.

Hoskin. Maybe he slipped through the bomb bay just after Crane.

Wenz. Sibert. Crane was almost certain they went down with the plane, but Wenz wasn't at his station. Did he jump before Pompeo?

Crane listened for any hint he was not alone.

Nothing.

As Crane cupped his hands around his mouth to shout again, he came to a crushing discovery. He had left his mittens on board in the rush to secure his chute. He knew how quickly the cold could freeze fingers. The medics and commanders at Ladd drilled that into the personnel from the moment they stepped off the transport plane. Crane tucked his hands under his armpits and tried to take stock.

Forgetting his mittens was a huge blow. But he had the silk parachute, which he could at least wrap around his hands and use as a makeshift sleeping bag. The rest of his flight suit was intact. He had three pairs of wool socks under his heavy mukluks, the Army's canvas version of the traditional soft boot of caribou or sealskin used by natives. Crane's were lined with felt and layers of burlap. He also had his flight helmet. And the luckiest bit of all: the matches he grabbed for Hoskin.

He had his Boy Scout knife, too. He always carried it. He liked the memories attached, such as a weekend camping trip at Valley Forge with other Scouts. Sadly, though, that was the sum total of his outdoor experience.

The sky was turning gray-blue. Nightfall was coming. There was no chance to reach the crash site in that time—if at all. Crane had taken a few stumbling steps. He realized immediately that the snow was atop a jumble of rocks that made walking near impossible. A broken ankle would be a certain death sentence.

Farther down the valley, Crane could see the outline of a frozen river. On the banks were piles of driftwood among the spruce groves. That gave him an idea. He spent the next hour cutting boughs to make an SOS in ten-foot letters in the snow. He added an arrow pointing in the direction of the wreckage. He figured that if the crash was spotted, the search mission would widen for any crew members who managed to bail out.

He thought back to the last radio contact with Ladd. This was not good at all. The call was at least an hour before the plane fell from the sky. That means the search area could be a radius of more than two hundred miles from their last known position.

And Crane wasn't really sure where he was. Somewhere east of Big Delta, for sure. But that meant nothing. Crane had only a vague notion of the area. The main point of reference for him was the great Yukon River, which begins in Canada and carves through the center of Alaska. He knew the names of some of the feeder systems. One of them is the Charley River valley. This could be the Charley, he thought. But it could just as easily be any of the other waterways spilling toward the Yukon.

Crane's hands were now covered in cuts from hacking at the spruce. Think, he told himself. You have no medical supplies and no mittens.

Prioritize. There was nothing more urgent than a fire.

It was clear that he had to get a blaze going, or he may not last the night. It was minus twenty and could easily slip past forty below before dawn. There was driftwood poking through the snow at the river's edge, left there from one spring flood after the other. Quickly, Crane gathered enough wood, made tinder-dry by the extreme cold and low winter humidity. With luck, he could have the fire burning through the long night.

He set out a bed of spruce and arranged a small cone of driftwood. His fingers were numb. Rubbing them and stuffing them into his jacket did almost nothing. He had little time. Precious minutes were spent just trying to pry off a match. His fingers seemed to be working in slow motion. Crane managed to strike the match, but the little flame wasn't enough to catch the spruce needles and shavings. Four matches—10 percent of his supply—did nothing but singe his fingertips.

Attempting to burn part of his parachute would accomplish little. Silk will catch fire, but not keep the flame once the source is taken away.

Wait. The letter, Crane thought. My dad's letter! He still had it in his parka. Crane unfolded the paper and fed it into a stack of spruce trimmings and flakes of driftwood. The fifth match worked. The fire rose among the spruce needles, sputtered for a second, and then caught.

Crane let the flames thaw his fingers before wrapping them in his parachute. Then he rolled himself in the chute.

During the night, two fires were the only things cutting the darkness: Crane's small blaze and the orange flames from whatever was left to burn on the B-24.

The clouds never broke. Crane lay back. As he listened to the fire, he thought about what would happen if rescue never came.

How long, he wondered, would it take to die?

TWO

DECEMBER 22, 1943

Charley River

By the time the sky began to brighten on his first morning alone, Crane's driftwood fire was down to orange embers.

He squatted close, trying to warm his hands yet mindful not to scorch his parachute. Mercifully, there was almost no wind. Even the high, thin fingers at the tips of the spruce were still. Cold and dry air can carry sounds well over long distances. But there was nothing to be heard. This was a deeper silence than anything Crane had known.

He became aware of his own internal hum. He could make out the soft, steady static of his inner ear. The sound reminded him of the shells he pressed to his ears during boyhood trips to the Jersey shore. It was reassuring, a sound of life and memory. He made it through the night. That alone seemed an accomplishment. There was something else, however, embedded within the awesome quiet. It somehow had its own special gravity, a force he hadn't really encountered before. The silence pressed on him, humbled him. It draws out honesty better than any truth serum.

Crane again ran through the odds of rescue. They certainly were no better than the day before. Without a last-minute radio call, Ladd's rescue planners would have no idea where to send the planes. They would, of course, circle over Big Delta, the location of the plane's last contact with Ladd. But they might as well be looking in Siberia. Crane was well off to the northeast—even if he didn't know exactly how far. And what if search planes never came? What were the chances of survival then? It looked bleak from any angle.

Start, Crane told himself, with the positives. It wasn't all grim. On the plus side, he had matches and the parachute. And don't forget: silk is an excellent insulating material and handles the deep cold well. His parka was in good condition, and the mukluks, so far, kept his feet warm.

There, too, was no problem with water. Even at the subzero temperatures, it gurgled up from fissures in the river ice. This was enough to keep him alive for a while. He also was in reasonably good shape except for his hands. Crane wiggled his toes. They were still nimble and warm enough. But how long, he asked himself, would that last?

For whatever reason, the radio operator, Wenz, hadn't indicated their heading from Big Delta in his last transmission to Ladd. And, in another baffling oversight, he had failed to make another call. Protocol was for radio contact at least every thirty minutes. If Wenz had kept to the schedule, there would have been a call to Ladd just before the B-24 went into its spin. Even if the plane was out of range, the message might have been heard at Big Delta.

But clearly, something must have happened to keep Wenz from making the radio call. Crane knew enough of Wenz to consider him deeply reliable. At thirty-one years old, Wenz was by far the oldest member of the crew. He had a nine-year-old daughter back in his native Nebraska. Even though the marriage didn't take, Wenz made arrangements to have some of his military pay put aside for his child. Wenz also was well aware of what it meant to be out of reach for help in the wilderness. Before coming to Alaska, Wenz spent time in Pinedale, Wyoming, not far from Jackson Hole. He opened a barbershop with his brother. In his time off, he was drawn to the solitude of the Rockies. Wenz hiked alone into the mountains and camped for a week or more. Relatives remember him playing with chipmunks and his curious choice of adopting a pet badger.

Crane figured that if Wenz could have made one last radio call, he would have. Something happened to him, Crane guessed. It couldn't be good.

Without the radio contact, Crane knew search teams had no road map. For all Ladd Field knew now, the *Iceberg Inez* could have pushed due east and gone down near the Canadian border. Or it could have looped back toward base. Or it could be any other direction. The normal search map began, obviously, with the last known position and expanded into widening circles if the plane's flight path was uncertain. That would give, at best, perhaps one or two passes that could come even close to Crane's location. So many variables would have to fall into place just to have a prayer of being spotted. There's the overall visibility, which is rarely good in winter. Then a host of other factors kick in: the angle of the sunlight, whether the plane was banking away or pulling up, whether a tree blocked the line of sight, whether the spotters were tired, hungry, bored, daydreaming, or just figuring the whole thing was a lost cause.

Think of trying to spot a button tossed at random on a football field. This is what search teams were sometimes told by their commanders trying to emphasize the need to stay sharp during a search. Then multiply it many times over with fields in every compass direction and no clue as to which one holds the prize. Crane was the button. This was no longer science. It was pure needle-in-haystack stuff. Technology offered no real help. It was too soon. At the time, over the border in Canada, a fellow aviation engineer and tireless tinkerer named Harry Stevinson was experimenting with a crash-resistance radio beacon whose beeps would be like a trail of virtual cookie crumbs for rescuers. Yet it would be well after the war until prototypes were tested.

Of course, the smoldering crash site also might hold some advantages as a search target, Crane thought. He looked up to the slopes. There were no more inky plumes. The wreckage must have burned itself out overnight. That would definitely lessen the chances of being spotted. Crane also wasn't sure whether the debris was plastered on a spot easily seen from the air. He racked his memory. He thought it was a relatively open patch. That was good. But he also recognized that he pulled the rip cord far lower than the altitude of search planes, which would have to stay thousands of feet up to avoid the highest peaks. Crane was also looking frantically for his plane as he floated under his chute. Searchers, however, would have no idea they were even near the wreckage and to keep their eyes peeled.

Crane's mind was clicking in the same way as when the poker-night pots got deliciously big: who knew what and how that knowledge—or lack of it—could influence the next move.

The short daylight also allowed precious little time for search planes from Ladd. The planes would be in the air by now, Crane guessed. He knew the drill. He hadn't taken part in any extensive search missions out of Ladd since arriving ten weeks before, but he had heard enough from the Cold Nose Boys. The hunt in winter was measured in days, not weeks, before it was called off as pointless.

Crane tried to take his mind off the worrisome logic of the search. He turned instead toward the embrace of simple dumb luck. Nothing could be more contrary to his scientific nature. But there were few cognates to his old life anymore. Crane's world was rewritten the moment he left the bomb bay. It seemed to him almost surreal. "It's all a dream," Crane told himself as he scanned the wilds. "It doesn't make sense." There was, however, still luck. That remains, no matter what. He already had amazingly good fortune to have his father's letter and the spur-of-the-moment matches. Stay upbeat, he told himself. It's rather amazing you are sitting here at all.

There was always that possibility of just the right path by a search mission and just the right gaze on just the right spot. It happens. Newspapers and magazines, pumped up with wartime propaganda, were full of miracle rescue and survival stories. Back in the summer, while Crane was wrapping up flight training, the papers carried the story of a Chinese-born steward named Poon Lim, who leaped from the torpedoed British merchant ship SS *Ben Lomond* and floated for 133 days on a wooden lifeboat in the Atlantic before being picked up by Brazilian fishermen. The lifeboat had basic supplies and water, but not nearly enough for more than four months. He resorted to fishing and catching rainwater. "The amazing Mister Poon Lim," said the clipped tones of a British newsreel showing his arrival in England to receive the British Empire Medal from King George VI. "To all intents and purposes, Mister Poon Lim is a dapper little Chinese one might meet anywhere. But now let's tell you something. He's a twenty-five-year-old merchant seaman who, after his ship had been torpedoed, lived for 133 days on a raft in the South Atlantic. Over four months adrift in midocean!"

And don't forget Pompeo. Crane even had his own rabbit's-foot guy on the *Iceberg Inez*. The crew chief, Pompeo, had been pretty much written off as dead two winters before. Crane heard it right from the source. Pompeo took an immediate liking to Crane because of their shared Pennsylvania roots. Pompeo grew up near the Appalachian Trail in Mount Holly Springs, southwest of Harrisburg. He gave Crane special renditions of his life on the Alaskan tundra and meals of caribou meat and dried fish. In January 1942, Pompeo and another airman were forced to make an emergency landing on a frozen river after getting lost en route to Whitehorse in the Canadian Yukon. The plane's radio was knocked out in the hard landing. They waited by the aircraft for two days and then set off on foot. In a phenomenal stroke of luck, they ran across some native trappers who arranged for them to be handed off, trapper to trapper, on a fifty-mile dogsled relay to Fort Yukon, an outpost on the Arctic Circle. The Army lauded them for "resourcefulness, fortitude and soldierly qualities." The pair arrived back at base, it said, "apparently in excellent condition."

"Pompeo!" Crane yelled again, half expecting him to come swooping up on a dogsled.

"Hos! Hoskin!"

Crane didn't even bother calling out for the others anymore. There were those odds again. If they didn't get out, the chances of surviving a nose-first slam into a mountainside and then escaping the fire were, well, it just doesn't happen. Crane had a hard time believing Hoskin made it out. But that parachute he saw *could* have been Hoskin's. What harm is there in allowing a little hope?

Crane gave his overall condition another check. He was stiff, and his hands were developing a pasty, white look—the first signs of frostbite taking hold. He tried to keep them wedged in his parka pockets as much as possible. But when the fire needed tending, there was no choice. He had to gather more wood. Frostbite would mean a quick death if he lost the use of his fingers. He already thought about the ways to accept the end on his own terms if left with no other way. Well, his Boy Scout knife was certainly sharp enough to slit his wrists.

He blinked away the thought. He wasn't even close to that point. The chance of rescue from the air was depressing, yet there were other elements in his favor. He could walk. And maybe a settlement was just down the river.

Crane gathered his parachute, dotted with burn holes from sparks exploding off wet patches in the driftwood. He checked the matches. Just thirty-five left. He had to be careful. The chemical reaction atop those small sticks—a mix of red phosphorus, potassium chlorate, and sulfur—was now the centerpiece of everything. No fire equaled no chance. Crane then looked at the river. It was frozen bank to bank. But, in sections of fast-flowing water, the ice was much thinner. Here, Crane could see the current running on the other side of the glass-clear sheets. He carefully tested a section with his boot, adding a bit more weight second by second. Hairline cracks started to spread. It was far wiser to walk in the snow along the banks.

His decision was made. Crane would head downstream. If nothing else, the reasoning was solid. It would eventually have to drain into something—the Yukon River, he guessed—and somewhere along its banks there was a chance of finding trappers or others riding out the winter. He knew it was wrong to stray too far from the crash site. The military procedure was to stay with the wreck to boost the chances of rescue. But he felt he had to explore a bit. Sitting around brought nothing except anxiety.

He set off. It took hours just to cover a mile. The snow would suddenly swell into waist-deep drifts and then fall away into a slippery crust of ice-coated rocks. Crane kept the river to his right shoulder. The low winter sun—in the rare moments it broke through the clouds—brought ashen shadows over the hills. Crane had no idea of the landmarks around him. On the other bank, the hills folded toward a smaller waterway called Copper Creek. If Crane had even these scant bearings, he could have worked out his spot: near the headwaters of the Charley River and a twisting, nearly ninety-five-mile course north until its clear waters merged with the muddy Yukon. The nearest road was at least seventy-five miles away.

He knew none of this. There was just what he could see: a frozen river snaking north.

When hunger came, it surprised Crane with its intensity. There were no small pangs as warnings. Now, suddenly and desperately, he was hungry.

He hadn't thought much of food since the crash. He had been living off adrenaline and the counterintuitive nature of sudden and extreme exertion. Crane's body was churning through calories, but not immediately sending signals to replace them. Instead, it was cashing in stored energy accounts—glucose and fat—and putting aside the demand for food until later. For Crane, this was the later. He scooped up a postage stamp–size dash of snow, trying to keep his hands buried in the sleeves of his flight suit. He knew eating too much raw snow was a losing proposition. The potential damage to the sensitive tissue inside the mouth was often more than its benefit as a water source. But Crane's hunger demanded something, and this was his only answer.

He let the small bit of snow melt against the roof of his mouth. It helped a little. He also remembered stories about people sucking on stones to help drive away thirst and hunger. It just wasn't worth digging through the snow to test the idea. Every moment with his hands exposed, even a little, was inviting disaster.

The medical files back at Ladd were full of sobering lessons on how quickly cold can claim its victims. Crane received the standard briefings and was issued the cold-weather protection manuals given everyone shipped north. If he was more curious—and some pilots were—he may have thumbed through real-life accounts in the medical records on base. They were written with the precision and attention to detail of any military report.

The case file of JLB (names were kept confidential from other service members) would undoubtedly have held Crane's interest. JLB was a twenty-five-year-old crew member on the first of Ladd's back-to-back B-24 calamities in February 1943. His plane went down after sundown about thirty miles south of Ladd Field. The crew survived, but JLB was pinned under a dislodged bomb-bay door. He took off one wool glove and began digging in the snow with his left hand in an attempt to get free. It was minus forty-five. His hand was fully exposed for about twenty minutes. Frostbite, however, had set in. It took a week of treatment at Ladd to save his fingertips.

Then there was WP, a twenty-seven-year-old pilot whose P-36 fighter developed engine trouble about fifty miles east of Northway, Alaska, on November 5, 1942. He brought the plane down in a clearing. He had only rudimentary winter gear and wore leather shoes inside his fleece-lined flight boots. He attempted to walk through foot-deep snow to the top of the nearby hill in an effort, in his words, "to get a better look at things." After four hours of walking, and failing to reach the crest, he returned to the plane and started a fire. The temperature that night bottomed out at about minus fifteen. His feet ached from the cold, and the insides of his boots were caked in ice. When the rescue ski plane arrived the next morning, WP's frozen shoes had to be cut away. "The skin of both feet was reddened, swollen and shiny and all of the toes were bluish-gray," wrote Ladd Field doctors. They treated his feet with tepid compresses and a spray of something called Pickrell's Solution, a diluted mixture of an antibacterial compound and an organic emulsifier used in products such as cosmetics and sunscreens. It wasn't enough. WP lost four full toes and portions of others. On January 18, 1943, he hobbled out of the Ladd hospital with the help of a cane.

The follow-up report reprimanded WP. "He should have remained near the shelter of his plane and immediately built a fire and kept himself warm," it read. Crane did not have the first of those options.

The sky was darkening. God, the daylight just races by, Crane thought. He remembered the winter solstice the day before. There was a bit of nature's malice in this yearly pivot. The sun nudged a bit higher off the horizon each day, but the worst part of winter was still to come. Crane wanted to find a place to build a fire before nightfall. That would at least give him time to collect driftwood and arrange some boughs over the snow as a sleeping mat. There was no chance of moonlight. The lunar cycle was ending, and the new moon wasn't for five days. It started to snow for the first time since the crash. Small, delicate flakes sprinkled from the low clouds.

Crane saw a promising spot. It was level ground in a clump of tall white spruce. Plenty of driftwood was scattered about. There were also some bigger logs with gnawed sections that could have been from beavers. A bit of fast-moving water bubbled through a blemish in the ice. Crane's thirst took over. He stretched out flat, trying as hard as he could to distribute his weight over the ice. He used the toes of his mukluks to slide forward, inch by inch. His lips met the water. He drank until he almost felt full. A sheen of ice formed around his mouth.

There was still the urgent business of the fire. He wished that he hadn't burned his father's entire letter the night before. It took a few more matches to get some tiny flames going in the spruce needles and shavings. At this rate, he would have just a little over a two-week supply of matches. That is, if he could keep them dry. By the fire's warmth, he finally took time to give his hands a thorough inspection. It was frightening. They were crisscrossed with cuts from the spruce. Color had drained from the fingertips. They were numb, and every movement felt sluggish.

It was insanity to try to walk farther, he realized. His hopes of a nearby cabin seemed dashed. It was better to listen to the military's guidance and at least wait close enough to the crash site to hear a rescue plane.

He told himself he would make camp here for at least the best portion of a week. That's about the time Ladd would call off the search. If he still had the energy, he'd start walking again.

At least he would know it would be the only choice left.

THREE

DECEMBER 23, 1943

Ladd Field

Results negative.

For two days running, the words were typed at the end of each search report. More than twenty search missions had been made from Ladd Field since late December 21, beginning about eight hours after the last radio contact with the *Iceberg Inez*. The first night covered the normal flight path between Big Delta and Ladd. All knew there was little chance of spotting an intact plane in the dark. And visibility that night was reduced to near zero at times— what some bush pilots called *blotto-botto* conditions—with areas of snow squalls and heavy ground fog. The crews on the search planes scanned mostly for signs of a possible burning crash site, a telltale glow in the murk that might mobilize a ground patrol.

Results negative.

It was the same conditions and same outcome the following day as the search area widened around the frozen Tanana River. The weather outlook improved slightly on December 23. A blast of dry and superchilled polar air cleared out the fog. The cloud ceiling moved higher. In Fairbanks the temperature clicked below zero at sunset and kept falling. It was soon minus twenty-three. The search planes made wide passes over Big Delta in a gradually expanding radius from the B-24's last reported position. They had no way of knowing, however, that the missions were not even close.

Crane and the wreckage were at least sixty miles to the north-east from the nearest reconnaissance plane. It's doubtful the searchers even caught a glimpse of the Charley River valley on the other side of the Tanana uplands.

Results still negative.

The head of Ladd's search-and-rescue unit, Major R. C. Ragle, looked over the weather forecasts and maps. They were hand drawn, with wavy isobars, arched fronts, and wind-speed arrows flowing like schools of fish. Winds were still kicking up around the search zone, lifting the light snow into near-whiteout conditions in places.

The Ladd forecasters predicted an overall drop in winds the next day, Christmas Eve. The skies should be about as clear as they ever get in the eastern Alaskan winter.

Ragle walked down the wide stairwell from the second-floor weather office at Hangar 1.

Let's cover as much ground as we can while the weather holds, he told the flight scheduling officer. Sixteen planes were assigned for the Christmas Eve search.

The officer looked up sheepishly.

What is it? asked Ragle.

Well, we're not finding anything so far around Big Delta, sir. You think we should expand the search?

To where? Ragle snapped. We can't be flying blind around Alaska looking for a plane. We have to stick with what we know. And we know they were just east of Big Delta on the last radio call. Schedule the flights the way it was planned. We don't have a lot of time.

Ragle didn't have to state the obvious. If these missions came back empty-handed, hopes of finding survivors would quickly erode. It then becomes more about the duty of finding bodies. No commander—especially outside a war zone—wants to report that a plane was lost without a trace. But the searches cannot go on indefinitely. That's just how it went. At some point—usually less than a week in the winter—the chances that anyone would be alive were too slim to justify keeping planes on full-time search patrol. Aircraft and crew were valuable. They would eventually be diverted to other tasks.

Every bush pilot, Ragle included, knew that. The struggle between the ambitions of aviators and the rigors of the interior Alaska winters had been going on since a barnstorming couple, Lily Martin and her husband, James, shipped a biplane from Seattle for the first flight in Fairbanks in 1913. The grandstands were packed for the debut, a July 4 extravaganza arranged by local merchants. Everything went well and the crowds were wowed. The Martins then shifted into the real reason for the exhibition. They tried to sell the plane to the highest bidder. But there were no takers, despite the appreciative applause as the plane swooped by at forty-five miles per hour. This was all impressive in midsummer. No one, however, believed it was possible to fly once the long winter set in. And besides, who was crazy enough to wing off into the bush on one of those flying machines?

It wasn't until about a decade later that some pioneer pilots gave it a try.

Ragle's parents bestowed him with the regal name Richard Charles, but he was known to nearly everyone in Fairbanks as R. C. or Dick. That suited him fine. He liked the casual, frontier ways of Alaska. He also took well to the demands of backcountry flying, where confidence and caution had to be applied in just the right balance. Too much of either could bring nasty results. This was Ragle's niche at Ladd Field. He was the resident expert on the risks of Alaskan aviation.

Ragle came north with his wife and young son in 1938 after landing a professorship in geology at the University of Alaska in Fairbanks. The campus was then a handful of buildings with one notable work-in-progress landmark: the art deco aeronautics building dedicated to a local flying legend, Carl Ben Eielson, who was anointed the "Arctic Lindbergh" for his 1928 flight over the polar cap. The following year, Eielson and his mechanic were killed while trying to rescue passengers—and a load of valuable furs—from a three-mast schooner, the *Nanuk*, trapped in ice off Siberia. The *Nanuk* survived the winter and was later sold to Metro-Goldwyn-Mayer and used in swashbuckling films such as *Treasure Island*.

Ragle's academic expertise may have been very much earth-bound, but he seemed possessed with the soul of a flier. He was born in Colorado Springs—the future home of the Air Force Academy—and finished his master's degree in the early 1930s while serving with the Army's Flying Cadet Program in Texas. It was an exciting time. Military aviation had left behind the days of fragile biplanes and was racing toward the era of high-performance prop fighters and giant bombers.

Once Ragle climbed into an Army plane for the first time and skimmed over the Texas sagebrush, he never looked back.

For a few summers in Alaska before the war, he ran a civilian pilot training class for university graduates and students. The rules in those days were anything but rigid. Just about anyone who had the white-knuckle nerve could find something to fly—and then confront the sometimes greater challenge of figuring out where to land in a territory with few formal runways. The normal onboard bush-pilot kit included a rake and shovel to help maintain the landing strips, which often were little more than packed snow in a field in the winter or a spit of gravel along a low-running river during the brief summers. But the fliers took the hazards and hassles in stride. They were the costs of doing what they loved. When a member of the first family in early Alaska aviation, Ralph Wien, died in an October 1930 crash near the Bering Sea, the tributes poured in from the seen-it-all fellowship of bush pilots. "He died a man's death," said a letter of condolence from another famous backcountry figure, Sam O. White. "God help me to die as nobly as he did."

Ragle was quick to seek a slice of the growing air-ferry business that was opening up Alaska's interior. He called his company the Trans Alaska Corporation. It was a mighty name for an outfit with just a few secondhand planes and a flight school run out of small buildings on skids known as wanigans. But the timing was impeccable. Pilots were in great demand to service the ever-expanding network of rustic airstrips. Planes were slicing out of the sky in places that often had more sled dogs than people. One route advertised in the *Fairbanks Daily News-Miner* linked Fairbanks and Koyukuk, a Yukon River town about 275 miles to the west. The hardscrabble stops along the way included Stevens Village (population about seventy), the fading gold rush town of Myrtle Creek, and a flyspeck called Wiseman, whose few rugged hangers-on were profiled in a 1930s best seller, *Arctic Village*. A classified notice on the same newspaper page gave more hints of Alaska's diverse needs at the time: *Morrison's has guns, typewriters and vacuum cleaners for rent. 50 cents a day.*

Aviation opened up interior Alaska to the modern world at a breakneck pace. An airstrip, no matter how rocky and gritty, meant access to a previously unimaginable cornucopia. There were mail-order goods, books, clothes, booze, and even just the wonders of sending an ordinary letter. Sometimes people scribbled messages on the outside of the plane for a recipient at the next stop. "No post office fees," said Pete Haggland, curator of the delightfully eclectic Pioneer Air Museum in Fairbanks.

The planes, too, brought links to Alaskan seaports or bigger airfields. And, from there, the rest of the globe. The role of Alaska's bush pilot cannot be overstated. They were—and remain—couriers, counselors, emissaries, guides, and anything else that fits the moment. Once a pilot hauled back a crated polar bear cub and became its temporary nursemaid, feeding the animal hamburger and raw eggs in his backyard before it was shipped south to a zoo. In many ways—big, small, comical, tragic—bush pilots helped create modern Alaska.

Yet the early decades of Alaskan aviation certainly were not for the timid. It was a stage for pilots with nicknames like "Mudhole" Smith and "Big Money" Monsen and planes running the Jacobs Radial L-4 engine, a loud but reliable machine known affectionately as the Shakey Jake. The wooden planes in the 1920s could be blown into mountains or disintegrate in an emergency landing. The sturdier aircraft that followed fared a bit better, but Alaska's weather claimed them at a steady clip.

Ragle became a familiar sight in Fairbanks, dressed in a jumpsuit with his goggles propped atop old leather aviators' headgear. Ragle always kept a comb handy. He paid close attention to his thick straw-colored hair, which topped him like a plush carpet. It would have been easier to crop it off, as did many pilots. He wouldn't hear of it.

He lived close enough to walk to Weeks Field, the crushed-stone strip that served as Fairbanks's main airport. Weeks was a modest affair, but had one grand moment. It was part of the Fairbanks tour by President Warren G. Harding in July 1923 after driving a ceremonial fourteen-carat spike to finish the last stretch of the Alaska Railroad. Harding later fell ill. Two weeks later, he dropped dead—reportedly in the middle of a conversation with his wife in the presidential suite of the Palace Hotel in San Francisco.

On the day of the Pearl Harbor attack, Ragle and his wife heard the news on the radio at home. About the same time, a local radio engineer named Augie Hiebert—who would go on to become a paragon of Alaskan broadcasting—caught the same bulletin from a San Francisco shortwave station. Augie beat the Pentagon's own internal network. He called the commander at Ladd Field, Colonel Dale Gaffney, to give him the world-changing news. "He was sort of a party guy. He had been up the night before," Hiebert recalled. "I got him out of bed, and I asked him, 'Did you know there was a war on, Dale?'"

Ragle's wife, Jane, was too shaken to remember to thaw out the milk delivered to the front porch. The kids were served something like latte Popsicles with dinner that night.

Ragle was soon called back to active duty. His combination of bush-pilot experience and hard-charging optimism won him honored status at Ladd, which was bulldozed out of the taiga and opened in 1940. The base was named for a military flier killed in a South Carolina crash. The choice angered some locals, who wanted it named in honor of a late Army major born on the "outside," but considered a friend to Alaska. Ragle was a newcomer, too, but never seemed to have any problem winning over the locals. Everyone knew if someone at Ladd was lost, it was Ragle, the wing rescue officer, who would oversee the search, set its boundaries, and decide when to call it quits. His reputation was further bolstered by a number of military combat awards and a curious bit of wilderness diplomacy that won him additional accolades.

The summer before the *Iceberg Inez* went down, a strange call came from Nome in early July 1943. The Soviet crew flying a loaned A-20 Havoc fighter-bomber reported that one of the crew members was missing. The plane was okay. The airman was, um, simply gone. It appeared that Lieutenant Constanta P. Demianenko got bounced out of an open hatch somewhere between the central way station of Galena and Nome, the last U.S. jumping-off point for planes heading to Siberia. Less than a week earlier, two A-20s collided in flight along the same route, killing four Soviet airmen.

Ragle joined the search team in a pontoon plane capable of landing on lakes. Right along the flight path, they spotted Demianenko's yellow parachute, which was likely hooked to a static line and deployed when he toppled out. Ragle's plane made a water landing, and Demianenko started to pick his way through the soggy moors. One of the American airmen who got out to help—a grocery store owner from Iowa—sank to his armpits in a bog and later told reporters he expected to be swallowed alive in the muck. "I thought I was a goner," he said, "and, believe me, I was really scared." They eventually pulled aboard the wayward Soviet, who looked like a pincushion from mosquito bites.

Ragle had also seen action in Alaska. This deeply impressed airmen such as Crane, who arrived after the Japanese had been driven from the Aleutians.

The Japanese assault began in Dutch Harbor, the sea gateway to a relatively small but strategic U.S. base far out on the Aleutian archipelago. The inhospitable site was protected by antiaircraft batteries and made livable for soldiers with diversions like Blackie's bar. Whiskey was fifty cents a shot. Blackie's was always so crowded that one veteran noted that "regardless of how drunk we got, there was never enough room in the place to fall down." Tables and chairs were removed because, as many Alaskan saloon owners of the day could attest, the splintered wood could become choice weapons in bar fights. One enterprising sergeant always had a big wad of bills handy to make loans—with interest, of course—for the endless poker games.

U.S. code breakers had intercepted Japanese chatter indicating a probable Dutch Harbor attack. While the intel appeared good, it was widely regarded as a diversionary tactic by Japan to draw away U.S. forces from the main battle looming in the Pacific at the Midway atoll. There was even a good idea about the size of the force Japan could deploy in the Aleutians: possibly two carrier groups. But American combat reinforcements sent north were left at a relative trickle. There simply were other, more pressing, demands in the Pacific theater. And the military infrastructure in the Aleutians was alarmingly basic in many places. Some of the U.S. planes arrived in the Aleutians skidding on a secret airstrip made of interlocking iron sheets. Grass and wildflowers poked through the seams.

Japanese naval forces had already shown they could take aim on U.S. shores. In February 1942, a Japanese sub shelled the Ellwood oil field near Santa Barbara, causing only minimal damage but succeeding in stoking the West Coast paranoia level. It eventually contributed to disgraceful measures such as ordering Japanese Americans into internment camps.

The Dutch Harbor Naval Operating Base was under attack before dawn on June 3, 1942. Japanese air raids took a quick toll. The radio tower and oil storage tanks were destroyed. Among the dead were about twenty-five soldiers killed when bombs blasted their barracks at nearby Fort Mears. The Japanese bombing and strafing runs were so low that American forces later said they could make eye contact with the attacking pilots.

U.S. counterattack options in Alaska were limited. Personnel were scarce. But on hand were the Cold Nose Boys at Ladd Field. They were rapidly mobilized. Ragle found himself as copilot in an old B-17B bomber, an early model of the Flying Fortress. They headed east through broken clouds over the treeless island chain. His family and other military households in Alaska, meanwhile, were ordered to pack up. There were fears the battle could widen to the mainland. Ragle's son and young daughter—the first of his children born in Alaska—headed to Colorado.

At one airstrip along the way, Ragle watched two B-26 Marauders limp back from a close encounter with a Japanese ship. The planes were peppered with holes from Japanese gunners, who had easy target practice in the Aleutian weather. American pilots were forced to make their bombing runs under the cloud ceiling, which pushed as low as 200 feet. It was not only perilous, but pointless. Some U.S. bombs needed a 600-foot fall to trigger. Any lower, and they just bounced off the Japanese destroyers and carriers. A black-humor punch line about flying below the Alaskan cloud cover went like this: "Stick your hand out. If it touches a ship's mast, you're flying too low." The erratic Aleutian weather, meanwhile, also played into Japan's hands for the moment. For several hours, the skies over Dutch Harbor cleared slightly, allowing higher-altitude bombing runs and long strafing passes.

Ragle's plane was fitted with four 1,110-pound armor-piercing bombs as big as refrigerators. Turning toward Dutch Harbor, Ragle and the pilot, First Lieutenant Jack Marks, brought the plane to the edge of the cloud ceiling at about 150 feet—close enough to make out fish in the seabed shallows. Soon, other aircraft began to drop through the clouds. Amazingly, Ragle's plane had meshed into a formation of seven Japanese warplanes heading back to the carrier.

Ragle set the plane's directional gyro to fix the course to the carrier. Then he called for the gunners to open fire.

"But, Lieutenant, I can see their faces," came the reply from one.

"That's a problem?" Ragle barked. "Just fire!"

Suddenly, a group of American P-40 Warhawk fighters poured into the middle of the Japanese formation. The single-seat fighters, just under 32 feet long, dipped and buzzed. The pilot Marks shouted into the radio. There's another American plane here, he yelled. Don't shoot us! The P-40s either got the message or recognized the fellow Yanks. The P-40s let loose with their .50-caliber Browning machine guns, picking off a Japanese plane.

The waist gunner on Ragle's plane lined up his own .50-cal. They were running alongside the long cigar-shaped body of a Nakajima reconnaissance aircraft.

"Got 'em," he roared over the radio. The Nakajima rolled to its side and then dropped into the sea.

A moment later, the pounding bursts of a .50-caliber echoed through the plane.

"We hit?" yelled Marks, already looking down at the sea for a possible place to ditch.

Then came more firing from inside the plane. "What the hell?" cried Ragle. The plane, though, seemed to be fine.

Word then reached the cockpit about what had happened. The waist gunner had noticed a Japanese plane closing from behind. The B-17B had no tail-gun turret. So the sergeant swiveled his .50-caliber back into the plane and stuck his head outside to aim. He opened fire and prayed. The spray blasted more than fifty holes in the tail, but remarkably missed any critical cables or flight systems. Even more astonishing—probably, too, for the Japanese crew on the receiving end of the barrage—was that the shots nailed them. Days later, the sergeant asked sheepishly if his pay would be docked for shooting up his own ship. Instead, he was recommended for officer candidate school for quick thinking in combat.

The Japanese planes peeled away from around Ragle's plane and the P-40s.

Marks and Ragle, however, still had a bead on the Japanese carrier group through the gyro settings. And there they were: the carrier and four other vessels about fifty miles off Dutch Harbor. But the cloud ceiling was far too low for the bombs and their six-hundred-foot minimum trigger. Marks pulled the plane into the clouds to hide while they worked out a plan. It came down to simple geometry, but it could work. They would fix the location of the carrier and then fly for three minutes in the clouds while climbing two hundred feet, take a ninety-degree turn and climb another two hundred feet, and then finish with a third leg. The maneuver should put them in line with the carrier with enough altitude to drop the bombs at two-second intervals.

Ragle checked the instruments at the end of the climb. They were at nine hundred feet; airspeed was ninety miles per hour. If their ambush plan worked, the Japanese warships should be right below. Marks put the plane into a dive. Just before six hundred feet, while still in the clouds, they dropped the bombs.

The first two 1,110-pounders detonated in the sea, kicking up monstrous columns of water. There appeared to be some slight damage to the back deck of the carrier, but far from a decisive blow. The third, and last, bomb had a quicker trigger and exploded above the vessels. As Ragle would later say: "All hell broke loose." The shock wave was strong enough to tip the tail of Ragle's plane in a queasy pirouette. They regained control, but the instruments had gone loopy from the jolt. It was time to get away.

They guessed the direction back to the Aleutians and rode in a cloak of clouds back to Umnak, a garrison island of volcanoes and geysers about midway in the Aleutian chain. Despite the island's awesome landscape, probably the most photographed site was the "Umnak National Forest": a single tree flown in for the enjoyment of a colonel's dog named Skooch.

For five more days, Ragle's B-17B limped around the Aleutians and into the Bering Sea on various search-and-destroy missions, once mistaking a flattop island for a Japanese carrier and later nearly crashing into a cloud-shrouded mountain. They had to pull up so quickly that some bombs broke away from their cradles and smashed shut the bomb-bay doors. There was not even enough downtime to plug the .50-caliber holes, which made the tail section look like a colander. By the time it was clear the bulk of the Japanese fleet was being pulled back from the Dutch Harbor offensive, the crew had a total of six hours of sleep. Meals were two thin sandwiches a day and rainwater dripping off the wings during refueling stops.

On June 11, pilot Marks was too exhausted to keep flying and was left at a base to rest.

I'll catch up with you later, Ragle told Marks. I'll take the ship back toward Anchorage.

Take care, Marks said from his cot. See you soon.

Ragle stopped for refueling on Kodiak Island. There were only a few aircraft at the field. Every plane that could get off the ground was farther down the Aleutians. Ragle's plane—holes and all—was just what the field commander needed. Ragle was put in charge of a slapped-together mission to help a Navy troop transport ship under attack from a Japanese submarine. There was just one hitch. There were no bombs or ammo for Ragle's plane. The munitions depots were emptied over the days of fighting. The only "weapon" on board was a heavy metal tool chest. Ragle cynically figured he could take out a single gun on the surfaced sub with a lucky throw. He decided on a bluff move instead. Ragle lined up the plane as if in a bombing run on the sub. Luckily, it worked. The sub dove and broke off the attack.

But the days of high pressure and little sleep were catching up. Ragle was having a hard time keeping it together. Spells of dizziness were increasing, and he often had to rest his head on the cockpit window until it passed. Back at Kodiak, Ragle collapsed in a bunk for some sleep.

Ragle awoke five days later in a hospital bed. He had fallen unconscious after his temperature sunk to critical levels. The nurse said they didn't think he would make it. Ragle was shipped back to Ladd Field for recovery. It would be ninety days before he was allowed back in a cockpit. During that time, Marks was back in the air. He died days later when his bomber was shot down.

Japanese amphibious forces, meanwhile, had staked out smaller targets while the Dutch Harbor battles raged, seizing control of two lightly defended Aleutian sites, Attu and Kiska. On Attu—near the western tip of the chain and closer to Sapporo than Anchorage—more than one thousand Japanese soldiers stormed a settlement with fewer than fifty people. One resident was killed, and the rest were sent to a prison camp in Japan. Attu schoolteacher Etta Jones said they passed the time sewing little silk bags for the religious items carried by Japanese soldiers. About a third of the Attu detainees died in Japanese camps. On Kiska, about two hundred miles toward the Alaskan mainland, a Japanese force of about five hundred marines came ashore and overran a U.S. Navy weather station with ten men and a dog. One soldier in the weather detachment managed to escape and survived fifty days roaming the island's back hills, eating grass, plants, and earthworms until starvation forced him to surrender. He weighed eighty pounds.

The Japanese held Attu for nearly a year, while the Americans waited until spring to stage a counterattack. They even told the Japanese it was coming. Japanese-language leaflets were dropped on the Aleutians during the long winter. They were among the most deviously creative attempts at mind games from the Army's Psychological Warfare Teams—and this time with unusual consulting help from the Brooklyn Botanic Garden. The messages were shaped like the brown leaf of a kiri tree. It's a powerful symbol of loss and regret for the Japanese. In the famous Japanese play *The Kiri Leaf Falls,* a fluttering leaf represents the end of the power-grab ambitions of the play's central characters. "The Kiri leaf falls," the U.S. message read. "Its fall is the ill omen of the inevitable downfall of militarism. With the fall of one Kiri leaf comes sadness and bad luck. Before spring comes again the raining bombs of America, just like Kiri leaves fluttering to the ground, will bring bad fate and misfortune."

It did little to shake the Japanese. More than two thousand Japanese troops were defending Attu when U.S. forces began a counteroffensive in May 1943. With little natural cover, the two sides were largely exposed to whatever was thrown at them. The Japanese, however, couldn't hold out indefinitely without fresh supplies. In the end, with defeat only a matter of time, Japanese soldiers raced at the American lines in banzai suicide charges. A U.S. Army photo shows the bodies of Imperial Army soldiers piled atop each other—mowed down in formation by U.S. fire—on an open stretch of crowberry and sedge. Only a few dozen Japanese occupiers were still alive to surrender after weeks of fighting. On Kiska, meanwhile, the Japanese force slipped away under cover of fog without a fight.

Back in the Ladd Field weather room, Ragle took the charts and ran his finger over the known course of the B-24.

The exchange with the flight scheduling officer had him thinking. The officer was right in one sense, of course. It was futile to keep looking in the same area for the plane. But it also was a foolhardy strategy to have the searchers winging off in random directions.

Ragle scanned the map. A spine of mountains runs to the east of Big Delta. The Charley River is on the other side. Ragle wondered if the *Iceberg Inez* could have veered off that way. Maybe. But it was too risky to send planes over in questionable weather. One crew lost was enough. Let's not compound it. More often than most, Ragle faced the quandary of rescue leaders anywhere: how to balance the scope of a search against the risks for the searchers. There's one fundamental rule: don't turn one tragedy into potentially two.

No, thought Ragle, the search will continue in the Big Delta area. Maybe if the weather predictions are accurate, they can use the greater visibility to expand the search perimeter in the coming days. But he also knew what it meant as the "results negative" reports piled up. It was becoming a total crapshoot.

We're looking for a bit of luck now, he told the crews at Ladd. We need it.

Ragle knew what he was talking about. Finding wrecks, as well as possible survivors, is not easy even when searchers know where to look.

With Crane's B-24, they didn't even have that. But Ragle tried to stay upbeat. The B-24 is a big target. The wing area alone is almost 1,050 square feet. That's more than some two-bedroom apartments. The glass turrets in the nose, tail, and top can glint sunlight as well as any signaling instrument.

Ragle filled out the flight roster for the Christmas Eve search missions. All were still directed toward Big Delta. Ragle looked it over again. He then crossed out one route and redirected it north, the opposite direction from Big Delta.

It was against his instincts to send a plane on a long shot, but time was fading and the Big Delta runs were bringing back nothing. Ragle assigned Lieutenant Arthur Jordan, an airman from Maine, to head toward Fort Yukon. The winds were coming from the southeast the day of the crash. Maybe, Ragle guessed, the B-24 was pushed toward the Yukon.

"A desolate, God-forsaken part of the world," Jordan later wrote in his diary after returning from the December 24 run. "We were able to see very well. Most of our area was clear. It was cold up there, flying close to the ground and straining our eyes for any glimpse of distress signals or wreckage.

"The job is beginning to look hopeless now. I think the ship either blew up for some reason or rammed into a mountain trying to get below the overcast. Went to midnight Mass tonight. There was a big attendance."

In Washington, it was nearly sunrise on Christmas Day. The newspapers carried accounts and analysis of the president's third yuletide address since Pearl Harbor. This time, Roosevelt wanted to reach beyond the morality play of freedom versus tyranny and remind Americans of tangible gains on the battlefield. The year 1943 saw some Allied setbacks. German U-boats also continued to menace Atlantic shipping routes. But there were strategic Allied gains in Sicily and North Africa and on the Russian front. In February on the Pacific island of Guadalcanal, the last Japanese units abandoned their posts after six months of battles against U.S.-led forces on beaches and in jungles. In August, north of Bucharest, refineries were blasted by B-24s flown out of Libya in a bold mission that degraded some of Germany's oil lifeline, but Axis gunners were waiting and American losses were heavy.

As Ragle plotted the search for Crane and his crewmates, British Lancaster bombers—the Manchester-built cousin of the B-24—were leading another raid on Berlin.

"But on Christmas Eve this year, I can say to you that, at last, we may look forward into the future with real, substantial confidence that, however great the cost, peace on earth, goodwill toward men can be and will be realized and ensured," Roosevelt said in his radio address, reaching Ladd Field via Fairbanks's KFAR radio. "This year I can say that. Last year, I could not do more than express a hope."

"American boys are fighting today in snow-covered mountains, in malarial jungles, on blazing deserts," he said near the end of the address. "They are fighting on the far stretches of the sea and above the clouds, and fighting for the thing for which they struggle."

That night in the Yukon, Crane watched the purple and green ribbons of the aurora dance through the breaks in the clouds.

FOUR

JUNE 23, 1994

Yukon–Charley Rivers National Preserve

A helicopter banked over the Charley River valley in late June 1994. From this height, the water glistened silver-gray among the spruce and birch.

"There it is," said the pilot, maneuvering the chopper closer to a hillside about 120 miles due east of Fairbanks.

Below, shining in the same metallic hues as the river, was the resting place of the B-24D, whose paint had been burned away by the fire in the crash. Decades of subarctic weather scrubbed away whatever was left, leaving only the gleaming raw steel and other metal. The wreckage spilled over slabs of granite, ancient greenstone, and quartz-laced shards churned up by the same tectonic forces that formed Alaska's ranges and drained away teeming Jurassic seas.

The nose of the *Iceberg Inez* and its two inner engines were shattered and scattered as if lopped off with a giant hammer. Other parts of the wings, incredibly, withstood the impact. Some of the wing lines were as sharp and clean as the day the plane left Ladd Field. But two huge spaces—like missing teeth in a smile—were gouged out from the wings when the outer engines ripped away. The steel propeller blades, dinged and scarred from slicing into the rocks, stood like sentinels on the edge of the debris field.

Portions of the bomber's internal frame jutted from the twisted and folded metal.

It all spoke of details that Crane couldn't have seen as he watched the plane pinwheel into the snow. The B-24 apparently struck nose first. The force sheared away everything down to the wings. But the *Iceberg Inez* must have been falling flat enough to avoid disintegrating the rear sections and was likely skidding to a stop when fire swallowed the entire wreckage.

The prop specialist, Sibert, was farthest back in the plane. He could have had a minuscule chance of surviving the crash, but apparently had no way to get out. He could well have perished as the flames spread during the plane's plummet. The space where Crane last saw Hoskin struggling with his chute was obliterated. If he didn't bail out, then he was certainly killed when it struck the hillside.

The starboard wing, the side where Crane sat, pointed downhill toward the river. Over the decades, a few trees sprouted around the crumpled fuselage.

From the helicopter, local National Park Service historian Douglas Beckstead pressed his face to the glass. He had, of course, heard about the crash site as he researched the rich lore of the wilderness preserve, which covers the entire Charley basin and a portion of the much bigger Yukon River, stretching to the Canadian border. The region has been home to prehistoric nomads hunting caribou, Native tribes hunting for fishing grounds, and prospectors hunting gold. And one crash site where an iconic bomber from World War II dropped from the sky.

War is always a negative-sum outcome. It subtracts, removes, empties. No one who has witnessed combat can, with any honesty, describe it another way. "We know more about war than we know about peace," said five-star general Omar Bradley in an Armistice Day address a few years after the end of World War II, "more about killing than we know about living." Think of it like this. For every soldier's grave in places such as Arlington or Anzio or Normandy, there are more forgotten burial sites for civilians—parents, children, newlyweds, and newborns—claimed in some way by the same fighting.

Digital-age warriors can tap the precision of microchips and lasers to try to pinpoint attacks. But old-style firepower—with wide and random killing range—still occupies arsenals around the world and will be there for a long time: missiles, mortar rounds, artillery, and bombs for air strikes. Combatants die and suffer. So do people caught in the middle. No euphemisms—such as counting civilian casualties as "collateral damage"—can cloud this fact. Another phrase coined from the battlefield describes a nation's fighting forces as its war machine. This one is on point. The science of warfare is, at its core, about finding ways to build new tools to scare, shock, and raze.

Never have the world's industrial giants been more focused on that task than during World War II. Japanese powerhouse Mitsubishi produced the feared Zero fighters; Kawasaki developed a light bomber that later was converted to the infamous kamikaze craft near the end of the war. Germany's Krupp manufacturing dynasty built U-boats. The United Kingdom responded by cranking out more sub-hunting Corvette escort ships from the Harland and Wolff shipyards.

Nothing, though, compared with the wartime audacity of the B-24.

It literally cast a huge shadow. The hulking, fearsome glass-nosed bomber came to exemplify the American war effort as much as buying bonds or collecting scrap metal. Airpower had redefined conflict in the short decades since the first gun was bolted onto a plane. Control of the skies quickly became as important in the overall strategy as holding a line or capturing a hill. World War II made every military look skyward. America's government vaults were thrown open to keep pace. Suddenly, there was a generation of airmen to train and new fleets of planes to build. No expense seemed too high, no plan too outrageous. The B-24 literally rode into the skies on this spirit of urgency.

In the popular mind, meanwhile, the plane became indelibly linked to the blitz of wartime propaganda. Homespun actor Jimmy Stewart flew missions in Europe in one. The always-suave Clark

Gable, then a first lieutenant, posed for publicity photos aboard a B-24 while on military assignment in England, making Army combat films with a B-17 squadron. But perhaps the biggest feel-good bonanza was a fictional character, Rosie the Riveter, the archetype of the bandanna-clad woman doing her part to build fighting machines for the men on the front. The song "Rosie the Riveter" became a hit in 1942, and Crane and his crewmates certainly knew the words:

> Keeps a sharp lookout for sabotage
> Sitting up there on the fuselage
> That little frail can do more than a male can do
> Rosie, brrrrrrrrrrr, the riveter

The precise origins of Rosie are blurry. Some believe it was based on a woman from a California factory line. Others think a Canadian gal was the inspiration. In May 1943, Norman Rockwell came up with his own vision: a muscled-up Rosie for the *Saturday Evening Post* with a rivet gun on her lap and her penny loafers resting on a copy of *Mein Kampf*.

But the American government—hand in hand with Hollywood—wanted to cast the *right* Rosie for a short inspirational film. Scouts blanketed the country. On the list was Michigan's Willow Run Aircraft Factory, built by the Ford Motor Company specifically for the B-24. The eighty-acre assembly-line floor was pumping out B-24s at a furious pace and with some novel innovations. Flight crews slept on factory cots so they could get airborne within hours of the last bolts being tightened. A team of midgets—as they were called then—was put to work crawling into tight spaces to buck some of the plane's more than 313,000 rivets. Women were part of every step of the B-24 construction. For those who had doubts about factory work, wartime film clips tried to sell the idea that it was well suited for a female touch. "The rivets are but the buttons of a bomber," said one pitch.

Somewhere on the factory floor in Willow Run, the movie talent scouts came across Kentucky-born Rose Will Monroe—auburn hair and plump cheeks—who became the indefatigable Rosie and the face of the home front in a morale-boosting clip seen by millions.

But Crane, the aeronautics engineer, was likely far more impressed by another B-24 backstory. This one involves a genius in aviation design, who remains a largely unheralded hero in how the war was waged on drafting tables, wind tunnels, and test sites.

Isaac Machlin Laddon—known as I. M. or Mac to everyone, including the U.S. Patent Office—joined the U.S. military's experimental aviation division in Ohio in 1917, just fourteen years after the Wright brothers skimmed over the sands at Kitty Hawk. For the young I. M. Laddon, fresh out of Montreal's McGill University by way of New Jersey, the cutting-edge aircraft at the time were models such as Boeing's CL-4S biplane, whose 100-horsepower engine was capable of just over seventy miles per hour. Quickly, however, Laddon was among the handful of Roaring Twenties engineers—in age and era—pushing the boundaries of what could get off the runway.

In 1922 he helped design the first all-metal plane. Patents bearing his name marked new steps in aeronautics: enhanced braking systems and more reliable landing gear. Laddon's improvements continued with the "flying boat" that would evolve into the storied PBY Catalina, a fat-bellied craft that was used in World War II in all-purpose roles, including rescues, reconnaissance, and attacks. In the Atlantic, a Catalina flown by the Royal Air Force reported the location of the German battleship *Bismarck* before it was sunk the following day. In the Pacific, Catalinas painted the color of airstrip tar conducted nighttime "Black Cat" raids on Japanese ships.

Just as the Catalina design was getting its final touches, Laddon was working on another project at the San Diego headquarters of the Consolidated Aircraft Corporation, one of the first major industrial-military marriages of the aviation age. Laddon's team was asked to muscle up a companion for the B-17 Flying Fortress, whose development in the 1930s rewrote the book on aerial warfare. The goal was a new bomber capable of longer range, bigger payloads, higher speed, and more defensive guns bristling out from the nose, center, and tail. Oh, and did we mention that it all needs to get done in a matter of months?

One breakthrough was already in the bag. It came via the sheer chutzpah of an aeronautical engineer, David R. Davis.

To anyone who would listen in the late 1930s, Davis was peddling his new wing design. It was basically a longer and more tapered shape that, he boasted, would give less drag and greater lift. But this was still the Depression. Who had the cash, or the gumption, to take a chance on an untested design? The answer, of course, was just about no one. The more Davis faced rejection, the clearer it became what he had to do: somehow finagle a meeting with Consolidated. Its owner, the aviator-turned-tycoon Reuben Fleet, had the right combination of deep pockets and soaring ego to try to get one over on his rivals. After all, he seemed to like a challenge. In 1918 Fleet managed to cobble together the country's first airmail service between New York and Washington after a series of embarrassing false starts, including planes running out of fuel in midflight and leaking tanks that had to be patched with corks.

Davis managed to set up a meeting with Laddon and Fleet. It took place in Fleet's office, which oozed confidence with its hardwoods and leather. Fleet tried hard to embody his signature slogan: "Nothing short of right is right," which was painted in huge letters outside the company's Plant No. 1. This was Davis's moment. He had to sway Fleet and show that his wing design was *right*.

Davis made his pitch to incorporate his wing into the Catalina. Fleet's reply: Interesting, but no thanks. Not so quick, advised Laddon. He was still intrigued. He persuaded Fleet to give the wing a test in the Caltech wind tunnel. It delivered everything Davis promised in a slimmed-down style that was longer in length than the B-17 but with less overall wing space. Laddon was a believer. So was the Army, after reviewing tests on planes refitted with the Davis wing.

The Army contract with Consolidated was awarded in March 1939. Before the end of the year, the prototype B-24 Liberator made its first flight with the new Davis wing. In between was Germany's invasion of Poland. The United States was still officially a neutral party in the widening war, but it was not lost on anyone that Washington could be forced, someday soon, to make a choice. The timing was right for a companion to the B-17. Laddon's plane, though, still had some serious growing pains. The first batches of the B-24, sold to Britain in 1941, were too vulnerable in the flak-filled skies in Europe. The performance of the Davis wing degraded quickly once it started to sustain damage. Also, the B-24 lacked self-sealing fuel tanks. It was like painting a bull's-eye for the Luft-waffe aces. The Royal Air Force shifted the early B-24s to maritime patrols. Laddon and his team got to work on doctoring the design.

But there wasn't much they could do at this point about how the B-24 responded once off the ground. The overall shape of the plane—especially its Davis wing and the rear stabilizers that stuck up like twin billboards—gave added lift. The price was that it simply didn't cut through the skies as elegantly as the B-17. It took muscle to keep the B-24 Liberators in line. It was said there was an easy way to spot a B-24 pilot: his bulked-up left arm, which got a workout steering the plane while his right arm dealt with throttles and other levers. Aircrews quickly cooked up other colorful jabs for the boxy Lib: the flying brick, the pregnant cow. The nicknames came from both the B-24 crews that liked the slightly underdog image of the new bomber and the B-17 flyboys who wanted nothing to do with it. One quip went that the B-24 pilots had to fly the crates that the B-17s were shipped in.

Such talk only deepened the loyalty among many B-24 crews. "There were lots of jokes about the B-24," said a radio operator, Bill Gros, who flew it in combat missions in Europe and as a sub hunter in the Atlantic. "But I had a lot of faith in that airplane."

The B-24 also was unmatched on the assembly line. Its success can be expressed in one stunning number: more than eighteen thousand variants of the B-24 were produced from 1941 until September 1945 in San Diego, Willow Run, and plants in Texas and Oklahoma. That's about 315 a month on average. Or more than 10 a day.

On that June day in 1994, Beckstead was getting his first look at the B-24 wreckage, but certainly not of a downed plane.

A plane wreck in the Alaskan wilderness is sadly common. The B-24 is just one of hundreds of mangled airplanes dotting Alaska.

Pilots need no additional reminders of the perils of their home skies. But the fallen planes serve as sobering points of reference in the same manner of shipwreck notations that dot mariners' charts. Some of the crashes even carry a kind of stark beauty. Bush pilots heading north out of Fairbanks often snap photos of a nearly intact Cessna T50 floatplane. Its wooden skin has been weathered away since a forced landing near Fort Yukon in the 1960s. What's left are its internal frame and struts. From the sky, it resembles a delicate silver fish in a muskeg sea.

But for Beckstead, whose job was to research the Yukon–Charley Rivers National Preserve, the B-24 was much more than a wartime scrap heap. The wreckage would become a personal mission. It was the biggest crash site within the preserve's borders and, without doubt, had the best story attached. Beckstead combed military and civilian records. He also began developing his own theories behind the crash. Over the years, he would amass boxes of notes and documents and twenty-five hundred photographs. He once boasted that he got to know every rivet and piece of wrenched metal.

But before all this, there had to be formal introduction between Beckstead and the wreckage. It took place in 1994 after he escorted archaeologists to the preserve. Beckstead had dropped them off and was flying alone with the pilot. Beckstead had heard of the B-24 crash site, but knew little more. He asked the pilot if he knew the location.

"Sure," he said. "Want me to stop?"

Beckstead, a barrel-chested man with a carefully trimmed beard and wire-rim glasses, wandered amid the shattered B-24 and the jetsam in front for about an hour. He came across some personal items: spoons, a tin can, the rubber sole from a boot that inexplicably escaped the flames.

As the helicopter lifted off, Beckstead looked down again. He no longer saw just a spray of war-era relics. He was surveying a patch of wilderness he knew would draw him back. What he didn't know yet was how his obsession would change the lives of a family on the other side of the continent.

FIVE

DECEMBER 25, 1943

Charley River

Hunger can be an unpredictable companion.

At times, it gripped Crane with angry, clawing need. That usually hit hardest just after he woke, when he pulled away the parachute and felt that first full slap of cold. Small scoops of snow helped a little, but did almost nothing to curb his thirst. Crane had quickly learned one of the monstrous ironies of the Far North. The seemingly inexhaustible supply of water is an illusion. It takes huge amounts of powdered snow—melted or warmed into slush—to satisfy thirst. Even so, Crane didn't have a pan. He was left to paw at the ring of watery snow on the edge of his fire.

Only in the most desperate times will Natives of the northern tribes turn to eating snow. Gobbling down too much snow can actually increase thirst by inflaming the mouth's mucous membrane and irritating the tongue. It can also bring on cramps and accelerate hypothermia. Thirst is wretched, but trying to satisfy it with huge servings of raw snow can make it even worse.

Crane knew enough to lap at whatever river water seeped through the ice. Still, he found it rather surprising how the hard wiring of the body could be fooled even as he drifted into the first stages of starvation. He would imagine a milkshake, one of his favorite indulgences. Somehow, he could coax his taste buds into the same fantasy. A drop of snow, for just a few seconds anyway, tasted faintly like the shakes back at Ladd.

Other times, for reasons he couldn't quite grasp, the hunger faded to almost nothing. Crane, in fact, would feel fine, even weirdly energized. During these surges, he busied himself. He built another SOS in spruce branches on the river—being careful to keep his hands exposed for only seconds at a time—and arranged a more permanent camp under the trees. He thickened his mattress of flattened boughs and replenished his supply of driftwood until it was waist high.

In biological terms, Crane was experiencing eons of evolution. It's an acknowledgment of the importance of mind over matter for the human species. Our long-ago ancestors seemed a rather pathetic lot as hunters at first glance. They couldn't come close to matching the speed or stealth of most of their prey or competitors for food. What they did have on their side was ingenuity. Basically, they developed the ability to outwit the wilds. So when the flow of calories stops, a distinctive survival mechanism kicks in. It puts the brain near the front of the line for the body's glucose reserves and proteins while, at the same time, shifting the gray matter into energy-saving mode. The formula seeks to keep a person's mental state as sharp as possible for as long as possible. A starving person's best tool, nature is saying, is their head.

Still, the clock was ticking for Crane.

An American study conducted in the early 1960s on the effect of semistarvation was not pretty. The tests were, in fact, very similar to Crane's predicament stranded near a river: ample water, but no food. Participants shed a daily average of nearly three pounds at the beginning. Blood volume decreased. So did blood plasma, red blood cells, and serum electrolytes, which influence a range of processes, including blood acidity and muscle function. Before a week is out without food, the body is typically breaking down muscle protein to keep vital organs going. Cramps begin as body salt levels drop. By the tenth day of the study, the researchers described a group of healthy men leveled to "very poor condition." The most troubling signs were that their minds were moving toward surrender. Memory became spotty. There was a general apathy toward any kind of taxing mental or physical acts. The men were thrown into a sort of hunger-induced stupor.

And this was in a lab setting. Calorie burn is increased by cold weather and, obviously, by activity. Crane had the natural energy of a fit young man. But a bit of pudginess could have helped him about now. Fat is the main calorie source when food intake stops. Crane likely didn't know it, but his slim physique—an advantage in most settings—was a liability here.

Time, too, started to toy with Crane. The scant daylight hours seemed to fly by. Just taking fifteen minutes to scan the skies for a rescue plane was a considerable chunk of the winter day. The nights, on the other hand, felt endless and bled together in ways that already made it difficult for Crane to keep track of how long since the crash.

He counted each dawn. Was it four? Yes, that's right. Well, that made today Christmas.

The holiday passed without too much special notice at home when he was a boy. His parents held tight to the Jewish traditions of the Old World even as they embraced nearly everything else about American life. Christmas, they told Leon and his siblings, was for the Christians. Let them have it. We have our own holidays. The cycle of the Judaic calendar—Hanukkah, Purim, Rosh Hashanah, and so on—was observed fully in the Crane household. Keeping the connection was important to Crane's parents, even if they gave some slack with Yiddish, allowing their children to get by with just a smattering. The kids didn't resist their parents' wishes. Yet they also couldn't ignore the overwhelming salesmanship of yuletide in the land where they were born. Like many of his Jewish friends, Leon didn't advertise his religious roots. It didn't seem necessary to try to carve out a separate identity in West Philadelphia. The neighborhood itself was their touchstone. You didn't just live in West Philly. You were *from* West Philly. Besides, Crane liked to look forward, not back. The equations and physics in an engineering textbook held far more interest than the parables of the Torah. One neighbor didn't even know Crane's family was Jewish. He was puzzled why the Cranes would go to *church* on Saturday.

The first night of Hanukkah was Crane's first night alone in the wilderness. At Ladd Field, a small menorah was lit in a corner of the chapel. Crews were still building a multidenominational center. It was intended for all faiths, but nevertheless looked a lot like a chapel at home overlooking a classic New England common. Some Jewish soldiers at Ladd headed into Fairbanks to join Hanukkah events at the home of Robert Bloom, a Lithuanian shopkeeper who reached Fairbanks via Ireland. Bloom, along with his wife, Jessie, became an anchor of the town's Jewish community. But Crane had been more involved in the preparations for the turkey and trimmings that would be served for Christmas. He had helped fly in some of the birds on runs to Anchorage.

The Thanksgiving menu at Ladd was lavish. Christmas might just beat it. A diary entry from a Ladd airman described a Thanksgiving feast in loving detail: *olives, vegetable salad, Thousand Island dressing, celery hearts, mixed sweet pickles, shrimp cocktail, chicken soup, roast turkey, giblet gravy, chestnut stuffing, mashed potatoes, peas, yams, cauliflower in cream, corn on the cob, rolls, hot mince pie, pumpkin pie with whipped cream, plum pudding with brandy sauce, fruit cake, grapes, apples, oranges, salted nuts, mints, coffee, tea.*

Crane knew he must figure out, and very soon, how to find something to eat. He couldn't undertake any kind of serious expedition along the river with just its water to sustain him. A tough overland hike can burn six thousand calories a day. Walking in the snow, in deadly cold, would demand more. A few days of that and he would simply collapse.

The rub was that he wouldn't know whether someone was near unless he set off to look.

He had no map, no firm idea where he was, and only a guess on the name of the river. He assumed it was the Charley, based on their flight time from Big Delta and the fact that the river ran north. Many other rivers carved through the hills, but not all ran northward. On the western side of the uplands, they flowed back toward the Tanana. To the east, others wandered off in that direction to meet the Yukon on the Canadian portion of its long run. So if this was the Charley, Crane knew just one certainty: he was somewhere south of the Yukon River.

Don't get sidetracked, he told himself. Keep sharp. Stay on the problems you can address. There has to be a key to surviving here. He ran though the list. Fishing was impossible in winter. Hunting was doubtful. What could he bring down with only a pen knife? Okay, anything else? The military manuals gave this advice: you can consume anything green that animals eat as long as it doesn't have an intensely bitter taste.

He'd seen plenty of red squirrels, one of the few animals that do not migrate or retreat into hibernation during the interior Alaskan winter. But Crane couldn't be sure whether the little squirrels were foraging for new food or eating whatever they gathered before the freeze. There were clumps of moss poking out from under the snow. This was worth a shot. Crane hacked away with a branch until he reached the frozen ground. He ripped up a cold, spongy handful. Just prying it loose felt like needles piercing his frozen fingertips. He jammed a wad into this mouth. The taste wasn't awful, at least. In fact, it had almost no taste at all. It just sat in a soggy lump no matter how much he chewed, something like an earthy paste. He managed to swallow a little, but it stuck in his throat. He gagged and tried to wash it down with snow. Clearly, this was not the answer.

He thought again about the squirrels.

They were a constant presence. The animals were fearless. Crane might well have been the first human they had come across. They flitted down the spruce branches to investigate the fire and gaze with their black-marble eyes. Their curiosity could be my meal ticket, Crane reasoned. A plan began to hatch. He turned to inspect the driftwood. He picked out a sturdy arm-size piece that made a nice club. Crane walked beneath the trees and waited for the snowy branches to stir.

One squirrel came into view. It dropped down a few more feet. Then a few more. It was now so close he could make out the details of its ruddy coat and its tiny claws grasping the branch. In Crane's right hand—throbbing from the cold—was the driftwood bat. Closer, Crane silently willed the squirrel. Just a little closer. He swung. But the squirrel's hair-trigger reflexes were too fast. He was already bolting up the tree before the club hit the branch. Frustrated, Crane tossed it away. There was no way he could swipe a squirrel off the branches. Crane wrapped himself in his parachute, slumped near the fire, and dozed off to try to forget the hunger.

He awoke with a start. Another idea hit him.

He decided the trick was more power and a greater element of surprise. His engineer training also offered up a maxim: if the right tool doesn't exist, design it. Crane broke off the straightest branch he could find among the driftwood. This could make a spear, he thought. Crane took his Boy Scout knife and began whittling down a point. He dipped it into the coals of the fire to char and harden the wood. The spear point probably wasn't sharp enough to skewer the little animals, which chatter away with a *churr-churr* call when frightened. But the spear could certainly wound a squirrel and maybe leave it writhing in the snow long enough for Crane to pounce. The squirrels were still leaping around the lower branches, maybe ten feet above the ground. He took aim.

He missed by a foot. The spear flew wobbly and slow. The squirrels barely flinched.

Maybe a sneak attack is better, Crane figured. He pressed himself close to the tree trunk and waited until a squirrel was on the lowest branch, which was close enough to reach the animal in one thrust. Wait. *Wait.* A squirrel moved a little closer. *Now.* The jab was on target, but struck the branch right under the squirrel, sending it rocketing up the tree. That wasn't too bad, Crane thought. He had come close. This could work. He waited again until another squirrel came within his killing zone. Another thrust. This time, it was just to the side of the creature. Crane kept at it until the light began to wane. He never managed to even graze his prey. In the concentration of the hunt, however, he lost track of how long his hands were exposed. Crane knew he couldn't keep this up without risking more serious frostbite.

What else?

Crane looked over his parachute. He couldn't hack away at it too much. The wrap he fashioned every night was one of the reasons he was still alive. But there were rubberized cords that had no role in keeping him warm. Crane tossed some more wood onto the fire and got to work. The spear would become a bow and arrow. Crane slashed off a four-foot length of parachute cord and tied it around notches in each end of the spear. It was taut and gave a weak twang when plucked. Step one. For arrows, he trimmed down two sticks and made cuts in the end to affix spruce needles in place of feathers. He gave it a test. The arrow lobbed harmlessly about twenty feet and skidded on the snow. Ridiculous, Crane cursed. What am I thinking? He didn't even attempt to shoot at the squirrels, which were now eerie little chiaroscuro figures flashing between the yellow light of the fire and the complete darkness.

It was five o'clock on Christmas Day at north latitude sixty-four degrees, forty-nine minutes.

Crane's breath came in puffs of frozen vapor. The temperature was minus twenty and dropping. The frustration of the day was building. For the first time, Crane felt a genuine panic rising. Idea after idea had failed miserably.

The chattering of the squirrels now seemed to him maddening, mocking. He cut away a short strand of the parachute cord attached to the harness. A sling shot might do it. He made them as a kid and had his share of broken windows to show for it. This had a shot. Crane loaded the contraption with frigid rocks of just enough weight. It might stun a squirrel long enough for Crane to dispatch it with his knife or wring its neck. He pulled back the cord. Even his modest effort seemed to test the limits for his sluggish fingers. The pebbles flew toward their mark, but no faster than a gentle toss. There just wasn't enough recoil in the cord.

Damn it! Crane was panting. Suddenly, the Alaskan Yukon seemed to be closing in.

He raged in return. He was beyond caring. Crane grabbed rocks as big as baseballs with his bare hands and started hurling them at the animals. You little bastards, he yelled. Go to hell. He screamed as loud as he could, from a place inside that was deep and primitive. Days of fear and fatigue and frustration poured out. Crane, the man who dropped from the sky, shouted back at the heavens—in fury, in helplessness, in a primal act of submission to nature as the life giver and, now it seemed, the life taker.

Just as quickly as his unwinding occurred, Crane stopped. Get a grip. Don't be a fool, he told himself. You are just wasting energy. He slumped into his bed of spruce branches and tossed fresh wood on the fire. It would burn for several hours. Crane wrapped himself in the parachute. Above, steel-sharp stars dotted a sky awash with the pale purple gossamer of the northern lights.

Crane slept, feeling beaten and truly lost for the first time. Instead, the opposite was true.

He just wasn't aware of it yet.

It's not an easy concept to translate. But, like many things of deep substance, it can be understood without many words. It just is.

For the Native tribes along the Charley and surrounding rivers, it's part of their ancient codes in a place where life is a fragile bargain in the best of times. In their world, nature rewards. It also punishes. To mock it—with greed, insincerity, arrogance, or any number of human failings—was to guarantee an unpleasant sting in return. It might not come right away. But it will come. The clans of the Athabascan people, cast across the Yukon basin and beyond like seeds in reluctant soil, built their beliefs around the most towering truth they knew: the spirits of all things, from man to minnow, are bound in a chain of *yega,* or souls, going back to a time when all creatures spoke a common language and understood each other fully.

There are many ways to stumble. Animal spirits are displeased by a hunter not utilizing an entire carcass. Water spirits are angered when someone takes more fish than they need from the rivers. The payback comes later. The spirits might make the caribou herds disappear or the salmon stay away from the nets, and the winter will be heavy with hunger. To abuse the land with needless fire or reckless tree chopping might also close the door to the Athabascan afterlife, which some imagine as a place so plentiful and joyous that the flowers trill sweet songs.

The Athabascan world, however, is not just about dread. Like most faiths, the righteous have the last laugh. One often-told story begins with an Athabascan man who lives in full harmony with nature. As a reward, the spirits bestow him with a dream: a moose sitting on a particular spot where he hunted. The next day, the animal was there waiting for him and his weapon.

Learn to listen to the wilds, the Natives say, because it is always listening and judging you.

"You just can't go out and kill a bear and let it rot, you know," an elder from the Alaskan town of Beaver told researchers compiling a 2012 study on Athabascan culture. "It will be no good and you could feel bad about it. . . . Some of it you give back to the land. Some to the water, set some aside for the wolf, and the camp robber [gray jay]. . . . Put some back in the river, even just a little piece of fat in that water."

It's a lesson told in endless variations, including some much closer to Crane's home and traditions.

The nature philosophers of the nineteenth century looked for answers in places beyond the touch of man—even as the industrial age was selling the idea that a better future was being forged on factory lines and inside inventors' workshops. Nature's rhythms and continuity, the transcendentalists believed, are reminders of the humility we must retain and the innocence we cannot let slip away. "Nature grows over me . . . and I have died out of the human world," wrote one of the guiding lights of the transcendental movement, Boston-born essayist and lecturer Ralph Waldo Emerson, in his journal kept while contemplating the New England woods, "and come to feel a strange, cold, aqueous, terraqueous, aerial, ethereal sympathy and existence."

Emerson lived in a time when the world was shrinking at an astonishing pace. The dots and dashes of the telegraph had killed off the pony express. Railroads made it possible to have breakfast in Manhattan's Gramercy Park and dinner in Rittenhouse Square in Philadelphia. Whaling ships set off from New Bedford and other ports on yearlong voyages into the Pacific and far-flung seas. Other vessels headed north, their hulls reinforced with foot after foot of oak planks and captained by explorers and mercenaries driven by the promise of glory.

Their goal was the Northwest Passage linking the Atlantic and Pacific. But even for the fast-expanding nineteenth-century mind in Europe and America, the truly Far North was still an other-worldly place of mystery and fantasy. In salons, lecture halls, and universities, there was boundless speculation about what lay at the top of the world. Some believed the ice floes of the Arctic were like sentinels encircling a temperate North Pole sea. Other theories sounded more at home in the Dark Ages. They spoke of worlds within a world. Some self-appointed "experts" packed auditoriums with crowds eager to hear musings about the hollow earth. The pole, they claimed, opened into passageways, leading to a verdant Eden lit by a subterranean luminous sky—which sometimes spilled out into our outer world in the form of the aurora borealis.

Yet the crackpots and their critics were linked by one undeniable element. The Far North is truly as unforgiving as the deep desert or high peaks. It offers no pity to those who fail to understand it. Emerson, even from his comfortable Boston-centric world, recognized the dangerous arrogance of those who thought they could simply bully their way through the world's harshest corners. "Nature is a language," Emerson told audiences, "and every new fact one learns is a new word; but it is not a language taken to pieces and dead in the dictionary, but the language put together into a most significant and universal sense. I wish to learn this language, not that I may know a new grammar, but that I may read the great book that is written in that tongue."

This reality was sinking in, too, for Crane bit by bit.

He had already time-traveled on that Christmas Day, plunging back to impulses that could get no more primeval: a hungry man throwing rocks at food. He knew he would have to rebound and be more cautious, more attuned to what the wilderness could share rather than what he could plunder. Perhaps it could be some kind of plant that survives the winter or the gift of coming across a frozen animal carcass. Crane figured he would have to be more like the squirrels that remained just beyond his grasp: more watchful, more nimble.

The wilderness education of Crane was swift and, in many regards, unusual. There is a long tally of those who have struggled in the tundra and ice. But the list is populated mostly with adventurers, explorers, roamers, fortune hunters, and hired hands. They sought out the Far North or at least signed up willingly for the ordeal. Few were instant castaways like Crane, who had to face the wilds alone and unschooled.

It's likely that Crane, in his young days, came across the short story "To Build a Fire" by Jack London, who himself tried a stint in the Yukon prospecting but came away with less than five dollars in gold dust. London's doomed wanderer in the story was given no name. He didn't need one. He represented everyone—rich or poor, erudite or illiterate—foolish enough to underestimate the cold. It is among the great levelers. Crane understood that now.

After giving up on hunting squirrels, he spent the next three days in a kind of hibernation.

Crane would climb out of the parachute cocoon to feed the fire and drink from the river. The temperature never moved much above minus ten. The hole in the ice from the gurgling Charley River was closing. At least it wasn't snowing. A blizzard would have been a huge blow. All Crane's energy was funneled into making sure the fire kept burning, day after day. On the one-week mark after the crash, December 28, Crane experimented with trying to signal with smoke. He threw healthy spruce boughs into the flames. The smoke was weak and thin. It blew away before it reached the treetops.

"Freezing to death must be a queer business," wrote one of the star-power names in polar exploration, Rear Admiral Richard E. Byrd, who was also a lightning rod for controversies over weakly supported claims of points reached. Nevertheless, there is no questioning what Byrd endured. Crane knew it now, too: trying to survive in a place that does everything in its power to crush that hope.

"Sometimes you feel simply great," Byrd went on in a memoir. "The numbness gives way to an utter absence of feeling. You are as lost to pain as a man under opium. But at other times, in the enfolding cold, your anguish is the anguish of a man drowning slowly in fiery chemicals."

The logic of remaining on the spot was now gone. No one was coming.

Crane knew he would have to walk out.

SIX

DECEMBER 29, 1943

Philadelphia

All eyes were on the boy. It was like this always.

The attention used to unnerve him. Gradually, it became just a part of the job. It takes a certain detachment to do it right, the boy had figured out. By now, he was an old hand. He had delivered hundreds of Western Union telegrams issued by the secretary of war. The news, naturally, was rarely good. He learned to keep his gaze forward as he rode his bicycle, focusing only on the address in question. But he could sense the nervous pause as he passed. Barbers' scissors would freeze in midsnip. Clothespins would stop snapping on laundry lines. Fingers would pull back curtains just enough to get a look. The prayers were all the same. It was as if he could hear them: *Please, please, please don't stop here. Keep on pedaling.*

Morning affairs were in full swing along Baltimore Avenue, the busy Philadelphia leg of an old colonial route that sweeps down into Maryland. At the fire station, the day crew was wiping down the engines after an overnight blaze. At the Ambassador Theater, the neighborhood's grandest movie house with the urn-and-laurel trimmings of a Greek temple, the marquee was being changed for the upcoming Spencer Tracy film *A Guy Named Joe*—planned as the first big movie of 1944—about a dead pilot who becomes a guardian angel for another airman. Commuters heading downtown huddled on corners for the streetcar, stamping their feet on the pavement to stay warm.

It was just below freezing, but a stiff wind made it seem far more biting. The boy was glad the snow held off. Even a few inches made getting around on his bike a treacherous proposition.

He glided to a stop. He leaned his bicycle against a metal sidewalk fence at the bottom of a small dip on Baltimore Avenue. There was no need to lock it up. Who would steal a bike in winter? He checked his cap. Western Union had rules for the messengers' image down to the smallest detail. Flapping shirttails and sloppy shoes could cost you a promotion when it came time to select applicants for an office job. "Your Appearance and Your Future" headlined the section on grooming and presentation. It advised that the Western Union cap should be worn at a slight angle, with the visor just over the eyebrows. The cap's brass-colored company emblem gave the messengers the look of a scaled-down cop. Also make sure your uniform is pressed and clean, the company advised, and your tie should have a tidy four-in-hand knot. The leather puttees around your calves must be shined to a chestnut gloss.

The irony was unavoidable. These fresh young kids, dressed up snappily and with their lives ahead of them, had the gloomy task of carrying the worst news possible.

The boy checked the address again: *5464 Baltimore Avenue. Crane, Louis, Mr.*

He walked up the four steps from the sidewalk. Then five more until he was on the porch. To his right and left, a long string of steps and porches—some with hardy winter plants, some with chairs, some with fancy ironwork—stretched down the block of row houses. The Cranes' door was straight ahead. The metal outer door was decorated with floral swirls. It made a tinny clang when the boy knocked. Crane's mother pulled open the inside wooden door, sucking the metal one shut with another rattle. Sonia Crane was a sturdy woman, just short of fifty, who favored plain dresses and the simplest jewelry. It was Wednesday. Her husband, Louis, had already left for work at the auction company. He had learned the business well. Louis would sometimes buy entire failed businesses, right down to the office watercooler, and put them on the block bit by bit to the highest bidders. The Cranes rarely received telegrams, though. This one made Sonia's heart pound. She knew what it likely meant. She saw the black armbands worn by fathers on the trolley and the gold-star banners of grieving families in home windows. All her sons were in the military. Morris, whose high school friends once called him Muff, was in Europe. Nathan was in the Pacific. Leon was the youngest.

Western Union policy urged messengers to remain on an even keel. The company portrayed it as an almost patriotic act. "You are entrusted with one of the most important jobs of Western Union's war service," the employee manual reminded. If the telegram causes a "shock," the messengers were instructed to ask: "Is there anything I can do?" In cases where the recipient has a severe breakdown, the messenger should offer: "May I call someone or ask a neighbor to step in?"

Sonia Crane was not the type of woman to fall to pieces. She'd seen far too much in life already. With a deep breath, she took the telegram: eight-by-six-and-a-half-inches of newsprint with a two-way fold to fit into the envelope. She read the block letters.

THE SECRETARY OF WAR DESIRES ME TO EXPRESS HIS DEEP REGRET THAT YOUR SON FIRST LIEUTENANT LEON CRANE HAS BEEN REPORTED MISSING SINCE TWENTY ONE DECEMBER IN ALASKA.

There were a few more words after that, but no more details. Crane's family knew he had been sent to Alaska and was at times testing planes. But was this a crash? Or some other type of mission? Was he alone? Were they still searching? The telegram, however, offered nothing more than just promises to pass along more information if it became available.

The boy turned. He left the Cranes' porch and got back on his bike for the next delivery. There were always more.

Around the country, similar messengers on similar bikes with similar telegrams were also making their rounds with news of events that had taken place on that first day of winter in 1943.

On Audubon Road in Montgomery, Alabama, the parents of Marine Corporal Thomas Carl Alford were informed he was missing in action on December 21 in a South Pacific battle. In Syracuse, New York, the family of Army Air Forces First Lieutenant Norman English learned he was last seen during fighting in the Italian campaign near Florence. In Long Island City, the telegram said Seaman First Class Joseph McGovern was washed overboard off the New England coast while attempting to hoist the colors on the bridge of the submarine USS S-17.

At 12 Lincoln Street in Houlton, Maine, Mary Hoskin had to sit down after reading the telegram about her missing husband. She was shaking and gasping for breath as she read and reread the words, almost as if she was trying to will the message to change. Mary instinctively ran her hand over her belly. She was five months pregnant and tried to calm herself. I have to think of our baby, she told herself. Stay steady. She tried to walk off her nerves in tight circles around the living room. She started scrubbing the kitchen counters. Cleaning always calmed her. Just then, she thought of how she liked to make dinner for Harold. She put down the cloth and broke down in tears at the kitchen table. She was so lost in her grief that she never remembered her mother making the call to Harold's parents or being helped into bed to try to sleep away the sad afternoon.

The next correspondence she received was her own letter to Harold, dated December 19. The note inside ended: "All my love to the dearest husband and daddy in the whole world." Outside on the envelope it was stamped *Returned to Writer*.

More than thirty years earlier, on a September afternoon in 1913, the steamship *Prinz Adalbert* pushed north against the Delaware River current. The thousand or so immigrants on board had finally cleared their medical screenings and general vetting downriver at the Marcus Hook reception center, which was having its busiest year processing newcomers bound for Philadelphia. The clearance documents for the American arrivals included all-purpose affidavits from the ship's officers. They pledged that the émigré in question was not "an idiot, an insane person or a pauper, or likely to become a public charge or is suffering from a loathsome or a dangerous contagious disease."

It had been a relatively easy crossing from Hamburg. The late summer can be complicated if a tropical storm kicks up. This time, however, the ship stayed ahead of a low-pressure system spinning up the center of the Atlantic. The *Prinz Adalbert* headed toward Philadelphia on a magnificent day. A few puffy clouds dotted the sky, but not enough to block the sun for long. There was just a hint of the coming fall, carried in a breeze from the north that kept the temperature in the midsixties. The immigrants crowded the deck under the shadows of the ship's triple smokestacks. Exactly seventeen months before—from a point on the same deck—the ship's chief steward snapped a photo of a passing iceberg marked with a scar of red paint. Some believe it was among the last sightings of part of the berg that carved the fatal gash in the side of the *Titanic*.

When Philadelphia's busy wharves came into view on September 15, 1913, the excitement onboard the *Prinz Adalbert* rose. The dominant chatter was Hungarian. But there were groups of Austrians, a few Poles, and pockets of Yiddish-speaking Jews leaving behind the frightening insecurities of czarist Russia. Among them was a twenty-year-old yeshiva trade school student from central Ukraine and his teen bride. The young Karagodskys were getting the first look at the place where they would reinvent themselves as Louis and Sonia Crane.

As they stepped onto the cobblestone docks, the couple entered a city that had become one of the great, and most turbulent, centers of Jewish immigration in little more than a generation.

A seminal moment in the city's Jewish legacy came on a raw winter day decades earlier, in February 1882. An immigrant-packed ship, not unlike the *Prinz Adalbert,* dropped anchor off Philadelphia. On board the SS *Illinois* were more than two hundred Russian Jews, the first major group of eastern Europeans to arrive in Philadelphia, seeking refuge from rising mob violence. The pogroms—a Yiddish word meaning destruction—had expanded sharply the previous year when false rumors spread that Jews had a hand in the St. Petersburg bombings that killed the reformist czar Alexander II. Jews who had the money and connections to flee were doing just that.

Shortly after the arrival of the *Illinois,* a VIP gathering convened at Philadelphia's Academy of Music under its fifty-foot crystal chandelier aglow with 240 gas flames. Among the notables discussing the plight of the Russian Jews that night was Pennsylvania's governor. At one point, a firebrand activist rallied the assembly—and drew applause from Jewish leaders—by insisting it was the city's duty to offer haven for "people in exile, chased out of their homes, robbed of their possessions and murderously treated." His words were prophetic. After the *Illinois,* ship after ship arrived carrying Jews from places such as Kiev, Odessa, and the Karagodsky homeland, Shpola, a crossroads of Jewish culture in Ukraine. By 1904 the Jewish population in Philadelphia had grown more than fourfold to about seventy thousand and would continue to swell for another decade and begin to rival New York as a hub of Jewish scholarship, commerce, and enterprise.

But there were growing pains. The established German-speaking Jews—whose ranks included Thomas Edison's rival Siegmund Lubin and other luminaries—began to bristle as the demographic scales tipped in favor of the Yiddish masses. One night, disgusted crowds stormed out of a Jewish theater performance when actors performed in Yiddish instead of German. It was once said the German Jews contributed the money; the Russian Jews contributed the tuberculosis. It wasn't too far off the mark in some respects. Many of the city's Yiddish-speaking arrivals in Philadelphia congregated in a wrong-side-of-the-tracks jumble of boardinghouses, street hawkers, and sewage-fouled alleys. After downpours, the streets flooded so badly that some people kept rowboats on hand to get around.

At the same time, greater strains were emerging over what it meant to be Jewish in this new land.

Some factions, such as so-called Jewish anarchists (they called themselves the Knights of Liberty and other names), were finding their voice in Philadelphia. Their messages emphasized workers' rights and had little room for Jewish solidarity. They cast the city's Jewish leaders in the roles of proxy oppressors. To the angry upstarts, the prominent rabbis and the Jewish gentry were on the side of bankers and factory owners who had no interest in improving the lots of the newer immigrants. Soapbox speakers at the piers would harangue newly arrived immigrants to turn their backs on the Jewish establishment and traditions. Instead, they would urge, throw your support to the fledgling unions and other groups challenging the old order. They emphasized their disdain for tradition at every opportunity. They would hold dances on solemn Yom Kippur and loiter outside synagogues on Saturday, blowing cigarette smoke into the faces of those going to worship. "The atmosphere," wrote one local Jewish historian, "was poisoned."

When the future Louis and Sonia Crane passed through the last checkpoint, they were atop the crest of an immigration wave. The year 1913 marked the peak of the eastern European influx into Philadelphia and many other seaboard cities. More than twenty ships arrived in Philadelphia in September of that year, bringing thousands of immigrants who stayed put or began the next leg of their trek overland. Newspaper classified sections were packed with help-wanted offers: cooks, plasterers, dishwashers, maids, waitresses. A basic room in Philadelphia's teeming Jewish quarter could be found for as low as $1.50 a week, and, for those who needed cash, pawnshops were ready to make a deal. "We buy old gold, silver, false teeth," one promised. The automobile—virtually unknown in provincial Europe—was already a semiaffordable dream in Philadelphia. A used 1910 Thomas Flyer Runabout with 50 horsepower under the hood was going for $650 or best offer.

The immigrant flow wasn't to last, however. World War I erupted the next summer. It brought passage to America to a near halt. But for those who arrived in the city before the doors slammed shut, new areas were opening fast.

One reason was the humble streetcar.

Electric-powered trolley lines started to snake into leafy West Philadelphia across the Schuykill River. New homes and stores quickly followed. By the time the row-house developers reached the corner of Baltimore Avenue and Fifty-Fourth Street in 1925, Louis and Sonia Crane had formally adopted their new names, had taken the oaths as new citizens, had honed their English, and were parents to three boys and a girl. A dozen years after arriving in Philadelphia, it was time to move, Sonia insisted.

She wanted out of South Philadelphia, which was close to Louis's auction company but also drawing Leon's older brother Nathan into some unsavory street gangs. Sonia took the lead. She got on the trolley and found their new house on Baltimore Avenue.

Leon Crane pushed his way through the crowd. There was never much excitement on his sleepy end of Baltimore Avenue, miles from downtown. Or at least it all seemed too sedate for an eleven-year-old who liked to imagine he was designing newfangled planes ready to soar off on travels and adventures. But this sidewalk hub-bub near young Crane's house was definitely something different. Newspaper hawkers were selling out fast. People were talking about a place Crane knew well, the local Ambassador movie house, and something he could hardly imagine: the faraway French Riviera.

What's going on? Leon asked.

Kid, someone chimed in, you don't read the papers? The tycoon who used to own the Ambassador was killed by his wife in France. The court said it was self-defense. Check her out, kid. The girl is a knockout.

Crane hurried to class. It wasn't worth being late and risking the wrath of his parents, who expected nothing short of excellence.

He got the rest of the story later. Turned out that Philadel-phia theater mogul Frederick G. Nixon-Nirdlinger, whose empire included the Ambassador, was fatally shot by his newlywed wife, a former beauty queen named Charlotte Nash. It all happened in a fancy hotel room in Nice two months earlier in March 1931. Nixon-Nirdlinger was wildly jealous. He hired detectives to follow his young wife—despite the fact that he had conveniently left out some details of his own life before they were married, such as: he already had a wife and a pregnant mistress. A fierce argument erupted after Charlotte was accused of being unfaithful. She pulled out a pistol stashed under a pillow. Two shots hit their mark. Fred was dead. A French jury, however, needed only ten seconds for its decision. They agreed with the defense claims of self-defense. "She is too beautiful to be bad," her attorney said as he wooed the sympathetic jurors.

But what gripped the schoolboy Crane more than the lurid murder tale from France were the descriptions of the couple flying around Europe in the latest planes. Crane simply couldn't get enough of aviation. He constantly doodled pictures of mighty Zeppelins and long-distance aircraft such as "Lucky" Lindbergh's *Spirit of St. Louis*. Leon, or Lee as he was called, didn't dream so much about being in the pilot's seat. What fascinated him were the mechanics and engineering of getting the thing off the ground. The Depression was narrowing dreams and expectations everywhere. But aviation seemed immune to the imploding economy. New planes and ideas kept on coming. Record books were being revised before the ink could dry.

Lee Crane thought endlessly about the boundless skies, but his own world was very small in comparison. It revolved around West Philadelphia, the cramped bedroom shared with his two brothers, and a trip now and then to the New Jersey shore. At the same time, the backdrop of Crane's boyhood world was changing rapidly. The Jewish influence in the neighborhood was giving way, as migrating southern blacks gained footholds in West Philly. Other groups soon joined them, as Philadelphia's streetcar suburbs became a patchwork of languages and backgrounds. The high school's athletic field, once a vista of white kids on green grass, became the home of Negro League teams from 1931 to 1935 and featured such dynamos as the rail-thin flamethrower Stuart "Slim" Jones. Years later, at the tail end of the Depression, Jones ended up penniless and died before his twenty-sixth birthday.

Crane's parents didn't get too involved in synagogue or community affairs. The internal rifts within Philadelphia's Jewish world were not their problem. Tradition, however, was paramount. Passing on Jewish life to their family was taken far more seriously than getting involved in the passing political storms. The Crane children had private Hebrew and religious lessons. Bar mitzvahs were more than just coming-of-age parties with cash and frivolous loot from relatives. The gifts from Louis to his boys were prayer shawls known as tallit and small boxes called tefillin containing Torah verses and worn with leather straps during weekday morning prayers.

Meanwhile, Louis and Sonia were busy staying ahead of the Depression.

Sonia brought in money as an accomplished seamstress. She turned her back on the fledgling unions and negotiated her own pay, demanding—and getting—the same as her male coworkers. She didn't bend easily. Sonia had learned from an early age how to take care of herself and protect her family, which lived on the poorer side of the Jewish district in Shpola. When the local Cossacks got drunk, they often raided the Jewish neighborhoods. Anyone unfortunate enough to be in their path—especially a young girl—might suffer unspeakable abuses. When it was time to hide, Sonia and her two sisters stashed themselves in a hidden room under a closet floor. The Cranes eventually had enough money to bring over relatives, including Sonia's sisters.

That's because Louis, highly educated and even more highly motivated, had found his footing in Philadelphia in the auction business, sometimes traveling as far as North Carolina to buy up failing businesses. The family had it better than many. There was even enough money for music lessons for the kids. Leon picked the clarinet. Old brother Morris gravitated to the violin. Louis bought a car, a noisy contraption with faulty headlights. He rigged up a flashlight on the steering wheel to help guide his way.

By the time Leon was in West Philadelphia High School, his interest in aeronautics was sealed. "There were a lot of aeronautical firsts," he would say later in life. He wanted to be part of it. He graduated in February 1937 with fanfare that included high honors, kudos for his stint as yearbook editor, and a laudatory send-off toward greater things. "Best in everything he undertakes," the yearbook inscription reads. "Leon has justly earned the position of best student." Still, there were Jewish quotas in place for admission at some of the most prestigious colleges. Older brothers Morris and Nathan managed to get into medical schools—with a little help, in Nathan's case, of five thousand dollars slipped to the right person.

Leon was short a few math credits, however, and made them up during a spring semester at the University of Pennsylvania. The term ended just as Amelia Earhart and Fred Noonan set off on their ill-fated round-the-world flight. Sonia wanted Leon to follow his brothers into medicine. But Leon had other plans. He was bound for MIT and the labs that were pushing the bounds of aeronautical engineering.

In Cambridge Crane quickly found his niche. He joined the "Jewish" fraternity Phi Beta Delta and immersed himself in campus life and its brainy pedigree. A freshman-year frat photo shows Crane, looking dapper in a dark suit and striped tie, standing near future Nobel Prize–winning physicist Richard Feynman. They became poker buddies. And it's very likely they chewed over their shared paths as whip-smart kids from down the coast (Feynman's home base was Far Rockaway, New York) who were now somewhat awed as small fish—the smallest, in fact, as freshmen—swimming the intellectual currents of MIT. Crane and Feynman fell into what Feynman would later call the "studious" group of the fraternity. The others were the "wild social guys." Each had a role. The bookworms would help with the schoolwork as in-house tutors. The partygoers would, well, get parties going. And that required some preparation where needed. Feynman recalled that some of the more outgoing frat brothers taught him to dance. Once that was done, they moved on to setting him up with a blind date. It was a girl named Pearl. "So I was from New York, so I said, 'Oh, Poil, Poil.' They said, 'No, you must say Pearl, because she'll be horrified if you say Poil,' and so on," Feynman recounted in a 1966 oral history. He managed just one properly enunciated "Pearl" at the beginning of the date before slipping back into his New Yorkese.

Crane also had a front-row seat to some of Feynman's pranks, such as the time Feynman stole the door to a frat-house room that was a favorite study site. Crane, meanwhile, also gravitated toward some of the more innovative minds on the faculty. One of his advisers was Manfred Rauscher, who had visions of moving the daily commute from the roads to the air. He codeveloped an everyman plane, playfully named after the flightless Dodo, with folding wings for easy garage parking.

Inevitably, Crane figured that if he wanted to design airplanes, he should learn to fly them as well. He earned his private pilot's license through a university training program and entered the Reserve Officers' Training Corps. That led to a stint in the summer of 1940 at a military installation in Virginia, learning how to handle guns and artillery. Although America was still officially neutral, telegrams calling up reservists kept flowing out of Washington. Crane's came in late 1941, just months after he graduated from MIT. He was told to report to Wright Field in Ohio, near the site where B-24 designer I. M. Laddon began tinkering with plane designs in the 1920s. At Wright Crane was happy to see a dozen old faces from MIT, including the extra good news that one of the crew had brought his 1936 Olds so they could tool around off base.

On a raw Sunday in December, they listened to the radio reports of the attack on Pearl Harbor. Within months, Crane was shipped off to Alabama to begin military flight training, and the wartime industries were making planes as fast as they could drive rivets.

The future *Iceberg Inez* came off Consolidated's San Diego assembly line years later, May 31, 1943. Its price tag for the Army was $297,627. The plane was flown June 2 to Tucson to install additional equipment such as radios, which were not part of the factory-line procedures out of concern such detail-oriented work would slow down production. From there, 42-40910 passed through Wright Field in Ohio, where Crane was first posted after being called up. The B-24 touched down at Ladd field on November 19, 1943, on an unusually mild day outside Fairbanks. It didn't last. Soon it was well below zero.

Back in Philadelphia, as the war in Europe dragged on, Crane's parents struggled to get any scraps of news from Shpola. They knew the Nazis had control over nearly all of Ukraine. But only fragmented reports made their way to West Philadelphia. What they heard was hard to fathom: whole communities wiped out or herded off to camps by the Einsatzgruppen death squads. A photo taken in 1913—perhaps about the time Louis and Sonia left for America—showed a group of young Jewish militiamen organized to protect against the pogroms. Their rifles are pointing defiantly at the camera. Louis Crane now wondered what had happened to them and their children if the stories of the Nazi killings were as horrible as they sounded.

They were. By the war's end, only remnants remained of the once flourishing Jewish community in Ukraine. In Shpola there was almost no one left. One young boy, Iurii Pinchuk, managed to slip away from a concentration camp just before a mass killing in 1942. His mother couldn't manage the escape.

Before the extermination, a man had approached Pinchuk's mother and asked if she had a spare piece of fabric.

"I remember him well," Pinchuk told filmmakers five decades later. "He was skinny and had a thin neck and big ears that stuck out. He said, 'Give me a piece of this fabric.' She asked why. He said, 'I want to hang myself.'"

SEVEN

DECEMBER 29, 1943

Wilderness

Harold Hoskin pulled up a chair. Dinner was served. The plates were heavy with juicy steaks and mashed potatoes swimming in butter.

You look good, Crane told the pilot.

I'm fine, Hoskin replied. But we need to eat fast, he continued. We've got to get out of here.

Crane nodded. You're right, Hos. I was thinking the same thing.

Then they ate, digging into the meal and savoring the tastes— especially the warmth.

It all seemed so real.

Leon Crane was dreaming the dreams of a starving man.

Night after night for more than a week, such scenes visited Crane. Each time was more vivid than the last. The food was always hot and plentiful, the settings cozy and inviting. One meal was imagined so fully that Crane thought he could feel the warm grease from a lamb chop running down his fingers. In that half-way space straddling sleep and waking, he thought how bizarre it all was. It was punishing and pleasant at the same time. His sub-conscious was playing tricks. That was clear. But he enjoyed the ruse nonetheless. He allowed the wonderful fantasies to play out. If nothing else, it was a nice escape from the strangling cold.

The feast with Hoskin was a bit different, however. Crane hadn't dreamed much of the crew since the crash. Now, Hoskin had appeared. He looked healthy and calm and was carrying a message: move and move quickly. Intellectually, Crane recognized that this, too, was nothing more than a reverb of his decision to leave the river and strike off overland. But hearing it repeated by the reliable pilot—even if just a dream—offered some uplift that he had made the right call.

Crane had set his course. He would head west into the wilderness. That was the general direction of Big Delta. Crane, of course, had no way to judge the distance. He was only sure that somewhere out there was Big Delta base. It wasn't a lot to go on, he knew. But the river, on the other hand, was a total cipher. If I'm going to walk, Crane told himself, it might as well be toward something certain. There was also something psychologically fortifying about that. At this point—with no food and just about no hope of rescue—Crane felt he needed to do something bold before he was too weak or broken.

Certainly, the plan involved a gamble. Crane was comfortable with that. The alternative was far worse in his mind. Crane did not want to die meekly without attempting some bid to save himself.

He waited for first light to set off. He figured he could fix his path west in relation to the rising sun in the east. He would have to sit tight for a while, though. Dawn was still two hours away. He tried to sleep, but couldn't doze off. Crane lay deep within his parachute wrap and wondered how he would handle being on the move. Since his brief trip downriver days before, he hadn't traveled much beyond the twenty feet between his camp and the ice. Thankfully, there were no further injuries. His fingers, however, were clearly worse. They were growing unresponsive. It took supreme effort to make a fist to try to squeeze some blood past his knuckles. Crane forced himself to keep at it.

Frostbite works like a shoplifter. It comes quietly and pilfers bit by bit. The losses begin small, but continue to add up until it's impossible to replace what's been taken.

At first, as the outer layers of skin cool, the body goes into self-preservation mode. It does not want chilled blood pumping around. So it constricts the capillaries and veins near the cold tissue. There's still no major dilemma. Warming the areas can restore circulation without anything more than a pins-and-needles rush. But that grace period doesn't last long. At some point, if the exposure persists, nerve synapses shut down and ice crystals begin to form between cells. Now, it's far more serious. There is still a chance to counteract the damage with gradual thawing, but the recovery can be acutely painful as the nerves snap back to life and the warming skin erupts in blisters. The deeper levels of frostbite sharply narrow the chances for such recovery. Healthy cells dehydrate and freeze. Here, it's moving beyond the point of no return. At some point, there is little left for doctors to do except reach for a scalpel. During Napoléon's retreat from his disastrous Russian campaign in the winter of 1812, his chief surgeon, Baron Dominique Jean Larrey, reportedly amputated hundreds of frostbitten limbs from soldiers. It was a gruesome, but important, education. Larrey went on to become one of the first physicians to attempt to scientifically document frostbite's causes and progression. Among his groundbreaking conclusions: it's far better to keep skin covered and at a relatively stable temperature—even if still cold and unpleasant—rather than go through repeated cycles of fireside thawing and then freezing.

Crane somehow understood this. He wisely kept his hands buried deep inside the parachute or drawn into his parka sleeves whenever he could and avoided placing them too close to the flames. There was something else starting to worry him, however. And, for this, he had no obvious remedy. In fact, he couldn't really give it a name. It started with just a few passing moments of disjointed or meandering thoughts. He had to consciously snap himself back to reality. At first, he wrote them off as mental drift caused by hunger. But they were coming more frequently in the past days. Sometimes he would lose track of the fire and let it burn too low even as he sat just feet away. Other moments, he would find himself in a daze and wonder how long he had been staring into space. Crane felt himself slipping. His judgment was fraying.

Experts in wilderness survival often cite the timeless "enemies" of survival. They include pain, cold, thirst, hunger, fatigue, boredom, and loneliness. With the exception of thirst, Crane ticked all the boxes. Starvation, of course, will ultimately claim its victims. In the wilds, however, tragedies are often hastened by decisions made as hunger takes hold or panic takes over. An expert in sub-arctic survival, Gino Ferri, advises clients at his northern Ontario camp to watch how the extreme cold "plays tricks on your psyche."

"Your reptilian brain takes over," he said. "It is telling you, 'I got to get the hell out of here at any cost.' That is when disaster is looming."

Crane's periods of cloudy thinking also suggested he was moving into the next stage of starvation. At this point, the body is shifting into crisis measures. Muscle tissue is being converted into fuel to maintain blood sugar levels and feed critical organs, especially the brain. The liver, too, is in overdrive. Fatty acids are being turned into something called ketone bodies, which is the biological equivalent of a reserve tank. But, like most end-of-the-line options, there are shortcomings. Among them is a chance for panic-induced decisions. The brain, getting a taste of the ketone bodies, tells itself that things are getting desperate.

Alaska is a clearinghouse for such stories. In 1942, a year before the *Iceberg Inez* went down, the U.S. military embarked on a comprehensive study of Far North survival techniques. Dozens of Alaskan old-timers were interviewed. Nearly all recounted some bad-news tale about people striking off blindly into the wilderness. One veteran bush pilot from Nome told the Army envoys about a group of fliers who tried to hike back from their downed plane. They wandered in circles for eight days and were found, near death, just a few miles from the crash site. In another interview, a dogsled mail carrier described how hunger and cold can bring on fatal miscalculations in the wild. There's a "strong tendency to fight his environment by roaming" until the point of exhaustion, he told the Army team.

At sunrise, Crane tossed his last twigs on the fire. He gathered up his chute, turned his back on the river, and began blazing a trail through shin-deep snow.

Crane had no concept yet of the magnitude of his blunder. Big Delta was at least 70 miles to the southwest in a direct line—and probably close to 150 miles of hiking even by an experienced Alaska hand with a compass and knowledge of the terrain. In between is a mountain ridge capped by the more than 6,500-foot Mount Harper, which has an indirect but tragic connection to Crane's distant Philadelphia. The peak is named for an Irish-born Yukon explorer and trader, Arthur Harper, whose marriage to an Athabascan girl produced eight children. The youngest, Walter, gained mountaineering immortality in 1913 as the first person confirmed to reach the summit of North America's highest point, then known in the Western world as Mount McKinley and now widely called Denali, after one of the Athabascan names, meaning the Great or High One. In 1918 Walter and his new bride set off for Philadelphia—ten months before Crane's birth—where Walter planned to attend medical school. Their Seattle-bound steamer struck a reef near Juneau. The couple were among more than 340 passengers and crew members lost at sea.

There were no villages in the Harper mountain chain and perhaps only a few scattered cabins. This, too, Crane could not have known.

It took just a few minutes, however, for him to discover that overland travel would be nothing like following the river, whose banks were at least a level grade. The land rose gently from the riverbank, but even this modest incline was torturous. Each step meant he had to plow aside snow. With surprising speed, numbness began to spread downward from Crane's knees. He could still move his toes inside the mukluks. But that wouldn't last indefinitely.

"Ack," he cursed, stumbling again on the rocks hidden everywhere under the snow.

Not a single stride landed easily. Crane had to adopt a stutter-step cadence to avoid toppling over and exposing his hands. He let his boot sink halfway into the snow, pause a second, and then push deeper, slowly feeling for the rocks. Progress was ridiculously slow. He had to stop every ten paces just to catch his breath. His heart pounded, and he could feel drops of sweat trickling down his back. It's minus twenty and I'm sweating, he almost laughed. But he knew the perils.

Any kind of moisture could freeze into a potentially life-sapping armor. The cold material siphons off the body warmth and clears the way for frostbite and other complications, such as gangrene. Natives of the Far North understand this well. Typically, undergarments are avoided or worn in the lightest possible materials. In the era before mass-produced clothing, Natives of the frigid Bering Strait hunted in the winter wearing an inner parka of skin from a month-old fawn and an outer layer of skin from a reindeer killed at the height of summer when the hair is at its most fine. In interior Alaska, the most prized skins for clothing came from the hides of pregnant moose killed in late March. Only in extreme cold would they add undergarments made from squirrel hide or woven rabbit fur.

The rock dodging also sent Crane zigzagging off course. Every few minutes, he needed to check his bearing against the sun. Sometimes, he'd be so turned around that he faced south instead of west. At midday, with the winter sun hanging about thirteen degrees over the horizon, Crane stopped. He looked back at his tracks and could still see the river below. In more than two hours, he made perhaps three hundred feet. I'm simply marching to my death, he thought. At this rate, he'd be lucky to make a half mile a day. Even if Big Delta was close—which, in his heart, he knew it wasn't—it could be months of hiking. He had fewer than thirty matches left.

And no one would ever find his body.

The idea of wolverines or birds picking at his corpse seemed to Crane the ultimate insult, the parting shot of the wild. He did not want to end up like that. It was, however, increasingly hard to imagine another outcome. More and more, Crane was envisioning his own end. Everyone does in some abstract way. In wartime the images take on sharper relief. This was particularly true among the Cold Nose Boys. In battle there was any number of ways to get it. Here in the Alaska skies, everyone pretty much knew what trouble looked like. Either the plane would seize up in the weather, or a storm would clobber it. No one at Ladd had climbed aboard a plane for a winter mission without thinking whether this could be their last one.

"This is a bad place to be out in the wild, lost," Maine airman Arthur Jordan wrote in his Ladd Field diary.

"I wonder if the mystery of what happened to it will ever be explained," Jordan penned in reference to the fruitless hunt for the *Iceberg Inez*. "The only hope, I guess, is that some trapper may come upon some bits of twisted steel some time and report his find."

Crane was shuffling into the past tense.

His family knew this. But they refused to describe him as gone. Hope was kept within reach, although a bit more of a stretch as each day passed. To anyone who would listen, Sonia Crane insisted she could sense her Leon was still alive. Call it a mother's intuition or simple stubbornness. No one dared to contradict her.

But the facts couldn't be ignored. The Army telegram said he was missing for more than a week. Anyone surviving the crash would stand little chance in the winter. Being homeless during a rough patch of Philadelphia winter could be harsh enough. What were the odds in Alaska? At Ladd Field, the bunks and lockers for Crane, Hoskin, and the rest of the *Iceberg Inez* crew were still untouched. That would change soon. The personal items would be packed up and eventually shipped south to the next of kin in the Army files.

Crane guessed the telegram was already sent to Baltimore Avenue. He pretty much knew the words, too, written in the military template: *Missing since Dec. 21. . . . Searches have failed to find crash site or survivors. . . . We will keep you informed of any developments.* It won't say what really matters: it's minus fifty some nights in the backcountry or that the military is no longer going to devote much energy to the hunt.

In hearts and minds, Crane was being reassigned to the rolls of the dead. He was turning into a living ghost, an invisible pilgrim.

Crane found a special cruelness in this in-between world.

There were no walls or barbwires cutting him off as with prisoners of war (POWs). He wasn't pinned under wreckage. Only space and the winter stood in his way. That was more than enough, of course. But, at times, he seemed so connected, so heartbreakingly close, to what was on the other side. This waxing crescent moon over the Alaskan Yukon in late December was the same one that rose over Ladd Field and Philadelphia and Boston and Berlin. The constellations decorating the sky were the same ones seen from outside some warm and well-stocked cabin maybe just over the horizon. The wind stinging his cheeks was pulled around the globe by weather cells that mingle and collide—all seamlessly connected—from continent to continent.

These were curious thoughts for Crane. He was not a man of poetry. Crane was shaped by machines and their power. What he most admired was how these creations could shove aside nature and natural limits. As a boy, he studied the steamships that crossed oceans without relying on the winds. He dissected the workings of automobile engines that shrank distances and made the horseman a quaint obsolescence by the time he was born. In his eyes, though, air travel was the ultimate expression of man's mastery. It fulfilled dreams as fundamental as dreams themselves. Leonardo da Vinci sketched his ideas of taking flight. Further back, the Greeks wrapped stories and morality tales around the wings of Daedalus. Even earlier, the awed Ezekiel of the Old Testament watched the spinning wheels that carried aloft heavenly creatures. At MIT Crane's science-for-the-people avionics mentor, Manfred Rauscher, was hailed for figuring out how to get earthbound hardware off the ground. "He makes them fly," said the caption under Rauscher on Crane's senior yearbook.

Crane's interests leaned toward speed. He concentrated on pushing the limits of the relatively new science of jet engines. Now, his world had contracted to the pace when the skies were out of reach. His pace below was one step at a time.

He paused on the hillside. There was perhaps ninety minutes of light left. He could probably make it over the next ridge. He wouldn't have the stamina to turn back to the river after that.

Setting off into the hills was an obvious mistake. Crane was now forced to confront what to do about it. Is there any point in continuing other than the blind hope that some kind of settlement sits just over the hill? And, if there were, wouldn't they have noticed the crash and tried to send some kind of rescue party? Far more likely is that it's more wilderness, and more beyond that. Rivers were the real highways of the Alaskan interior. He knew that much and cursed himself for forgetting it. The rivers are where people lived, trapped, fished. Think as if this is a poker hand, he reasoned. Would you bet on drawing the right card from the hills or the river?

Crane did not take another step away from the river. He turned around and headed downhill. He followed the meandering snow rut he had plowed with his numbing legs. He could have walked a straighter line to the river. But there was no sense in fall-ing over a rock and risking an injury. If he had any chance—any at all—it would rest on making the right choices. He could not afford another folly like striking off on a cross-country trek. A sprinkling of luck wouldn't hurt, either.

That came as he spotted his camp.

The fire was nearly out, but some of the wood still glowed. He coaxed flames from dried spruce needles. At least that's one match saved for later. Crane cloaked himself in the parachute for another night. The idea now was to set off downstream. There was no other way.

When Crane left his bivouac on the morning of December 30, he was certain he would not return. He would have to stick with the river until the end, whichever way that played out. Crane also chose to walk atop the frozen ice. There was a risk of breaking through, but it was faster than picking his way through rocks and gullies along the bank. Haste seemed important. Crane still felt relatively strong after more than a week without food. This surprised him. But there was no telling when his body would simply give way.

In many places, the Charley River separates into a braid of channels, known as sloughs, along a rocky bed. But Crane could have no sense of what was below and where the ice could be thin. It was only a white pathway winding through white hills. At each bend, Crane would tell himself: I'll turn the corner and there will be a cabin with a fire going and a family who will listen to my story while they feed me supper with steaming coffee. But, bend after bend, it was just more river, more hills.

About three o'clock, as dusk was giving way to evening, the river valley widened. Crane began to look for a place to camp. Just the thought of collecting more wood and starting a fire discouraged him.

He stopped. Hold on. What's that?

Crane squinted in the fading light. It looked like a tent perched on a platform. *Impossible*. Is it really? Crane took a few steps closer. It was certainly something.

"Hey," Crane yelled.

"Anyone there?"

He wondered for a moment if it could be some sort of North Country mirage. Could the cold be fooling him?

But the closer he got, the more the tent silhouette sharpened. It's real.

"Hello. Hello!"

Crane began running. Then, to his right, something bigger came into view. A cabin? Crane found it hard to believe. Yet there it was: a log cabin, half covered with snow, on the river's edge.

Crane stumbled over rocks, running and yelling, not caring that his hands were covered in snow.

He cleared away a drift from the door. It was more like a hatch, about three feet high. He grabbed the handle. The door swung open.

Crane tumbled inside.

EIGHT

DECEMBER 30, 1943

Phil Berail's Cabin

It took some time for Crane's eyes to adjust to the shadows.

The place seemed more cave than cabin. The floor was pounded earth, but hard as concrete in the subzero cold. Flakes of dust and dried moss and God knows what else floated in the shaft of yellow twilight that spilled through the open door. At the same time, it smelled enticingly of life: tobacco and sweat, candle wax and summer grass, and meat that sizzled in frying pans even if not so recently. After more than a week in the Alaskan Yukon winter—scrubbed clean of these warm, comforting scents—it was overpowering. Crane tried to sort out the different odors. Old fur. Wet wool. Meals cooked and eaten. Wood and canvas.

Gradually, Crane could see the dimensions: a rough rectangle, about ten feet wide and slightly smaller from door to wall. The ceiling was low, sagging in places under the weight of the traditional dirt-and-sod covering on the roof, but it still managed to peak at the center. The nearly six-foot Crane could stand upright with some room to spare. At one corner was a bunk built on a sturdy wooden base. Next to it sat a pile of wood and shavings. Crane looked to his left. A table was packed with burlap sacks tied tightly with twine. His frigid fingers couldn't manage to loosen the knots. Crane slashed the closest bag with his Boy Scout knife.

Out spilled something white. Crane dipped his fingertips and brought them to his lips. He gasped. Sugar! The rest of the satchels held gifts that made Crane's head spin: a tin of cocoa, another of dried milk, a half-dozen cans of baking powder, and a box of raisins.

Crane stuffed the raisins into his mouth. They were as cold and hard as pebbles, but quickly softened and gave up their juices and flavor. Crane chewed wildly. Just a few nights ago, he had dreamed of polishing off a steak with Hoskin. Crane thought that might be the closest he would come to genuine food. He was now chomping on sweet raisins with a roof over his head. It was almost too much to absorb. Just concentrate on eating, he thought. He grabbed more raisins, but stopped before he tossed them into his mouth. He suddenly felt full. Unbearably so. It was clear he needed to go slowly to give his body time to reacquaint itself with food. He checked the raisin box. There were plenty left.

But did that really matter? He figured he must be close to a village. Who would stock a cabin in the middle of the wilderness? Tomorrow, Crane assured himself, I'll be in a real home. Tomorrow, surely someone will know how to treat my fingers. Crane examined his hands in whatever light was left. The skin was bone white. Sensations in his fingers seemed muddled and muffled. He could still feel the rough wood of the cabin's table or the coarse weave of the sacks, but it was as if they were encased in a thick skin that allowed only the basic textures to come through. Crane would later describe it as though he was wearing boxing gloves. Crane's fingers, at least, still obeyed his commands, but slowly.

Crane knew enough about interior Alaska not to hope for a phone or telegraph office in whatever settlement he was certain was nearby. The only outside link at many outposts were two-way radios tuned to a bush-pilot frequency. He smiled—the first time since the crash—at the idea of putting on the headgear and letting the world know he was still among them.

While he was examining his fingers, a glint under the bunk caught his eye. He pulled out a small wood-burning stove and ventilation pipe. Things just kept getting better. He spotted a tin covering for the pipe in the roof and fitted it through. Soon, a fire was lit. Crane filled a frying pan with snow, and—as if all this cabin magic wasn't enough—within minutes he was wrapping his fingers around a tin cup full of hot cocoa. He still wasn't hungry. It would take a while to restart his appetite. But he managed to gulp down two cups.

There was enough light for one more exploration. Crane wanted to see what wonders sat under the tent on stilts he first spotted.

It was too high to hoist himself to the platform, but he found a ladder leaning against a tree. He sliced through the tent flaps. At least a dozen times a day, he thanked the fates that he had the Boy Scout blade tucked in his parka. Inside the tent, two heavy tarpaulins covered the stash. He pulled away the first. Underneath was an array of tools: hammers, drill bits, saws. He was careful not to touch the metal. He remembered the careless mechanics at Ladd leaving behind flaps of flesh. There also was a coil of sturdy rope, two folded tents similar to the one on the platform, and two big cans of rendered animal fat known as tallow.

Crane left the second tarp alone. He was too tired. That could wait. There were enough gifts already. Crane took a few moments to study the tools and tents. Could there be clues about its owner or the cabin's location? Not a thing he could see.

Crane was sure the folks in the village—the one he kept telling himself was right around the river bend—would know about the owner and he could offer proper thanks.

For the first time since the crash, Crane set aside the parachute. He wrapped himself in the canvas tents and dropped into the bunk. The cabin held the warmth from the fire remarkably well. The spaces between the logs were filled with nailed rope and wedged moss, which served as reliable insulation. The earthen-covered roof also helped trap the heat. What a luxury, Crane thought before sleep came.

Had Crane dug deeper into the cache, he would have found more supplies stored in boxes marked with the stenciled tag *Phil Berail. Woodchopper, Alaska.*

It was something of a message from an earlier era. Crane was the accidental guest of a man whose story reached back to a time before Alaskan bush pilots, before the railroad came, before the more genteel customs of the forty-eight states migrated north to interior Alaska.

A series of steamships, horses, and mule trains brought the young Berail to Alaska a few years after the turn of the century. Gold rush fervor was roaring back after discoveries in feeder rivers off the Yukon. Soon, a flood of strike-it-rich dreamers—and the inevitable schemers and merchants who followed—was quickly populating a frontier bazaar. Things were moving so fast that there was no time to remove the stumps of trees whipsawed down to build new saloons, stores, and flophouses. Many places have entertaining origin stories. Few can top Fairbanks's.

It begins with a stern-wheeler moving up the Tanana River in late August 1901. Aboard the *Lavelle Young* was a backwoods entrepreneur named Elbridge Truman Barnette, who came West from Ohio and had given himself the fabricated title of "captain." He had visions of setting up a new trading post along the Chena River, which branches off the Tanana. But the *Lavelle Young* was blocked by low water on the Chena far short of the captain's goal. E. T. Barnette and his wife were unceremoniously sent ashore in the wilderness, along with their merchandise. Barnette was furious. His wife—who had misgivings about the whole enterprise from the beginning—was sobbing.

Meanwhile, on a far hill, an Italian-born prospector and his Iowan partner, Tom Gilmore, were trying to find their way back to civilization. They had found a creek they believed was rich with gold, but now needed the equipment to dredge it out. The Italian, who had changed his first name from Felice to Felix, spotted the smoke from the *Lavelle Young* and used it as a guide to walk out of the bush. They found Barnette fuming and his wife fretting amid the crates and sacks. Felix asked to poke around. They made some deals with Barnette, including buying some winter gear for the fast-approaching cold. A city was born.

What came next was a breakneck blur of construction and con-
niving as gold was scooped from the creeks flowing into the Yukon
and Tanana Rivers. The tandem of Felix and Gilmore wasn't so
lucky. They never relocated their gold-flecked creek. Others struck
it rich, though. As Barnette's new town took shape, it needed a
solid name. A few were tried, but none seemed to stick. Finally,
a judge overseeing a huge swath of the Alaska territory, James
Wickersham, persuaded Barnette to call it Fairbanks after one
of the magistrate's political buddies, Indiana senator Charles W.
Fairbanks, who would go on to become the vice president under
Theodore Roosevelt. It was a blatant bid by the judge at gaining
some inside clout in Washington. Yet the newly minted Fairbanks
didn't really need much outside help to get off the ground. Gold
does that just fine. Within a few years, Fairbanks had more than
three hundred buildings, six saloons, and no churches. It was also
a place where few questions were asked. Pick a new name, new life
story, or just about anything as part of an Alaskan second chance.

Barnette, too, left out an important item from his past. It later
came to light that he was convicted in Oregon in 1886 of swin-
dling a partner in a horse-trading venture. His four-year sentence
was later commuted because of Barnette's political connections
in his native Ohio. He rode out that miniscandal, but wasn't able
to dodge trouble when his Washington-Alaska Bank went belly up
in 1911 after the boomtown days cooled. He was accused of flee-
ing Fairbanks with a fortune from the bank's vaults. Prosecutors,
however, could get a conviction only on a misdemeanor charge of
falsifying bank records. Protests broke out, and the word *Barnette*
became, for a time, a verb meaning "to swindle." Barnette never
returned to Fairbanks. Some believe he spent years holed up in
his Mexican hacienda with his girlfriend. Other sketchy reports
had him making his mark in the oil business in Montana. All
that's clear is that the disgraced patriarch of Fairbanks died in Los
Angeles in 1933 after falling down some stairs.

Barnette may have been vilified as the king of con artists in
Fairbanks, but small-bore crooks were everywhere in those early

days. Barkeeps were notorious for watering down their drinks. Fake maps were peddled allegedly showing the route to El Dorado–style riches. One pitchman tried to persuade gold rushers that a hybrid contraption called the "Klondike Bicycle" was the answer to their transport problems. The thing had four wheels made of solid rubber and served as a wagon, but two of its wheels could be retracted and it became a bike. Needless to say, it never caught on.

While others were chasing the siren call of gold, young Berail was knocking around Alaska doing what he could for a roof and meal. But he was also well aware he was a guest. He studied the Natives and their ancient rapport with Alaska. At the time, the followers of an Athabascan leader named Chief Charley were still following the age-old cycles of fishing and trapping. Two waterways—the Charley River and Charley Creek (now known as the Kandik River)—bear his name. It's unclear whether the chief took his name from the river or the other way around. Regardless, the whirlwind of the early twentieth century was a time of transition that left few untouched. The ways of the outsiders were leaching into the lives of the interior tribes. One photo shows Chief Charley flanked by two men, all wearing a cloth version of a porkpie hat and striped flannel shirts.

Their traditional wisdom, though, remained uncorrupted. Some of the newcomers, like Berail, bothered to listen. They learned such basics as how to best store a cabin's supplies to ensure they were safe for the next season or available to a traveler in need. The preferred place for the cache is an elevated platform to keep away unwanted scavengers such as bears, lynx, foxes, and porcupines. Floods, too, made the raised platforms a necessity. The annual spring high water on the Yukon River reached such levels that it swept away just about everything in its way. That included Chief Charley's settlement, which was lost in a great flood in 1914.

When Crane awoke, it was still dark. It took him a few moments to remember where he was. He reached out and felt the curves of the peeled spruce logs. The amazing events of the previous day poured back: the cabin, the raisins, the supplies. He rose quickly and fixed the rest of the cocoa, sugar, and powdered milk into a delicious, sweet concoction. Crane drank it quickly. He was sure this was his last day in the wilds.

He filled his pocket with the rest of the raisins, ducked through the cabin door, and set off downriver. Maybe the village will be close enough to get a real breakfast, he thought hopefully. Anticipation drove away any discomfort. He even forgot about his fingers. The morning on the last day of 1943 broke at minus twenty-five along the Charley River.

The river bent to the west. The slopes along the banks grew steeper. The valley narrowed. Crane hiked on, waiting for the outline of homes and maybe the smell of warming fires. Instead, there was just more wilderness. The next turn will be the one, he promised himself. Yet nothing. For hour after hour. The Charley was now straightening out into a near–due north path. Crane was walking into the wind. Eddies of whipped-up snow skittered over his cheeks.

By midafternoon, with the sun going down, Crane still pushed ahead. How could there be a lone cabin and nothing else? He hadn't lost faith that a village was near. To his logic, informed by the tight confines of the urban East, the idea of a far-flung cabin seemed outrageous and just plain unnatural. He refused to consider any other explanation. But there was always that background noise in his mind. It said: what made sense to the Philadelphia mind doesn't always apply in Alaska. He tried not to listen.

It was, however, true. There were no villages and no inhabited cabins nearby. Crane could not know this. He willed himself forward. Darkness returned.

Whatever Crane had learned about respecting his limits was tossed aside just days after his failed journey into the hills. He was again putting it all on the line.

A half-moon rose into a cloudless sky, dark as polished onyx. The North Star was dead ahead, tucked between the Big Dipper and Cassiopeia. It was much higher in the sky than when he had studied star charts during flight training in the South. The gossamer of an emerald-green aurora borealis flickered just below Polaris. It was really quite beautiful, Crane thought. For maybe the first time since the crash, Crane was taking in the majesty of the Alaskan wilds. He recalled the first time he saw the northern lights. It was during midterms at MIT in late January 1938 when some of the people on his block—just over the bridge from Cambridge—began pointing to the sky and rushing to their roofs after sunset. The horizon to the north was a deep red that shifted and flared as if coming from the glow of a huge fire. The next day, the papers were full of accounts of one of the most intense geomagnetic storms in decades, visible as far south as Virginia.

The clear Alaskan sky over Crane also brought more danger. With no cloud cover to hold in even the fractional amount of daytime warmth, the temperature tumbled downward. It was brushing against minus forty. For weather watchers, it's more than just a number. It's the only point where the Fahrenheit and Celsius scales cross. It's also near the freezing point for mercury. Below that, traditional thermometers are worthless.

Midnight was near. His buddies at Ladd would soon raise a glass to welcome 1944 and make the toasts of all soldiers in all wars: loudly to victory, but privately to the hope that the coming year would see them head home. Many still buzzed about the USO visit a few days earlier headlined by the elegant Ingrid Bergman, fresh off her latest movie, the Hemingway classic *For Whom the Bell Tolls*. Some others, like Crane's Mississippi roommate, Stud, might take a swig in Crane's memory. The clocks had ticked past twelve long before on the East Coast. No doubt it was more somber with his parents on Baltimore Avenue. Their son was missing somewhere in Alaska and, in the minds of many, would never return.

Crane stopped. Again, it was decision time.

Make the right one, he told himself. There is no room for error. Here's how it stood: To continue onward into the night was packed with perils. His hands were too numb to attempt to light a match for a fire. What if he dropped them in the snow while trying? It was colder tonight than any since the crash. It's unthinkable that he could ride out the rest of the night without a fire if he stopped walking.

The best move was the most painful one. Crane knew he had to turn around if he had any hope of returning to the cabin.

It was crushing to retreat. All his hope, which drove him ahead for twelve hours, drained away in an instant. He would not be saved. There was no village. No easy way home. He was alone. Suddenly, Crane felt the vastness of the wilderness again. This time, though, it was not to marvel at the stars or the shimmering northern lights. He now felt only small, vulnerable, and scared.

Crane remembered the raisins. He hadn't touched them since leaving the cabin. He dug into his pockets. Crane stuffed them in his mouth as he stood motionlessly on the frozen river. He then turned around to look at his tracks, which were a faint shadow in the eggshell-white snow.

It was 1944 now. The hours began to blur. Often, Crane wandered off course until he stumbled onto the rocks on the river's edge. Each fall was another punishment for his hands. He tried to keep them pulled deep into the sleeves of his parka. But instinct took over with every tumble. His hands would poke out as he tried to cushion his fall. The front of his parka was encrusted with ice from his breath. Icicles hung from his nose. It hurt too much to brush them off.

To stop was to give up. To give up was to perish. Crane had no idea how many hours had passed. His concentration was riveted on trying to follow the path of broken snow and keeping his legs moving. One breath, one step. Crane was like the machines he loved: all about function, movement, efficiency. There was no room for anything else. Don't think, just do.

Dawn came. That meant it had been twenty-hour hours since he had set off. Still, there was no sign of the cabin. He knew he couldn't easily walk past it since his outbound tracks were still clear.

But the landscape was no real help. Crane paid little attention while heading out, thinking he was only moments away from rescue.

It was close to noon—about thirty hours of walking—before Crane saw the cabin's outline.

Crane staggered through the small door. He stayed awake long enough to make a fire, using all his focus. He pulled out his parachute, which was tucked inside his parka for extra protection. He wrapped himself in its silk folds. Crane collapsed into the bunk.

He didn't leave it for forty-eight hours.

Hunger finally forced Crane to his feet. He took that as an encouraging sign. The raisins and cocoa must have been enough to stop his starved body from flipping off more biological switches. There were still the sugar, tallow, and baking powder in the cabin's supplies. He wondered what he could make that would be reasonably edible. Crane then remembered that he never looked under the second tarp in the stilt-raised shelter.

He climbed the ladder and yanked away the covering. There were two large boxes. Crane read the stenciled name. *Phil Berail.* Then the next line. *Woodchopper, Alaska.* He didn't remember seeing Woodchopper on any of his flight charts. Or was that even a town? Could it be this guy Berail's profession?

He used a hammer to pry open one box. Burlap bags were inside. He tore into them.

My God, Crane stammered. Why the hell didn't I look here before? It was, without exaggeration, salvation. The backcountry version of lifesaving flotsam to a shipwrecked soul.

The abundance was staggering.

- *flour, twenty-five pounds*
- *rice, thirty pounds*
- *dried beef and beans, thirty pounds*

The next box was perhaps more generous:
- *a bearskin*
- *a wool blanket*
- *two pairs of overalls*
- *long underwear*
- *three pairs of wool socks*
- *two pairs of mukluks (not the military-issue kind, Crane noted, but the superior traditional style)*
- *snowshoes*
- *a .22-caliber rifle with ammunition*
- *candles*
- *and more food: tea, dried eggs, powdered soup mix, dried onions, sugar, another can of cocoa*

What's this? Crane pulled out the last item at the bottom of the box: moose-hide mittens.

Crane carefully lugged the supplies into the cabin. The bearskin, blanket, and clothes were piled on the bunk. The food was stacked near the stove.

He then got down to making a meal. Tallow went first into the frying pan. He dumped in two handfuls of flour and some baking soda. In a second pot, he melted snow and brought it to a boil. He tossed in rice and sugar. Crane finished with hot cocoa.

He finally made his New Year's toast. It went to a stranger named Berail.

NINE

AUGUST 31, 2006

64 Degrees 49.072 Minutes North, 143 Degrees 31.361 Minutes West

Doug Beckstead watched the military forensic team move with crisp precision around the wreckage.

The dig leader, anthropologist Gregory L. Fox, wanted to set up camp as soon as possible and get work started. Their window was small. Snow was not impossible in late August. The weather in 2006 was already uncommonly threatening. Low temperatures were dancing around the freezing mark in one of the coldest snaps on record for this time of year in the Charley River valley. Sporadic rain—sometimes near the verge of sleet—rode in on north winds.

Fox wiped the lenses on his square glasses, covered with dirt kicked up by the two Black Hawk helicopters that had ferried them from Fort Wainwright, the former Ladd Field.

"Let's get going," Fox urged. "We have a lot of work."

The team didn't need coaching. They had been through this before many times.

A search perimeter was set up, fanning out from the shattered fuselage and wings. Tents sprang into place, sleeping bags were rolled out, and generators were switched on. Bits of debris and rocks—some coated with melted aluminum from the B-24's fireball—were cleared away from the first grid marked out for the dig.

Some members of the eight-person search team, wearing sweatshirts and fleeces against the growing chill, crouched close to the rocky soil at an elevation fifteen hundred feet above the Charley. Their trowels began to scrap at the ground, clearing fractions of an inch at a time.

The team planned to spend a week at the site. Then they were looking forward to some rest. The Charley River was the second leg of a summer mission in Alaska. Earlier in August, they were on Alaska's rugged Kenai Peninsula, south of Anchorage, at the crash site of a Catalina Flying Boat that went down during the Aleutian battles in 1942. It was a near certainty that the pilots' remains were at that site. It was just a question of finding them.

The wreckage of the *Iceberg Inez* had less clarity for the searchers.

Only Beckstead was convinced that Hoskin's remains were there. It was essentially a gut feeling, but one increasingly bolstered by his own research and evidence. Beckstead had uncovered bits of gear, including parachute buckles, during his visits to the *Iceberg Inez* since his first stop in 1994 on the helicopter trip. As his research piled up, Beckstead never bought into the theories that Hoskin could have bailed out at the last moment.

His persistence paid off. He sent some bone fragments to the U.S. military, believing they could be human remains. They weren't. But the parachute buckles and other items were enough to move the crash site high on the priority list. The Pentagon decided to send experts in field forensics to the site. The military also allowed Beckstead to tag along as an observer and National Park Service liaison. Still, there was nothing stronger to go on than Beckstead's hunches and his collection of random debris.

"It was one of those roll-the-dice situations," said Fox, a Nebraska-based expert who had led dozens of missions around the world for the Pentagon's Joint POW/MIA Accounting Command, known as JPAC.

The unit, pronounced *Jay-Pak,* is often the last of any American boots on the ground in many former battlefields and crash sites.

Their undertaking, in the widest sense, seeks to write wartime epilogues that were once out of reach. Until the twentieth century, a soldier missing in action most likely remained missing. The fighters knew it. So did their families. It had been that way since antiquity. Rarely were bodies returned for funerals. Instead, their battles and deeds were celebrated in poems, fables, or song. Students of imperial Rome know well the many tales built around the mysterious fate of the Ninth Legion, which was last seen during clashes with tribes in Britain in the northern reaches of the empire. Centuries earlier, Herodotus recounted a tantalizing head-scratcher about a fifty-thousand-strong Persian force that disappeared in the Egyptian desert.

And even if someone wanted to comb the old battlegrounds, the corpses hold their secrets tightly. Few soldiers before World War I carried formal military identification, and the dead often ended up in mass graves or were left where they fell. Some soldiers during the Civil War made their own dog tags from wood or metal disks. But the lack of standardized ID made identification a sketchy proposition at best. Modern advances in postmortem detection, such as dental records, offered new tools to give a name to the remains of someone missing in action. Vietnam was a turning point.

The Pentagon opened an identification lab in Thailand in 1973, focusing on MIAs across Indochina. There had been previous labs following the Korean War, but the Thailand-based facility was a chance to employ new forensic techniques. The lab shifted to Hawaii three years later. Its mandate also expanded to cover cases from all conflicts involving U.S. personnel, including the Cold War. Various units merged in 2003 to form JPAC.

Nearly all its cases are from World War II and conflicts since. But some reach back earlier. Just a few weeks after the JPAC mission to the Charley River site, the remains of a World War I veteran, Francis Lupo, were interred at Arlington National Cemetery. In the casket were fragments of bone and teeth recovered from a French field. JPAC labs have also analyzed the remains of crew members from the Civil War ironclad warship USS *Monitor,* which sank in a storm off Cape Hatteras on the last day of 1862. The pieces of bone and teeth were studied after a lengthy process to desalinate the remains and remove ocean sediment. It was determined they belonged to two of the sixteen seamen lost in the sinking—one likely in his late teens and the other in his thirties—but experts did not have enough evidence to pinpoint their identities.

More than eighty-three thousand U.S. military personnel are listed as missing in action or killed in action and not recovered since Pearl Harbor. The overwhelming majority—more than seventy-three thousand—were listed alongside Hoskin as veterans from World War II.

Beckstead stayed to the side as the investigators moved ahead with their work. Dirt was sifted through quarter-inch metal mesh. Some soil was still so saturated with oil from the crash that it was picked through by hand. A military photographer documented each step. Also on hand was an explosives expert in case the cold-weather test flight had munitions that were never listed in the military reports.

It was a moment of runaway emotion for Beckstead.

Since his first impromptu visit in 1994, Beckstead had pored over any material he could find on the crash, including a detailed 1944 account in the *American* magazine under Crane's byline but crafted from an extensive interview by a celebrity journalist team of Gerold Frank and James D. Horan. Frank pioneered the "as-told-to" biography whose subjects included Judy Garland and Zsa Zsa Gabor, who once said she told Frank "more than I would ever tell a psychiatrist." Horan was a prolific writer of historical nonfiction, including Wild West tales about desperadoes, lawmen, and Butch Cassidy and the Sundance Kid.

Beckstead returned to the crash site several times, poking through the debris and crash-rippled metal. Hoskin was always on his mind. The pilot remained the biggest question mark from the crash. The crew chief, Pompeo, bailed out. No one doubted that. The fates of the two other airmen, the radio operator, Wenz, and the prop specialist, Sibert, were known.

A military investigation filed December 22, 1944—a year and a day after the B-24 plunged from the sky—concluded that Hoskin and Pompeo "cannot be presumed to be living" and recommended their status be changed from missing to deceased. It further dismissed the speculation that Crane may have seen Hoskin's chute. The pilot, the report said, "would normally be the last to jump. He was still in the plane when Lieutenant Crane bailed out."

Most of JPAC recovery efforts are still in the jungle highlands and tropical coasts of Southeast Asia, but cold-climate missions occur with some regularity. In 2013 on a Greenland glacier, surveillance cameras probing thirty-eight feet under the ice sheet spotted cables believed part of an amphibious Grumman Duck aircraft that disappeared during a snowstorm in 1942 carrying three crew members. In June 2012 JPAC teams began work on an Alaskan glacier after a military helicopter spotted the wreckage of a C-124 cargo plane that went down in November 1952. Eleven crew members died in the crash.

In comparison, the site above the Charley River was easy despite the weather. The subfreezing chill was enough to keep away Alaska's dreaded summertime mosquitoes. "Cold, wet, windy," recalled Fox. But there were advantages. The soil has relatively low acidity, which aids in the preservation of human remains. The fire that engulfed the B-24 also served to slightly harden the bone fragments that were not burned to cinders.

One area of high interest for the forensic team was shielded by a bent strut from the fuselage. It acted as a bit of a canopy from the harshest weather and kept plants from taking root. Animals, too, were blocked from rummaging through the soil. Here, some of the most promising artifacts emerged.

More than 102 square meters—about the footprint of a small home—were covered by the JPAC teams, digging to an average depth of about 10 centimeters, or nearly 4 inches. Clear plastic evidence bags began to fill.

"Here's something!" one of the diggers shouted excitedly. The others rushed over to see. Dirt was brushed away from the object.

It was the eagle insignia from the cap of an officer in the Army Air Forces.

Leon Crane, right, with his father Louis, who emigrated in 1913 from Ukraine to Philadelphia along with his wife Sonia. Crane had a letter from his father in his parka when he bailed from the crippled B-24. The letter helped Crane make a life-saving fire as he waited for a rescue that never came. COURTESY OF THE CRANE FAMILY

Leon Crane during training as a military aviator. Crane was called up by the Army Air Forces in 1941 just months after graduating from the Massachusetts Institute of Technology. COURTESY OF THE CRANE FAMILY

The row house at 5464 Baltimore Avenue in West Philadelphia where Crane spent much of his boyhood with his two brothers and a sister. The neighborhood became a magnet for immigrants as the city's trolley lines pushed outward. AUTHOR PHOTO

Second Lieutenant Harold E. Hoskin of Houlton, Maine. Hoskin's wife Mary was pregnant at the time of the B-24 crash. The couple believed they would have a boy. Instead, Mary gave birth to a daughter who, as a young girl, imagined that her father would one day walk through the door. COURTESY OF JOHN AND MARY HOSKIN

Master Sergeant Richard Pompeo, the only member of the B-24's crew still missing. Pompeo bailed out of the plane just seconds before Crane, but was only wearing a plug-in flight suit that offered almost no protection against the cold. Courtesy of the Pompeo family

A B-24 bomber at Ladd Field outside Fairbanks. Ground crews were constantly advised about the dangers of winters in interior Alaska, where even brief exposure can lead to frostbite. US Army

The head of Ladd Field's search-and-rescue wing, Major R. C. Ragle, who came north to teach geology but became enamored by the adventure of Alaska's bush pilot culture before the war. Ragle's military career included air combat with Japanese invading forces in the Aleutians, the only major battle of the war in North America. Courtesy of John Linn Ragle

Staff Sergeant Ralph Wenz, the radio operator on the B-24. Wenz was no stranger to the rigors of Alaskan aviation. He worked on mail routes around the territory for several years before the war. Courtesy of Ann Chambers Noble and the Wenz family

The enlisted men's barracks at Ladd Field, where winter amenities were so sparse that they earned nicknames such as Pneumonia Gulch. US Army

An aerial view of Ladd Field during the war years. The massive Hangar 1 still dominates the base. US Army

An American P-39 fighter repainted with the Soviet red star as part of the Lend-Lease aerial armada. US Army

Fighter planes at Ladd Field at the height of the Lend-Lease program, which turned over U.S. warplanes to Soviet pilots to join the fight in Europe and elsewhere. The program transferred thousands of planes in one of the most massive movements of military equipment of the war. US Army

Soviet officers and airmen at Ladd Field, where they occupied half of Hangar 1. The Soviets' presence was also felt in Fairbanks as they scooped up American goods as soon as merchants could put them on the shelves. Stockings and chocolates were big hits. US Army

The wreckage of the *Iceberg Inez* above the Charley River. Crane landed about two miles away after parachuting from the crippled aircraft, but was unable to reach the site because of deep snow and loose rocks. PHOTO BY DAVID MYERS

Debris from the B-24 crash. An intense fireball burned away much of the paint from the plane and the equipment inside, but the lack of foraging animals and undergrowth helped preserve the wreckage largely intact for decades. NATIONAL PARK SERVICE

The remains of the Ames' family cabin, located near where the Charley River empties into the Yukon River. Albert Ames and his wife Nina raised a family in the Alaskan bush, trapping and fishing for food and money. NATIONAL PARK SERVICE

Leon Crane stands outside the Ames cabin shortly after coming out of the wilderness. One of Crane's first questions was whether the war was still going on. COURTESY OF THE CRANE FAMILY

A 1936 photo of Woodchopper, Alaska, a town that grew around a gold dredging operation that turned a modest profit before going under. Woodchopper is now abandoned. US GEOLOGICAL SURVEY

Story of Crane's return in the *Fairbanks Daily News-Miner* on March 16, 1944.

Headline in the *New York Times* on March 17, 1944, as word spread about Crane's ordeal. The 84 days includes the three-days' time spent in the Ames cabin and the travel to Woodchopper.

Leon Crane after his return to Ladd Field, still wearing his tattered flight suit. US ARMY

Crane enjoys his first meal at Ladd Field following his return. One airman wrote in his diary that word of Crane's survival spread like "wildfire" across the base. US ARMY

Former Yukon-Charley historian Doug Beckstead on one of his visits to the crash site. Beckstead's research was crucial in finding the remains of the pilot Harold Hoskin. PHOTO BY DAVID MYERS

The twisted wreckage of the *Iceberg Inez*. NATIONAL PARK SERVICE

The U.S. military's Central Identification Laboratory in Hawaii. The military lists more than 83,000 personnel unaccounted for in conflicts going back to World War II. The majority of the cases remain in the Asia-Pacific region. DEPARTMENT OF DEFENSE

The B-24 wreckage with the Charley River in the distance. NATIONAL PARK SERVICE

John Hoskin, the younger brother of Harold, at his home in Gorham, Maine, in late 2013.
PHOTO BY TOULA VLAHOU

Harold Hoskin's daughter, Joann Goldstein, being greeted at Arlington National Cemetery following the September 2007 burial ceremony for the remains of her father.
PHOTO BY BRUCE GUTHRIE

Doug Beckstead addresses mourners at Arlington National Cemetery at the funeral for Harold Hoskin.
PHOTO BY BRUCE GUTHRIE

Ethel Myers, the sister of Richard Pompeo, at the 2007 burial of Hoskin's remains. Pompeo's nephew, David Myers, traveled to Alaska to visit the crash site two years earlier.
PHOTO BY BRUCE GUTHRIE

The grave of Harold Hoskin at Arlington. The graves in the background include the burial site of another crew member from the flight, First Lieutenant James Sibert.
PHOTO BY TOULA VLAHOU

TEN

JANUARY 10, 1944

Wing Rescue Section, Seattle

With a winter warm front approaching, a military plane flew south from Ladd Field.

A classified mailbag was in the cargo hold. The documents aboard included a dossier of seven typed pages that recounted, in exacting detail, the hunt for Crane, Hoskin, and the others. It also marked another official step in the process to move them from the list of the missing to that of the dead.

The last search flights had gone out in late December, making their passes about ten miles south of Big Delta. It was a fitting and frustrating end to more than a week of searches that never came close. The planes were dispatched in the opposite direction from the wreckage and Crane's northward push along the Charley River. None of the planes, in fact, ever came within the general vicinity of the B-24's resting place. It's unlikely that crews even glimpsed the mountains around the headwaters of the Charley.

The search leader, R. C. Ragle, waited more than a week before writing up the cover letter for the report on the loss of B-24D no. 42–40910. Perhaps he was waiting for some miracle with the new year. Ragle was like that. He tended to hold out hope until the very end. He knew Alaska well. A big land sometimes produced big surprises.

But the file couldn't wait forever. Ragle wrapped it up during the first week of 1944 and got it into the mail sack tossed into a

C-47 carrying airmen for some R&R in the States. The flight left for Seattle just as a ridge of relatively warm air ballooned up from the south, pushing the thermometer in Fairbanks over the freezing mark for the first time in months. The report on the *Iceberg Inez* was bound for the Army Air Forces command in Washington via review stops in Seattle and Minneapolis. Ragle made sure to document the scope of the search and—in a possible attempt to anticipate questions from the higher-ups—noted that the B-24 gave no indication of its heading after the last radio call.

"Intensive detailed search was continued with from 9 to 17 aircraft through the days 21 December 1943 through 29 December 1943, with particular attention being paid to the area of the submitted flight plan," wrote Ragle in his personal style that kept punctuation to a minimum. "This area receiving coverage by each of not less than five separately assigned missions both day and night, until no reasonable chance existed that further search would locate the missing aircraft."

The search, in other words, was now formally abandoned.

Ragle was not only wrong about the proper search zone. He also misjudged the chances that anyone had bailed out. "The possibility of parachute escape," he added in a backup document, "appears to have been remote."

With nothing to go on, the theories about the crash leaned toward sudden and catastrophic structural breakup. What else could explain a plane that vanished without the slightest hint to Ladd Tower? Aircraft went down all the time in Alaska, especially in the winter. Some Ladd disasters unfolded in full view. Planes crashed moments after takeoff or returned with cold-fouled landing gear and skidded in a bloom of sparks and shredded metal. For the others, there was almost always some trail—a distress call or sudden storm—to offer clues on what went wrong. This time, the plane was just gone.

"The aircraft while conducting propeller tests in an area of known intense turbulence suffered structural failure which prevented use of radio and prevented escape of personnel," Ragle speculated in a December 27 report that was included among the paperwork sent to Washington.

"This conclusion is reached after consideration of the known characteristics of the members of the aircraft's crew and in consideration of the fact that no signs, signals, or other traces of personnel have been found during search of this operating area and between that area and Ladd Field," Ragle continued.

Ragle's report concluded with a bit of self-generated optimism, perhaps inspired by the stunning return of Pompeo and his crewmate from the wilderness in 1942. He noted that the prevailing high-altitude winds on December 21 peaked at about ninety miles per hour from the southeast. They *could* have pushed the B-24 off course, and Hoskin *could* have made an emergency landing in the Yukon River valley for some reason such as low fuel, and they *could* all be safe somewhere.

"Under the premise, the probability is that all personnel are safe and comfortably supplied and encamped," Ragle wrote.

He urged all crews to remain vigilant for signs of the plane during regular missions.

Such appeals were passed to the west side of Hangar 1. This was known by some as Red Square: the hub for hundreds of Soviet airmen, officers, and handlers sent to Ladd Field in one of the most far-reaching displays of Moscow-Washington cooperation during the war.

Neither side, though, wanted to talk about it much at the time.

To most outside Alaska, Ladd Field was little more than a distant point on the military map of World War II. It came up occasionally in newspapers as a dateline for USO tours or, as with Pompeo, the backdrop for inspirational stories about survival in the tundra. What was rarely mentioned, however, was the extent that Ladd Field was a linchpin site for the complicated relations between the Soviets and Americans during the war and, as it would turn out, a bit of a dress rehearsal for the Cold War to come.

Fairbanks was the handover spot in a long-distance feeder network to ferry American warplanes over the Bering Strait. From there, the aircraft headed across the vastness of Siberia to join the battles on the Eastern Front. The logistics were complex, but the premise was simple. America had the industrial clout to churn out planes and fighting equipment at staggering rates, while the arsenals of the Soviet Union and other Allied countries were drained dangerously low. A match was made. The United States supplied the hardware. The other countries strapped in their pilots or sent the made-in-America firepower to their ground forces.

It was known as the Lend-Lease program. Washington set the plans in motion months before the attack on Pearl Harbor. At the time, it marked a major shift from official American policies to keep some distance from the widening war. Not all were happy with the change. It brought a fierce backlash from proisolationist factions in Congress. One vehemently antiwar senator, Burton Wheeler of Montana, complained that Lend-Lease would drag America into the conflict, and "our boys will be returned— returned in caskets, maybe; returned with bodies maimed; returned with minds warped and twisted by sights of horrors and the scream and shriek of high-powered shells." He appealed to other lawmakers: "Was the last world war worthwhile?"

The views of Wheeler and others who favored neutrality took a dramatic U-turn after the Japanese attack on Pearl Harbor in December 1941. Many of the former isolationists, however, later paid a political price. In 1946 Montana voters sent Wheeler packing to end his long Senate career.

In the early stages of Lend-Lease, some U.S. matériel was shipped off to Britain and its European allies. But the mainstay of the program became the supply routes for billions of dollars in equipment—from Spam to submachine guns to the latest fighter planes— bound for the embattled Red Army. The reasoning in Washington and London was that it was money well spent. Think of it as a down payment to keep the Soviet Union in the war. "The most unsordid act" in history, said a welcoming Churchill. Some shipments crossed over from Iran and through sea-lanes to Soviet ports. The fastest, and most storied, transit was the Arctic air corridor.

The U.S. planes began the journey in Great Falls, Montana, where a small Soviet advance team logged the departures and sent word back to Moscow about what was on the way. Sometimes, the Soviet red star insignia would be painted over the stars and stripes before the trip got under way. American pilots razzed each other, saying they didn't know whether they were flying on behalf of the Soviets or the air force of the filling-station giant Texaco, whose well-known logo also was a red star.

The aircraft then puddle-jumped across western Canada, bound for Alaska, which was bought from Russia for about two cents an acre fewer than eighty years before. In the winter, just getting to Ladd Field could be a harrowing feat. The last leg between Canada's Watson Lake and Ladd was dubbed the "Million Dollar Valley" because of so many costly wrecks below. On one run in February 1943, the heater froze on Major George Racey Jordan's C-47 transport. The plane was fourteen thousand feet over the tundra after leaving Watson Lake. Jordan estimated it was minus seventy outside.

"I never knew a person could be so cold," Jordan wrote in his 1952 memoirs. "I nearly lost a couple of toes, and my heels are still sore. My nostrils cracked when I breathed and the corners of my mouth hurt like a toothache. I shut my eyes because the eyeballs pained so. . . . The pilot couldn't see out of the window because of his breath freezing on the pane. So we flew by instruments until the end, when we used lighter fluid to wash a hole to land by."

Jordan's book became something of a Cold War screed. His contention was that the Soviets manipulated the Lend-Lease program to help build up their military and gain important insights into U.S. military technology.

But Jordan's chronicles are more important as one of the most vivid descriptions of Ladd Field's Soviet guests. About eight thousand planes headed to the Soviet Union along this route, including craft such as the P-39 Airacobra fighter that was Crane's specialty. The P-39 had its drawbacks, including small fuel tanks that limited its range. The Soviets loved the P-39s all the same. It was deemed so good at low-altitude combat that it was given the name *Cobrastochkas*, or Dear Little Cobras. Some planes, however, never finished the trip from Alaska. An estimated 140 Soviet airmen died in Siberia-bound crashes after taking over various aircraft. Still, many Soviet pilots—so confident in their war-honed abilities—barreled off the Ladd runway sometimes with no more training than received when picking up a rental car. In one preflight briefing, a Soviet pilot climbed onto the wing of a P-40 fighter to quiz the American airman before flying to Siberia. His translator was on the other wing. Just four questions were asked: How do you start it? How many RPMs for takeoff? How do you keep the oil and coolant pressures in the right range? How does the radio work?

On many levels, Ladd Field became an ad hoc laboratory in East-West understanding. Soviet engineers used pantomime in the supply room to fill orders. A seat was made available for a Russian speaker in Ladd Tower. A civilian woman who worked at Ladd once invited two Soviets to a home-cooked dinner by her mom in Fairbanks. The woman prided herself on being a good chess player and wanted to show her skill to the guests. Well, it turned out she was good by Fairbanks standards. She recounted how the Soviets demolished her with just a handful of moves before checkmate.

The Ladd Field newspaper, the *Midnight Sun*, ran phrases in Russian such as transliterations of "Comrade Captain" and "I am your friend." Yet the airmen from both countries quickly found the common languages of drinking and bartering. A popular swap was American pinup beauties for Russian memorabilia such as coats, pins, and the classic Cossack-style trousers with their billowing thigh panels. Many of the deals were brokered by an American private, Frank Nigro, who moonlighted as a bartender at the Russian Officers' Club, where beer was a dime and a Hershey bar a nickel.

When Major Jordan arrived on the frozen tarmac from his bone-chilling flight, he was greeted by a buxom Russian woman mechanic. "Without inhibitions, the generous girl seized my head with her brawny arms and hugged me to her warm bosom," Jordan wrote. "She held it there until I could feel 'pins and needles,' which showed that the tissues were warming back to life."

Jordan was then led to the Soviet section, where he was plunged in a tub of cool water that "seemed hot" to his iced skin. Paper cups brimming with vodka soon arrived. "Russian medicine," one of the Soviets grinned. Jordan then got a rough rubdown with towels and received a dinner invitation from a slim, elegant man who spoke refined English. He looked to Jordan to have the ascetic features of a monk. It was, according to Jordan's account, the KGB's man at Ladd Field.

Later, when Jordan showed up at the officers' mess for dinner, it was the usual divide. The Americans kept to one side in a men's-only section. Only a few women nurses stayed on base at the time, and the Women's Army Corps, or WACs, didn't arrived until April 1945. The Soviets were on the other side, sitting with young women who served as translators and, according to many winks and nods from the Americans, possibly more. One of the Cold Nose Boys, Lieutenant Arthur Jordan of Maine (no relation to Major Jordan), waxed on in his diary about his flirtations with some of the girls in the Soviet entourage and how he got chummy with a Russian soldier who had a passion for singing American folk songs. His favorite was Stephen Foster's "Beautiful Dreamer." Jordan also got a "great kick" out of watching the Soviet crews guzzle bottle after bottle of Coca-Cola while trying their luck at slot machines. "They slam in hundreds of nickels, dimes and quarters," Lieutenant Jordan observed in his diary.

"They are getting a taste of the best democracy has to offer and they love it," he added in a bit of personal flag waving. "I guess they are not too eager to leave. . . . Can't blame them."

It all must have seemed a bit disconcerting for someone like Leon Crane, who was raised on stories of pogroms in Ukraine and the suffering of his parents and other Ukrainian Jews. Crane knew a bit of Russian picked up from his parents. If he decided to try it out on the Soviets at Ladd, he never mentioned the results.

As it stood, there was no official media blackout on the Soviet presence at Ladd. But American reporters in those days generally toed the line on information considered instrumental to the war effort. So the War Department had a firm grip over how much was said about the Soviet role at Ladd. That control extended to censoring letters from the public to remove references to the Soviets.

Yet there was no way to keep it secret from anyone who ventured to Fairbanks. The Reds had full run of the town—then about four thousand people with just a few paved streets—and explored all it had to offer. One well-known stop on the footloose trail was a rustic red-light district known as the Line, where the working girls would place a curtain over their front cabin window as a sign they were otherwise engaged with a client. The Line was surrounded by a twelve-foot clapboard fence to protect, the town fathers said, the "sensibilities" of women and children. It was a bit of chivalrous overkill. In 1940s Fairbanks just about every vice was in ample supply. It was hard to walk one hundred feet without passing a saloon. Bets could be placed on just about anything, including the day's temperature. For a slightly less tawdry outing, the list of nightspots included the Graehl-O-Bar, with "Fritz on the piano with old time tunes" and "Thelma and her accordion."

The Soviets also received special attention. A longtime bush pilot, Jack Jefford recalled how a representative for General Motors was sent to Fairbanks to keep in constant contact with the Soviets about their impressions of the P-39 engine, which was made by a GM division. The GM liaison knew his customers' tastes. He kept cases of Old Grand-Dad whiskey on hand. "His job was to keep the Russians happy as far as those engines were concerned," said Jefford. "And there's nothing like a case of Grand-Dad to keep a Russian happy."

For the Soviet troops, however, the star attraction in Fairbanks was the shops. Here was eye-popping abundance compared to the state-regulated life back home. They gobbled up Fairbanks's fare at a voracious clip: nylons, chocolate, lipstick for wives and girl-friends at home, and—the score of all scores—real denim jeans. Alaska, not being a state, was exempt from the wartime rations imposed elsewhere. One story says an American officer overheard a conversation that went like this:

Soviet officer: "I want shoes."

Store clerk: "What kind?"

Soviet: "All kinds."

Clerk: "What size?"

Soviet: "All sizes."

The merchants were more than happy to oblige. At a major Fairbanks department store called Gordon's, which stretched an entire block, it was hard to keep up with the consumerism of the Communists. Silk stockings, dresses, lingerie, skirts—it all went fast. One group wasn't so happy: the Fairbanks ladies. They groused constantly about the siphon-style shopping of the Soviets.

Irene Noyes, who worked at Ladd, went into a store for a pair of shoes. "The saleslady looked at me and said, 'Are you kidding? We've sold everything,'" she recalled.

"It is no strange site," wrote a Ladd captain, Richard L. Neuberger, "to see a stoic Russian pilot, who has downed his share of Nazis over Rostov or Smolensk, lapping up a marshmallow sundae with chocolate ice cream and chopped nuts at a Fairbanks drug store."

The Soviet cadre in Alaska also stirred all manner of cloak-and-dagger theories, including speculation of efforts to steal details of the U.S. nuclear bomb program. Such tradecraft con-spiracies fail to mention the huge improbability of Manhattan Project secrets trickling all the way to Alaska or Montana. But one incident opened some genuine intrigue.

It involved a U.S. private named John White, who was assigned as a driver for the Soviet officers. One day in July 1943, he took two Soviet officers on a tour of Fairbanks with a stop at the radio station KFAR. At the time, the station had a back room used to send secret military communiqués by the then cutting-edge technology of primitive fax machines. The tour ended at Ballaine Lake, outside Fairbanks. The Soviets said they went into the woods "to pick wildflowers." When they returned, they claimed White had vanished. Later, investigators found White's uniform folded neatly near the water's edge. Authorities drained the lake and found his body. The Soviets who accompanied White were believed to be intelligence agents. But they never faced intense questioning from U.S. authorities because of the international sensitivities and the desire not to disrupt the Lend-Lease flow. The cause of death was ruled drowning, and the case was quickly closed, even though White's friends said he was afraid of the water and would have never voluntarily gone for a dip. To this day, the case remains riddled with questions.

After sending off the reports on the B-24 crash, Ragle went home to his tidy four-bedroom log house on Cowles Street, separated from Weeks Field by a culvert. For the first time in months, it wasn't necessary to light a fire in the big fireplace made of river stones. The brief push into the low thirties felt downright balmy.

Ragle, though, was not in the best of moods. He hated to be beaten by Alaska's backcountry. The *Iceberg Inez* was out there, and Ragle was responsible for finding it. He wasn't at all pleased about writing an inconclusive report. At least his family offered him some domestic downtime away from the base and its pressures. While airmen and crews were playing poker or chasing the local women, Ragle was tending to the routine of all families: homework, bills, meals. And there was also the constant home upkeep of varnishing the peeled logs and replacing the oakum caulking.

His young son and daughter returned from Colorado after the Japanese were driven from the Aleutians. The family now had a third child and a collection of dogs, including a white Siberian husky with glacier-blue eyes. The den featured a wall for the family's firearms, including shotguns, .30-caliber rifles, and the favorites of eldest son John: a .22 Mossberg and Savage lever-action rifle. All the kids learned how to properly handle a weapon as soon as they were strong enough to lift it. Ragle's mania about drilling in the commandments of gun safety had a personal history. About thirty years earlier, Ragle's uncle was accidentally shot and killed when a hunting partner fired on a rustling bush, thinking it was a deer. Ragle told the kids: a gun is always considered loaded until you have checked three times to make sure it is not, and then you still treat it as if it's loaded.

While Ragle fitted comfortably into Alaska's frontier ethos, it was not so kind to his Chicago-raised wife, Jane, a statuesque presence who stood a few inches taller than her husband.

Their first-born, John, recalled how his parents diligently researched the demands of life just below the Arctic Circle and rigged up a sunlamp for wintertime doses of vitamin D—also possibly in attempts to ease Jane's seasonal doldrums. But Jane's body and soul seemed to clash constantly with the Far North. She suffered from long bouts of melancholy during the twenty-hour winter darkness. At times, she was so incapacitated that chores such as wood collection and meal preparations fell to John while still in grade school. Jane also couldn't quite find a social center of gravity. Base activities didn't interest her. The university was a welcome haven for a while. But it quickly seemed too provincial and predictable for her sensibilities, which were shaped by the activist energy of Chicago's Hull House community and its campaigns for social reform. After the war, Jane's treatments for depression nearly bankrupted the family and, at one point, brought Ragle to tears after he was denied credit at the local Piggly Wiggly market.

It was a rare breakdown. Ragle usually seemed to be in forward motion—doing his part to keep up with Alaska's eccentric spirit.

It's a kind of Alaskan palimpsest: the nonstop waves of adventurers, visionaries, and misfits. They bring renewal that overlays, but never fully erases, the past. Fur trappers made room for gold rush stampeders; dogsledders passed the torch to bush pilots. Each period, though, left its mark for the next. War footing in Alaska brought its own share of splendid originals such as military advisers on cold-weather survival and tactics.

There was a Canadian-born Arctic scholar named Vilhjalmur Stefansson. He avidly backed proposals to establish a Jewish republic in the Soviet Far East and once encouraged a small expedition to colonize a Siberian island. The only survivors were a Nome seamstress known as Ada Blackjack and the team's cat, Vic. Stefansson's former Arctic exploration companion, Australian adventurer and polymath Hubert Wilkins, also found his way into the ranks of the U.S. advisers. Wilkins led a failed attempt in 1931 to cross under the Arctic ice cap in a decommissioned U.S. submarine he named *Nautilus* after Captain Nemo's vessel in *20,000 Leagues Under the Sea*. In January 1943 Wilkins boldly—or maybe recklessly—wore a light coat and no hat while posing for photos around military personnel bundled up against the subzero.

Meanwhile, out on the Aleutians, a group of soldier-journalists was preparing the first edition of a base newspaper. The newsroom of the *Adakian* at the garrison on Adak Island was led by another singular personality brought north by the war: the dean of the hard-boiled detective novel, Dashiell Hammett.

Hammett's best creative years were already a decade behind, with *The Maltese Falcon, The Glass Key,* and *The Thin Man* coming in a literary burst in the 1930s. After that, he drifted along in socialist political currents, which carried him into the American Communist Party and, for a time, as a leading proponent of keeping the United States out of the war. At the same time, his lover, the prolific playwright and screenwriter Lillian Hellman, was dismayed by the Nazi's anti-Semitic policies and became a leading voice of alarm in America about the Third Reich.

Like many—including the original Lend-Lease opponents—Hammett's views on neutrality took an about-face after Pearl Harbor. He somehow wrangled a place back in uniform despite being emaciated and weakened from tuberculosis lingering from World War I. The now Corporal Hammett was shipped off to Adak and got permission to put out the mimeographed newspaper. The trial edition came out January 19, 1944, and Hammett soon recruited a staff that included future journalistic standouts such as Bernard Kalb.

About two months later, actress Olivia de Havilland made a morale-boosting stop in Adak and met with the crew from the paper. Hammett penned a letter to Hellman about the starlet's visit. "She seems nice," he wrote.

> As a matter of strict fact, she seemed a little more than that to me, but I'm not unmindful of the fact that she's the first woman I've really talked to in nearly nine months. The softness is what really gets you. Suddenly you realize that everything you've touched for months and months has been harsh in texture. . . . The snow here is granular, with a good deal of ice in it; the tundra is coarse; even the mud is gritty. Visually there is no softness here. I'm, if possible, more convinced than ever that this is the most beautiful part of the world, but it's an almost metallic, two-dimensional beauty with no warmth or gentleness to trick or woo you into liking it. Its great bleak loveliness is just there, hard and sharp, forever and ever.

ELEVEN

JANUARY 19, 1944

Charley River

For a full day, Crane watched the wind spin heavy snowflakes into a veil of white.

He drank cocoa, tended the fire in the stove, and stayed within the cabin's walls. By the door, he leaned a makeshift rucksack. It was fashioned from one of Berail's tents and a wool blanket, threaded together with rope. Packed inside were beans, rice, and other supplies to last several days. A frying pan was tied to the pack with parachute cord. Resting atop it all was Berail's .22 rifle, oiled and cleaned, along with boxes of ammo.

The only thing standing in the way was the storm. When it eased, Crane was ready to set off for the first time since his all-night odyssey nearly three weeks earlier.

In that time, he had healed.

His hands were the biggest concern. Crane first tried to massage them with warmed tallow, but its oils stung the cuts and scrapes. Instead, he devised an ingenious remedy. Crane melted candle wax onto his palm and spread it like a lotion until it encrusted both hands. He then tucked them into Berail's moose-hide mittens. For six days, he kept at it. Gradually, color and movement returned to his fingers. Meanwhile, he slept nearly eighteen hours a day. His body seemed to crave the warmth of the bear skin. When he woke, he feasted on all manner of pancakes: sometimes with soup vegetables stirred in the batter or fortified with strands of chewy jerky. Berail did not leave a mirror. Crane used his revived fingers to assess his condition. He felt the inward sag of his cheeks and the sharpness of his jawline. But he could also sense he was putting some weight back on and regaining strength. He felt strong enough to begin exploring the river.

Crane planned to hike downstream for a day or two until he reached the midway point of his supplies. Then he'd head back to Berail's cabin. The idea was to get a better sense of the terrain and, possibly, a clearer fix on his location without taking any unnecessary risks with the weather. No doubt it was far easier to stay put. Crane felt the instinctive hesitation when he thought about facing the wilds again. He pushed back, forcing himself to pack and prepare for the scouting run.

Fifteen years earlier, an ethnographer named Cornelius Osgood grappled with a similar inner struggle during a winter of research spent in far northern Canada. The inertia of the season set in. It seemed natural to stay put and hibernate. Why fight the elements? Why not just hole up in his cabin until the weather broke as long as the supplies held out? Osgood felt himself foundering deeper in his hermitage, with chores left unattended and cooking pans unwashed. "I would say to myself, 'For God's sake, do something!' . . . Hour after hour I would stay in the little room from which I could not see, alternately dreaming and hating myself," he wrote.

Osgood climbed out of the funk with a time-tested method of survival: narrow your goals. Concentrate on one specific thing— darning a sock, fixing a broken clasp—that helps keep the psychological gremlins at bay. Osgood called them the "little things, perhaps the unimportant things, the predicaments in the process of learning to stay alive."

Crane had always been a quick study. He intuitively deduced that it was crucial to stay busy and focused. Yet he still fought constantly against the urges to simply conserve his supplies and allow the days to pass. Crane found a 1938 calendar along with some old magazines in one of the cabin's many cubbyholes and crannies.

It was remarkable to think that perhaps no one had been inside the cabin in more than five years. Crane started a daily routine of punching a nail through each day on the calendar to keep track of his own time. In this way, too, he could calculate the date since the crash.

One morning, the calendar slipped from the wall. Crane noticed a simple map of Alaska printed on the other side. There was Woodchopper. Of course, Crane thought. It's a town, not Berail's job. The settlement was on Woodchopper Creek, just south of the Yukon River. That at least validated his suspicions that the river outside flowed into the Yukon. But was he on Woodchopper Creek or the bigger Charley River to the east? Regardless, Crane figured it meant that Woodchopper couldn't be too far.

The map was useful but crude. There were no suggestions of topography, and only the most prominent features were marked. Still, Crane thought, the river valley had seemed to widen during his near-disastrous trek on New Year's Eve. Crane had enough grasp of Alaska to know that the Yukon River cut a wide floodplain and the land on approach would flatten out.

The planning for his next trip downriver weighed every contingency. Crane's out-and-back New Year's struggle underscored how just one miscalculation, one overreach, can level a heavy price. This time, however, Crane was healthier and exceedingly better equipped. He'd become a rather good shot with Berail's rifle. His main target was the Arctic ptarmigan, a melon-size grouse whose feathers had molted from summer brown to winter white. Crane also exacted some satisfying revenge on the red squirrel population.

He was learning how to read the Alaskan bush. When he bagged one of his first ptarmigan, he noticed its stomach was full of a reddish brush. He found a grove about a quarter mile downriver and turned it into a private shooting gallery. Crane badly butchered some of his first prey—so much so that it looked more like road kill than freshly downed game. He had since become quite efficient in field dressing the birds and squirrels. The trick was to clean them and strip the fur before they froze solid. He'd toss away the guts and wrap the heart and liver in cloth to add to his evening stew.

Even some of the old issues of the *Saturday Evening Post* left behind by Berail played a part in Crane's backcountry education. A couple of the stories were about outdoor life and cowboy ways. Crane read them at night by a Coleman lamp he found under the bunk. He mined the articles for tips. One caught his eye: in wind, build your fire in a hole. Perhaps obvious, but it was another aha moment for the city-bred Crane.

Crane had planned to set off January 19. The storm killed that. The next day came up clear, but distressingly windy. The swaying spruce made creaking sounds that reminded Crane of huge door hinges in need of oil. Fresh snow kicked up in stinging gusts. Crane, however, had tired of waiting. He decided to give it a try. He passed his pack and gun through the cabin door. He checked his pockets for the bullets and matches. The snow was over his knees.

He turned north. It was minus thirty.

From the first steps, this was a wholly different experience than the mad dash weeks before. He was now something of an explorer. Crane took his time and stayed attuned for signs of habitation: the possible smell of burning wood or a path in the snow leading from the river. He also converted a burlap sack into a windbreaking tunic by cutting holes for arms and his head. He congratulated himself on the idea.

The first day out was uneventful.

He watched for places that attracted ptarmigan and noted elk tracks, mentally filing away the details in case they were needed later. On the second day, about five miles downriver from Berail's cabin, he came across another log shelter. In his last journey, he walked right past this place. It was in far worse shape than Berail's and was not brimming with supplies. But inside, Crane came across a heart-soaring find: a sleeping bag, musty and worn, yet still very serviceable. Outside was a canoe, whose shell had been eaten away by the elements. Its metal ribs were still sound, though. This brought more forward planning. If he was stuck until the spring thaw, he might try to repair the canoe with canvas and bark and attempt to paddle out.

The Charley is something of an orphan.

Once the first flakes of gold were found in eastern Alaska, just after the turn of the century, the floodgates reopened. It was the Klondike stampede all over again, with miners, assayers, and lonesome panners looking for pay dirt. The mania was spurred by a banner headline in Dawson City's *Yukon Sun* on January 17, 1903—about seventeen months after Barnette and his wife were unceremoniously offloaded from the stern-wheeler. "RICH STRIKE MADE IN THE TANANA," it trumpeted. The story— with breathless embellishments—was based on accounts from a Japanese-born Renaissance man, Jujiro Wada, whose Alaskan incarnations included cook, elite dog musher, ultramarathoner in prize races, and one of the surveyors who mapped out the famous Iditarod Trail.

During the boom years, the Charley certainly had its share of prospectors on the watch for "color"—meaning the telltale hint of gold in the riverbed. Nothing made them linger too long on the Charley. There simply were easier, and more potentially profitable, streams nearby to try to strike it rich. One was Coal Creek, which roughly parallels the Charley River about fifteen miles to the west. Coal Creek never coughed up major riches with the small-scale prospectors, but later was the site for a new big-dig method to look for gold.

The change started in 1933, when a Canadian industrialist and World War I general named Alexander McRae called the Alaska Agricultural College and School of Mines in Fairbanks. He had a proposition for the dean, Ernest Newton Patty. Help me find some promising gold mining spots, McRae asked. In return, you'll be a partner and maybe get rich in the process. Soon, they picked Coal Creek and began to buy up the claims of the old-timers who were scratching out a living with a combination of gold dust, fur pelts, and dried fish. Their frontier-style days were coming to an end. The new concept was a dredge, basically the marriage of a steam shovel and a washing machine. It scoops up the riverbed and then sprays, tumbles, and filters the haul until—fingers crossed—bits of gold are captured by sticking to blobs of mercury introduced into the process.

There was just one complication for McRae and Patty. There was no such machine around these parts. The partners ordered one from California for the then-princely sum of $156,000 and had it shipped in pieces to Canada. The crates then came down the Yukon River by steamer. While it was on the way, Patty left academia to turn his attention full-time to mining. He began traveling the backcountry, sampling the rough-edged charms of the Alaskan roadhouses—a bit like the bush version of a B&B. Sometimes they would offer a welcome touch of refinement, such as clean glasses and mattresses. Others could be little more than a hovel, with bare bunks and meals of whatever grub landed on your plate.

"Young man," one of the chow slingers at a roadhouse told Patty after noticing his decidedly urbane aura, "you are looking at the dirtiest cook in Alaska."

"My friend," Patty replied, "you are looking at the hungriest man in Alaska."

The Coal Creek dredge started churning in 1936. A year later, the two partners had a similar operation going on neighboring Woodchopper Creek, which got its name as a stop for steamboats to replenish their supplies of logs for the engine room.

Workers on the dredges came and went depending on the seasons, their moods, and their ability to hold their liquor. Drifters showed up looking for a place to hang their hats for a while and make some money. One skinny geezer refused to give his name and was known only as Man with an Ax. Another time, a deranged character rolled into camp calling himself the Devil. He had to be tricked onto a bush plane with the promise of a job in Fairbanks, where U.S. marshals were waiting to take him out of circulation. The cook at Woodchopper had the unenviable task of keeping up with the crews' bellies. He also did his part to keep the varmints in check. He liked to show off his daily catch of drowned mice lured into a bucket of flour and water.

Some diehards stayed year after year on the dredging rigs. Among them was Phil Berail.

The third day out from Berail's cabin, Crane found another hut. This one was little more than a ruin. Its ceiling had caved in. There was nothing but empty tins scattered about. Crane had no complaints. Just finding two more signs of life was hugely uplifting. Others had been here, and others presumably had made it out alive.

Crane checked his supplies. About half were gone. It was time to turn back.

The trip was a major success in Crane's mind. He returned to Berail's cabin with a sleeping bag, the location of a canoe frame, and, most important, a newfound optimism that he would find his way home.

For the next week, Crane struggled over his next move. His food and ammo wouldn't hold out until the end of winter. Any fresh attempt to hike out depended on having enough supplies and the ability to hunt. But again that question: why give up the security of the cabin for the perils of the open?

Two overriding reasons were Louis and Sonia Crane back on Baltimore Avenue. The image of them mourning his death weighed heavily. His daily routines kept his mind engaged for a while, but his thoughts always circled back to his parents. How, Crane thought, can I wait out the season when my parents have emotionally buried their son? Then there were his two brothers in the service. What if they were gone? Could his parents bear it?

Crane's health was nearly restored. His stomach was full, and his hands were as good as when he left Ladd. If he made another push downstream, it would be for his parents. And, to a lesser degree, the war. It had been so all-consuming before the crash. Like everyone, Crane pored over the reports of battles won and lost. He joined his friends in endless strategizing about what Hitler or Churchill or Stalin or Tojo had up their sleeves. It now seemed increasingly abstract. It was as if the newsreel of the war had somehow gone dark when he bailed from his plane.

It's a hard thing for any soldier to process. The bedrock of military order is that every job, every act, is a vital contribution toward victory. Certainly, there is fundamental truth in that. A slipshod mechanic may cause a plane crash that may lose a battle, and that may tip the fortunes of the wider war. Signs at Ladd Field reminded mechanics that every bolt and weld counted. But what does it mean to be suddenly yanked away from everything and everyone? Crane felt a natural sense of duty to get back. But to what? He had no idea what had happened on the battlefront since that last radio broadcast of December 21 on the Rhineland bombings.

What Crane had missed was some progress by the Allies. But no one was predicting an end to the war anytime soon.

In Italy, Allied forces were attacking German paratroopers holding the bombed ruins of the hilltop abbey at Monte Cassino. The Germans would eventually pull back, clearing the way for the fight to move closer to Rome, but not until inflicting heavy casualties on American GIs. Meanwhile, U.S. forces with the 45th Infantry Division—loaded deep with Oklahoma farm boys who lived through the Depression-era Dust Bowl—were being pounded by German gunners at the Anzio beachhead. Before the rise of the Nazis, the symbol of the 45th was a swastika, one of the common markings used by the Native Plains tribes.

To the north in Europe, the Red Army was pushing deeper into Poland. In the Pacific, British marines had taken a critical supply port in Burma, and Americans were preparing for the invasion of the Marshall Islands. At Ladd Field, the crews were enjoying what they called another warm spell, with the thermometer rising to a pleasant five degrees.

Crane couldn't stay put until a real thaw. There was at least some purpose in action. If nothing else, the knowledge that at least two other cabins dotted the river gave him hope that maybe he could simply cabin hop to civilization. The trouble was how to carry sufficient supplies for an open-ended journey that could be days, weeks—who knows. A sledge was the only real option. Crane got to work.

He took two old boards from the cabin for runners and pulled away the wooden frame from a Plexiglas skylight. He nailed a washtub to the skylight frame. Crane fashioned a rope harness that would wrap around his chest and under his armpits. Packed with supplies, Crane guessed the rig weighed about 120 pounds. He gave it a few tugs to make sure the harness held. It did.

He now waited for some sign it was the right moment to leave Berail's cabin for good.

TWELVE

FEBRUARY 10, 1944

Charley River

Crane was jolted awake. The sounds were both familiar and strange—like a language learned and forgotten.

Something was breaking, snapping. But this was not quite like anything he had heard before. At first, Crane feared the cabin was collapsing. He tensed, waiting for bits of wood and moss to rain down. The structure, however, held tight. He listened closer. This was coming from outside.

But what? It was too deep, too powerful, to be prowling animals. It reminded him in some ways of the sickening whine of wrenching metal when the tail systems failed on their B-24. An earthquake? Crane had felt a few tremors since coming to Fairbanks. He heard firsthand accounts of a 7.3 magnitude quake in July 1937 and how roads near Fairbanks jackknifed and window glass popped from panes. But the ground wasn't shaking now.

Then it came to him. The river ice must be buckling.

For a few days, the temperatures had risen by a few degrees. It's the eastern Alaskan version of a winter warm spell. This modest, and fleeting, feint toward spring was enough to unsettle the ice layers on the Charley. In places, the ice was four feet thick and would not give up its hold until at least April. Alaskan bettors keep close tabs on such things. Near Fairbanks, the annual spring ice breakup of the Tanana River is a major event for wagering. The spring before Crane's arrival at Ladd, the official ice-break moment was set at 7:22 p.m. on April 28, 1943. It has occurred as early as April 20 and as late as May 20.

Yet, as Crane knew well, the ice was inches thin in other spots, with water percolating through some holes. Tons upon tons of ice were now rearranging in a creaking, groaning, pressure-easing churn.

Such fluctuations in winter temperatures are common even in Alaska's icebox interior. Low-pressure systems or wobbles in the jet stream can pull warmer, more humid air from off the Gulf of Alaska—like the brief spell above freezing in January in the Fairbanks valley when the transport plane carried Ragle's crash report on the *Iceberg Inez*. These midwinter temperature rises are rarely high enough or sufficiently sustained to melt river ice. But they can weaken the seams and weak spots in the ice, setting up a domino-style movement, as one shifting section bumps against another.

In that instant, Crane's plans were changed.

After the burst of determination to build the sledge, Crane had moved back to his old rhythms at Berail's cabin: punching a hole in the calendar, slowly fixing his meals, hunting. The desire for an all-or-nothing push north hadn't faded. It just wasn't so easy to give up the predictability of life behind four walls. Crane carefully rationed his food and the fuel for the Coleman lantern. Some days he tried to convince himself that waiting until spring maybe wasn't such a bad option. The reply in this inner dialogue was always the same: You have no idea when spring will come and what it will be like. The river will certainly rise, and that could leave you cut off. Crane had gradually come to some understanding of the backcountry winter and what was needed to survive it. The great annual melt would bring a new set of challenges. For all he knew, it could be worse, with soaking rains and chill winds. Those are, after all, the main ingredients for hypothermia.

The morning of the angry ice spurred him back into action. Crane decided not to risk becoming prisoner of an in-between dilemma: still not spring, but the river ice becoming too fractured and fissured to handle him and the sledge. Now was the time to leave.

Crane began to pack the sledge. The pile soon grew higher than the experimental load when he had first tested his design. Every bit of gear, every morsel of food, suddenly seemed indispensable. Crane rationalized the extra weight. It was, he decided, an acceptable price for the security of being prepared. He knew the temperatures would sink back into minus double digits. And how could he be sure there were any cabins beyond the ones he found on his January scouting expedition?

Crane filled the washbasin that served as a cargo holder on the sledge: a sack of flour, beans, cans of dried eggs, two frying pans, soup pot, tent canvas, the sleeping bag, an ax, and more. Crane planned to mush with the snowshoes found in Berail's boxes. Yet he could make no sense of the shoe's ties, which were caribou-hide straps that wrap around the toe and heel. The design is simple and effective, but not obvious to the uninitiated. In frustration, he slashed off the binds and made loops of rope. That left the snowshoes without a toe anchor. They twisted in all directions with each step. Crane pitched over like a drunk. Forget it, he thought. I'll trudge along in the mukluks. He tossed the snowshoes onto the sledge, figuring they might come in some use later. If nothing else, he could toss them in a fire.

All was ready at dawn on February 12, fifty-four days since the crash.

Crane made one last hole in the calendar, ripped away the cover with the Alaska map, and looked around one more time at the place that had saved his life. He used some tent canvas to patch the skylight that was dismantled for the sledge. The weak winter daylight flowed through the gaps in the weave, making the canvas seem dotted with rhinestones. Crane had nothing except some charcoal to attempt to write a message. He abandoned the idea. I'll track down this Phil Berail later when I'm out, Crane thought, and thank him in person.

Crane pointed the sledge downriver and looped the rope harness around his chest.

He leaned forward. The rope snapped taut. His thighs tensed. The sledge wouldn't budge.

Crane tugged again. Still, not even an inch of progress. He leaned in, almost parallel to the snow. The sledge finally creaked forward. Crane hauled it over the riverbank and onto the ice. He had gone twenty feet and was already panting. Remarkably, MIT engineer Crane had disregarded basic physics. A flat-bottom sledge, something like a toboggan or the carriages used on dog teams, would have distributed the weight better and perhaps rode over the snow with less resistance. His addition of sledge runners would keep it on a straighter line, but at the cost of more struggle and exertion.

He pulled. The sledge dropped onto the frozen river. It was little easier going in places where the snow was blown off the ice. But these clear patches were tucked between drifts that could run waist deep. There was no way around. Crane had to muscle through and hope the sledge would do its part and hold together. He glanced back just before Berail's cabin disappeared from view around the bend.

He knew if he ever saw it again, it would be because he had failed.

Before the first hour was out, the agony of Crane's choice was clear. In the snow, the sledge's runners would sink as if in quicksand. It took leg-burning steps to keep it moving. The harness dug into his chest. He was making maybe one mile an hour. He refused, however, to ponder an alternative. The sledge's contents could never fit into a pack. It was either stick with the sledge or grab the essentials and make a headlong trek as long as he could hold out. For now, the sledge would stay.

It also became evident that the minithaw had reordered the ice sheet. Pressure bumps and jumbled blocks were everywhere. This definitely meant no travel at night. Snowfall, too, was as much an enemy as the darkness. Even a small coating could cover the patches of weak ice and turn them into traps that would swallow Crane or, perhaps even worse, claim the sledge and leave him alone with nothing. He learned to listen closely to cues from the ice. It gnashed and grumbled like some restless thing.

There were other sounds as well. Crane's time in the wilderness had retuned his senses, tapping into instincts long plastered over by city noises and city life. What he first thought sounded like a distant plane engine was, he learned, the communal clamor of wolf packs. They kept a distance for now. The closest brush was some paw prints in the snow Crane noticed while hunting far from Berail's cabin. It always made him rush back toward shelter. It's unlikely that Crane knew the risks of wolves attacking a person were extremely low. But, even if he did, it's not so easy to take solace in statistics. Fear is fear. The biggest threat is from wolves made aggressive and erratic by rabies. In May 1943, a rabid wolf fatally mauled a ten-year-old boy in the northern coastal outpost of Wainwright. The previous year, more than two hundred miles to the south, a rabid wolf attacked a Native hunter near Noorvik. The man later died of rabies. Yet attacks by apparently healthy wolves do occur around the world. In Alaska wolves killed a thirty-two-year-old woman in the southwest peninsula in March 2010 and fed on her body. An investigation concluded the wolves were not rabid.

For Crane, it gave some measure of comfort to keep the rifle and ax lashed to the top of the sledge and handy to grab.

For two days, he trudged northward. He was well behind the pace he had made in his out-and-back mission a month earlier. He remembered this stretch of river. The hills around the river were lower.

To the west, they climbed gradually toward the base of the more than mile-high Twin Mountain and the rugged land beyond. Winds moved fast and steady across this valley, pushing the snow into formidable drifts. More than the cold, the wind tested Crane's spirits. He had somewhat made peace with the subzero temperatures after finding the additional provisions at Berail's cabin. It was the wind—even at modest levels—that was hard to battle. It found its way through every faulty stitch or paper-thin gap in his hood. Crane dipped his head low—like every wind-buffeted traveler through the ages—and tried to muscle on. It was so with the Lewis and Clark expedition, where the relentless winds on the prairies became a challenge to their stamina and sanity. A future Norwegian immigrant to the same flatlands, Ole Rolvaag, used the winds in his novels as a metaphor for the puny struggles of man against the boundless powers of nature.

Ahead of Crane was another fin of snow. The sledge, without a curled-back bow to ride over the snow, became a bulldozer in the drifts. It piled up snow in front until it sometimes forced Crane to a full stop. He would then slip out of the rope harness and clear away a path.

Crane had been lucky so far. In a few places, the ice snapped in protest at the combined weight of man and sledge, but he never felt in danger of its giving way.

Crane leaned forward to build up some momentum to push through. He stepped into the snow.

His foot kept going.

He could hear ice cracking. His right foot dropped through with a sickening, bottomless sensation. Crane's reflexes were fast, but not fast enough. His mukluk was soaked. Instantly, ice began forming. The thermometer had fallen back. It was at least minus twenty. At this temperature, wet material can freeze in seconds. Crane batted off the ice with his ax and waited—his heart pounding—to see whether he could feel any seepage into his socks. Seconds passed. Then a minute. The water didn't penetrate.

Of all Crane's near misses so far, this one shook him the most. He would have to be more careful. The next time, it might be far worse. It was the same thought that ethnologist Osgood mused over years before as he navigated frozen Canadian rivers. "In the subzero weather, I revolted from the sight of deep flowing water as from a horrible and deathly trap," he wrote. "To burn in molten metal would be preferable to the torture of slipping into that rippling steel-blue torrent."

For two more days, Crane marched. His neck cramped badly from the harness. The sledge, to his surprise, held together rather well. But it was not built for speed. It fought back at each step. At least the strain took his mind off the cold, which stayed well below zero. His breath turned his now-shaggy beard and mustache into an ice muzzle that melted off only at night before the fire. At times, it felt that he was breathing through a pipe. Everything seemed to narrow. Crane's world was whittled down to the act of a single step. And then the momentary terror on whether the ice would hold.

Crane also was not the same man who thought about giving up more than seven weeks earlier. His engineer training—the ability to think through problems—perhaps helped to some extent in his rebirth as a survivor. But the ranks of the Arctic dead are full of men of science and reason, almost all with far more wilderness credentials than the pilot from Philadelphia. What Crane learned was gathered in increments, plucked like stray threads from crises and moments of doubt. His transformation bound him, in ways he probably couldn't yet imagine, to some of the greatest feats of resolve. In the words of one famous polar odds beater, it just comes down to putting one foot in front of the other.

Early-twentieth-century Australian explorer Douglas Mawson was fond of quoting a bard from the other end of the earth, Yukon poet Robert W. Service: "It's dead easy to die. It's the keeping-on-living that's hard." Mawson did just that. His early 1913 ordeal through the Antarctic has become a well-studied case in the psychology of survival.

Mawson was a geologist and veteran of Antarctic expeditions. He once joined the indomitable Ernest Shackleton onto the ice sheet. Mawson's grand plan, however, was to lead his own expedition in the antipodean summer to set up a research base and draft the most comprehensive scientific treatise to date on the frozen continent. On November 10, 1912, Mawson left the group's home base, bound for the Antarctic interior. He was accompanied by two others: an affable British army lieutenant who served in the Royal Fusiliers and a Swiss explorer and mountaineer named Xavier Mertz, who was a rare mix of bon vivant and rugged alpinist in his native Basel. In Mertz's signature, a line slashes through the *M* of his last name, as if to say nothing stood in his way.

About a month after setting off, the young British officer, Belgrave Ninnis, plunged into a crevasse along with a dogsled and most of their supplies. Mertz and Mawson yelled down into the blue abyss for hours, but heard nothing but the whimpering of an injured dog. The surviving pair then started a dash back to camp—about three hundred miles away—using dead reckoning and a surveyor's theodolite. What few rations they had were soon exhausted. They were left to cull the remaining dogs, one by one, for food over the next weeks. It also possibly exposed them to dangerous levels of vitamin A from the livers of the Greenland huskies. The dogs' names paid homage to the greats of their fields, including Shackleton, Franklin after the lost-in-the-Arctic commander John Franklin, and Pavlova after the Russian prima ballerina Anna Pavlova, who gave Ninnis a dancer doll as a good-luck token.

Mertz soon became disoriented and delirious, symptoms consistent with extreme amounts of vitamin A flooding the body, according to a 1969 study by the *Medical Journal of Australia*. Others cast doubt on the theory, suggesting Mertz had simply pushed himself beyond the limits of endurance. Either way, he couldn't go on. He had to be strapped to a sledge and hauled, like Crane's rig, by a human harness for several days. Mertz died about one hundred miles from base on January 8.

Mawson, too, was suffering badly from possible vitamin A poisoning, and his body was ravaged by the cold. His hair fell out in clumps, and his skin dropped off in sheets from his legs and hands. Some accounts say the soles of his feet became detached in minus twenty temperatures, and Mawson was forced to secure on the flapping flesh with cloth wrappings just to keep walking. But, like Crane, Mawson benefited from remarkable luck. Near death, Mawson stumbled across a cairn covering supplies left by fellow expedition members. He was now less than thirty miles from camp.

And, also like Crane, the ice was a constant concern. Mawson was haunted by fears of slipping into a crevasse like the unfortunate British lieutenant. Finally, it happened. The ice opened up. Mawson dropped into the abyss. Then he stopped. By sheer good fortune, his sledge was just a bit bigger than the mouth of the crevasse. That little differential kept him from plunging to certain death.

"There," Mawson wrote, "exhausted, weak and chilled, hanging freely in space and slowly turning round as the rope twisted one way and the other, I felt that I had done my utmost and failed, that I had no more strength to try again and that all was over except the passing. . . . There on the brink of the great Beyond I well remember how I looked forward to the peace of the great release—how almost excited I was at the prospect of the unknown to be unveiled."

Instead, he mustered the will to climb up the rope, wondering every second whether the sledge would hold.

When Mawson staggered into camp alone on February 8, 1913, he was unrecognizable from illness and fatigue. One member of the team was said to ask: "My God! Which one are you?" The expedition's ship, *Aurora*, had remained as long as it could with the southern summer ebbing. Incredibly, it had pulled anchor just hours before Mawson appeared. A small group was left behind to continue the search for Mawson and the two others.

They were forced to spend another winter in Antarctica—in one of the windiest spots on earth—before their ship could return.

It was all glory for Mawson when he reached Australia in February 1914. His story dazzled his homeland and fitted well into the age's narrative of "heroic" exploits at the poles. But later, whispers and rumors began—never proven and vigorously denied by Mawson—that he may have resorted to cannibalism and eaten parts of Mertz's body.

Mawson, instead, talked endlessly about the perils of the ice in speaking tours arranged to help defray the costs of the expedition. One wrong footfall, he told rapt audiences, and it could be your grave. Sometimes, the margin is decided by inches.

For Crane, it began like so many frozen misfortunes. With a crack.

Ice again folded under Crane's feet. This was different—bigger, louder—than when his foot plunged in several days earlier. Instinctively, he gulped a breath as he felt the surface give way. This was it, he thought. I am going under. Just like the suicide he contemplated two months before. Crane wondered, in what he guessed could be his last conscious thoughts, whether the current was strong and how far he would drift under the ice before blacking out.

Then it all stopped. His chest was squeezed by the rope harness. It pulled at his armpits like a parent dunking a child in a pool. The sledge, Crane realized, had halted his fall. That stubborn, irascible sledge nudged forward a few paces, but held its ground, just as it did for Mawson decades before. Had Crane built a more streamlined model, it might have saved him some hardships while hauling it. But it also could have cost him his life. If the sledge slid forward through the hole, or even just to its edge, Crane would have had no chance.

He twisted around and grabbed at the rope. He slapped at the ice with Berail's mittens, looking for some leverage. The ice around the hole creaked, but held his weight. Crane was soaked and panicked. He hauled himself out, watching always the sledge's runners and praying they held fast.

A skin of ice formed the instant the air hit his waterlogged clothes. He could feel water leaking through the tops of his mukluks and finding its way through layer after layer to every part of his body below his chest.

Crane was shivering uncontrollably and having trouble catching his breath. His body, literally, was wondering what had hit it. A sudden drop into cold water sets off a cascade of responses. Nerve endings fire wildly. Heart rate and blood pressure spike to the point that it can bring on pulmonary failure. Some survivors report feeling their breath knocked out of them as if punched in the gut. At the same time, Crane was on a fast track toward hypothermia. Water below seventy degrees robs body heat far faster than cold air. When the water is just above freezing, like the midwinter Charley, exhaustion and unconsciousness can begin to set in after less than fifteen minutes.

At least his head was dry. That bought him a few precious minutes.

Crane had to act fast. He yanked at the harness and ran toward the bank with the sledge in tow. It may have resisted a bit, but Crane couldn't feel it. He surged onto the rocky shore. Where are the matches? They were in a sack near the frying pan. Thankfully, there were dry pine needles and small branches scattered at the base of the trees. Crane was shaking so much he could barely strike the match. It caught. Soon, he had a fire. Each movement broke away bits of the ice film forming on his clothes. He was careful not to let them fall into the fire.

Now, a rope. Crane yanked it free from the sledge and strung it between two trees near the fire.

Where's the tent? He was having trouble thinking clearly. He forced himself to concentrate. There it was. The tent was right on top of the sledge pile.

Crane draped it over the rope, forming a shelter that was almost on top of the fire. There was no time to think about whether the tent would go up in flames. Crane yanked off his flight suit, long underwear, mukluks, and socks. He was naked and losing body heat. He wrung out the clothes as best he could and laid them near the fire. He eyes stung each time the breeze would push the smoke into the tent. For ten minutes or so—until he could see the moisture evaporating away in silky swirls off his clothes—Crane cowered naked, his knees drawn up to his chest. He let the warmth of the fire slow his shivering.

Crane was never an overtly spiritual man. He attended synagogue sporadically—and apparently without much enthusiasm—after his bar mitzvah as a young teen. But it's not unreasonable to imagine that Leon Crane, in that primitive tableau of flesh and fire along the Charley River, wondered whether there could be higher powers at work, protecting him and helping him survive. By rights, he shouldn't have lasted that first night. His father's letter and matches grabbed on the run gave him a chance. Then came the life-saving supplies and shelter of Berail's cabin. And now the sledge. Crane would have been excused if, for just a while, he put aside his prized logic and surrendered to the idea that something he couldn't explain wanted him to make it home. It's often said that most of the Arctic languages don't have a word similar to the concept of luck. The closest they come is what an English speaker might call fate, destiny, kismet. Death is in store for you at that moment or it's not.

Tears rolled down Crane's cheeks from the smoke. They froze as soon as he turned away from the fire.

Crane's clothes were still damp, but somewhat warmed by the fire. Crane dressed and hastily arranged his camp. He pushed himself deep into the sleeping bag and thought about the sinkhole in the ice. It was minus thirty at least. A fresh crust of ice would soon cover the break and the side-by-side gashes where the rope held him from sliding under.

The next day, Crane was back on the move. The Charley valley was narrowing and made big, sweeping turns. The land rose sharper from the banks, and the lines of frozen feeder creeks cut the landscape like scars. Still, there was no sign of the Yukon River.

Just before sunset, he shot a squirrel and roasted it until the meat was crispy and the tiny bones gave a satisfying crunch.

A week passed.

Crane managed no more than four miles each day. He knew the sledge must be growing lighter as he ate through his supplies. But he couldn't feel the difference. It seemed the same exhausting weight that pulled on his shoulders and forced him to bend forward to keep his balance. Crane's legs kept moving, but the steps would shorten to a near shuffle. It took only about an hour of pulling now before he needed to rest.

At times, he would stop for long stretches and just stare at the river. Was there any change in the landscape from the day before? If so, he could not recognize it. Without a landmark—a visible goal—Crane saw only sameness: more hills, more bends in the river, another subzero day and even colder night. He could now see how mountaineers muster the superhuman effort to keep going. The summit was closer with each foothold. The monotony of the river brought the reverse effect: it seemed to drain him. It was maybe as much a burden as the piles of gear and food on the sledge. Crane had read stories of shipwreck survivors tipped toward madness by the sharp horizons of the sea in every direction. At least, he thought, they didn't have to walk. Every time Crane stopped to rest, it was harder to rise again, strap on the harness, and push toward that next turn in the river.

After more days of walking, Crane came upon another deserted cabin.

It had to be many years since it was last occupied. The roof was partially collapsed, and animals had long ago scoured the pantry looking for any scraps. There were some things they couldn't get, though. Crane was amazed to find a few supplies left untouched. And more than that. Here were some incredible luxuries. There were canned vegetables and—Crane could scarcely believe it—a tin of Vienna sausage, which were jokingly called Yukon shrimp by some of the Alaska-based GIs. He gobbled them down and licked up the juices. He was grateful for the shelter. The temperature was falling again. The morning was as cold as he had felt since bailing from the B-24. It was near minus fifty.

It simply was too much to go on. He stayed in the cabin to rest.

Far away in Washington, letters had been mailed to families of the *Iceberg Inez* crew. The one addressed to Crane's father was dated February 16 under the reference of Crane's Army serial number: 0409175.

It begins with the mention of the terse December 29 telegram. Now, for the first time, Crane's family had more information. The letter, from the office of Colonel T. A. Fitzgerald, said Crane was aboard a B-24 out of Ladd Field on a "weather experimental mission."

"Full details are not available," continued Fitzgerald, whose lavishly looping signature seemed out of place on the thousands of bad-news letters during his five months at the Air Adjutant General office. "The report states that your son's plane was last seen when it took off from its base."

Fitzgerald noted the last radio contact shortly after eleven in the morning. "It has not been seen or contacted since then," he added.

Fitzgerald repeated Ragle's keep-hope-alive theory that fierce winds may have blown the B-24 off course and the plane was forced down somewhere in the Yukon Valley. The letter, however, closed with a grim reality check about the search. "Neither the missing craft nor its crew members were found," wrote Fitzgerald.

"The above facts constitute all of the information presently available," the letter went on. "The great anxiety caused you by failure to receive more details concerning your son's disappearance is fully realized. Please be assured that any additional information received will be conveyed immediately to you."

Fitzgerald added the names and addresses of the next of kin of the others on Crane's plane: Wenz, Sibert, Pompeo, and Hoskin.

THIRTEEN

SEPTEMBER 15, 2006

Hickam Air Force Base, Hawaii

Each piece uncovered from the crash site above the Charley River was cleaned with a soft brush and tap water. A full inventory was made.

Possible human remains from the B-24 wreckage were set aside. They would undergo study later. For now, the job was to catalog and photograph items tagged as material evidence.

- *one U.S. Army metal button cover, badly corroded*
- *one stainless-steel watch body, burned and stained*
- *one type A-11 watch body, known as a "Hack" model, burned and corroded*
- *one presumed watchband buckle, corroded*
- *one metal key ring with four keys, corroded but "Made in USA" mark legible*
- *two pocket knives, one corroded and burned, the other with blade open and less stained*
- *one U.S. Army officer's cap insignia, intact but stained gray-black by scorched soil*

The Hoskin case, file number JPAC CIL 2006–124-I-01, had moved from the chilly Alaskan dig site to a temperature-controlled room in Hawaii lit by fluorescent lights. The space is filled with tables holding carefully arranged skeletal remains and shelves with boxes containing other artifacts found at dig sites. The black flag honoring America's POWs and MIAs sits near a glass wall. The forensic experts wear white lab coats, making the room seem like something between a coroner's office and a biotech research facility. Their mission is a bit of both. It's here, at the Central Identification Laboratory on Oahu, that analysts hope to give an identity to the remains and relics uncovered in the search for missing American military personnel.

It wasn't often that evidence bags arrived from Alaska. Most of the JPAC missions are dispatched to Southeast Asia or the South Pacific in search of the thousands of American remains believed resting in forest lowlands or mist-covered mountains. In Alaska the MIA tally is tiny by comparison—around three hundred— mostly from aircraft or ships that went down over the sea during the Aleutian battles. Others, like the *Iceberg Inez,* were taken by storms or cold or malfunctions during flight. Usually, the Alaskan crash sites are in places so inhospitable and remote that military investigators need more than just a hunch to mobilize a search for remains. Any Navy personnel lost at sea, meanwhile, are considered "entombed" under the waves and are not part of the active JPAC searches.

Occasionally, though, Alaska gives up its secrets on its own.

In June 2012 the Alaska Army National Guard was conducting a training flight over Mount Gannett, east of Anchorage. As their Black Hawk passed over the Colony Glacier, a crew member spotted what appeared to be yellow life rafts and shredded metal exposed by melting ice. It was the spot where an Air Force C-124 cargo plane crashed in November 1952, killing all fifty-two people on board.

The Hoskin case had an added distinction. Amateur sleuths such as Beckstead are exceedingly rare. Without his dedication to scour the wreckage, the Hoskin file would likely have remained on the shelf.

When the evidence from the Charley River dig reached Hawaii, it was put in the hands of analysts and anthropologists who had no knowledge of Hoskin or the background of the case. JPAC calls it working blind. All the lead investigators at that stage are allowed to know is the approximate area and era of the site in question. The protocol is designed to prevent any subconscious bias from influencing the analysis. In other words, if they were told they were looking for the remains of Harold Hoskin—a tall, young airman—there might be an inclination to favor evidence supporting that conclusion.

Instead, the pieces from the Charley River site were examined for details such as whether they could point to a specific rank or were consistent with gear issued during World War II. If they added up, the case shifted to the next stage.

Anything tied to a World War II veteran carried special significance at Hickam Air Force Base, which in 2010 would merge with nearby Pearl Harbor as part of Pentagon base consolidations. Japanese planes bombed and strafed Hickam in a rearguard attack during the Pearl Harbor blitz. The Japanese sought to keep Hickam warplanes from joining the fight or chasing down the Imperial Navy's aircraft carriers. Some of the buildings at Hickam still carry the bullet holes and shrapnel scars.

It was not the first time that Hawaii was part of the Hoskin family story. In late February 1944, Harold Hoskin's kid brother John stepped off a transport plane from San Francisco and into the humid island night.

John was a newly commissioned officer. But that gave him no additional access to information about his brother. He knew only what everyone else did: Harold was missing in Alaska, and the search had come up empty. In his mind, the facts pointed in only one plausible direction. Harold was gone.

He kept those opinions to himself, however. His brother's pregnant wife, Mary, refused to entertain that kind of talk. She simply would not allow herself to contemplate the worst. Even as months went by—and the northern Maine winter drifted into pale green spring—she would tell everyone that she expected Harold to one day walk through the front door like he was coming back from a normal day at work. People would smile sympathetically at Mary's unflappable faith. Then, when Mary was out of earshot, they would shake their heads and wonder when she would come off her cloud and deal with reality.

That wasn't so easy. Mary seemed to have a charmed romance with Harold. Everyone in town knew it since high school. They just fit. Mary couldn't imagine it could all be over so soon, so abruptly.

Let's not forget, she'd tell herself, that sometimes good fortune has a way of shining through even amid tragedies. The story of her father and the insurance salesman was a case in point. Her dad was a potato farmer imbued with a healthy dose of Yankee crustiness. The insurance man had an equal measure of perseverance. He tried to pitch life insurance to Mary's dad, but was sent packing. He came back some months later with the same result. On the third visit, somehow the salesman got through. Mary's dad signed the insurance papers. A few days later, he was kicked by a bull and died. The insurance payout helped keep the family afloat.

So this is a lesson, Mary would say. The plane was missing, but her Hal could be fine and just trying to get back to her. It just may take some time. I have to keep faith, she told herself. Don't give up on Hal.

While Mary kept up her brave front, Harold's parents veered off on other emotional tangents. His mother accepted the news of the lost B-24 with quiet resignation. If she had hopes that Harold survived, she kept them to herself. Hoskin's father, on the other hand, was not at all satisfied with the meager details from the military. Every few weeks, his frustration would boil over. He'd get out his pen and paper and set up near the old Franklin woodstove, the warmest place in the drafty house at 5 Columbia Street in Houlton, just miles from the border with New Brunswick. In letter after angry letter, he demanded more information from the Army.

But something Harold told the family during his last visit stuck with them all. He had just received his Army wings in December

1942 and had a few days free. Everyone gathered in the living room to hear Harold's stories of life in the Army Air Forces and what it was like to be in control of the big B-24s. Some fresh logs were tossed into the Franklin stove. Younger brother John listened with perhaps the most interest. He was home for the holiday from college in Massachusetts. He wasn't going back, though. He had received his draft notice and had to report in a few weeks.

Harold began talking in more detail about the B-24 Liberator.

"Thing is," Harold told his family, "if there's a problem on the plane, I'm not getting out."

What do you mean? they gasped.

He said either the parachutes for the pilot and copilot were stashed behind the seat, or, often, they were sitting on them without them being fully hitched up.

"There's probably not going to be time to put it on and get out," he told the family. Then he shrugged it off with a joke. This was always his way. Keep it light. I'll be fine, he assured his family. I'll be back in one piece. Don't worry about that.

Harold left a few days later.

John, meanwhile, had been selected for officer candidate school, which picked enlisted personnel for intensive twelve-week courses that ended with promotion to second lieutenant. John got into a new branch training medical administrative officers, who would assist in field hospitals and help run the military's vast health care networks. Harold planned to come to John's graduation from officer school outside Abilene at Camp Barkeley. The camp is smack in the middle of Texas and, to the chagrin of the military, sported an extra vowel in its name. The site was named for a World War I hero named Barkley, but a clerical error is believed to have revised the name.

Harold couldn't make it to the graduation, however. He was already in motion to be shipped to Alaska. We'll see each other soon, he promised John.

John bounced around the West Coast for a few months until he got orders for Hawaii. All during 1944, soldiers were streaming into the islands. The military commanders were not saying much. But it didn't take a genius in strategy to figure it out. Word began to circulate about preparations for an amphibious assault on Japan—an attack bigger than D-Day—intended to end the war in one crushing offensive. The cost, however, would likely be unprecedented casualties on the Allied side.

The prediction was that Germany's surrender was imminent—it finally came in May 1945—and all resources would then be thrown into a ground campaign aimed at the industrial heartland in Japan. The planned assault was to begin with the "Olympic" front on the southern island of Kyushu. John Hoskin was part of this group. The intent was to divert Japanese ground forces before a second wave a few months later to storm Honshu and battle toward Tokyo.

As the date for Olympic neared, John Hoskin and his unit practiced beach landings on Oahu. Seasick soldiers puked on their boots. They tripped over each other in the waves. And they all knew—just like with Normandy—they would be splashing ashore amid intense enemy fire. For some reason, John wasn't too worried. This was a chance to finally end this war, get back to Maine, and, hopefully, find his brother waiting for him. "I was twenty-one," he said seven decades later. "Who thinks at twenty-one they are going to die, even in a war? 'I'm going to swim in the ocean. I'm not going to be eaten by sharks.' It was that kind of thinking."

John was making another training run on the landing craft when word came down of something that seemed hard to believe at first. There was a huge explosion in Hiroshima. It was more than huge. It was a bomb like no other. They were calling it an atomic blast. The soldiers spent the next days fixed on the radio reports and devouring every word in the papers. Then it happened again in Nagasaki. Days later, the war was over. Japan had surrendered. John Hoskin celebrated the end of the war under the coconut palms and Hawaiian hibiscus.

But John was still bound for Japan. He stepped ashore as part of the occupation force in Osaka. John's unit was billeted in a four-story girls' school. Perhaps because of his training in medical administration, John was now part of the U.S. military's drug-enforcement patrols. The job was a window into the inner workings of Japan's military.

It was well known that Japan had directed an extensive trade in opium, heroin, and other drugs for decades. The profits helped bankroll its military expansion and costly hold on Manchuria and other parts of China. This was not an entirely novel strategy. The British East India Company and other European colonizers in the nineteenth century made mountains of cash by controlling the opium flow into China. Japan reworked it into a military doctrine. It even opened clandestine plots seeking to get Chinese commanders hooked in attempts to dull their fighting spirit. But Japan's own forces were not immune to the lure of easy drugs. Opium and heroin use became an increasing problem. It reached such worrisome levels that a Japanese military manual included a jingoistic rant. "The use of narcotics is unworthy of a superior race like the Japanese," it said. "Only inferior races, races that are decadent, like the Chinese, Europeans and the East Indians, are addicted to the use of narcotics. This is why they are destined to become our servants."

At one point, an odd little man speaking English approached the school where John Hoskin was based. John was the ranking officer, so he was called to meet the curious visitor who called himself Dr. Yoshi. The doctor had studied in the States and returned to Japan before Pearl Harbor. He could not leave once the war began with America. The doctor was now living on a hill outside Osaka and fending for his family with what he could grow in his garden and whatever else he could scrounge. John quizzed the doctor about the opium trade. He seemed well informed, and they struck up a mutually beneficial partnership. The doctor offered information. He got American food and supplies in return. As a bonus, John and some soldiers scared up a turkey on Thanksgiving 1945 and had their meal with Yoshi and his family.

Back in Maine, Harold's wife was now a single mom living in her childhood home. The baby was called Joann, the name they picked just in case their intuition about a boy was wrong. They had been so sure of a son that Harold and Mary started calling the baby-in-waiting Dick.

Mary Roberta McIntosh was a year ahead of Harold at Houlton High School, where he was the yearbook editor and played trumpet in the band. Harold was considered quite the catch. Yet few of the girls bothered to try to turn his head. It was known to all that Harold was smitten with Mary. "The rest of us didn't have a chance," classmate Phyllis Ritchie recalled.

Mary and Harold were married in Tucson in January 1943 just before he was reposted as a flight instructor in Texas. They bought a slightly shabby 1934 Buick and christened it "Elizabeth." In July they drove into the mountains of New Mexico for a long-belated honeymoon. A newlywed photo shows Mary in a floral dress with her curly chestnut hair styled back in a pleasant tumble. Harold looks sharp in his uniform—green jacket and tan trousers—with a mix of maturity and innocence that brought comparisons with the budding screen idol and fellow New Englander Van Johnson. By the fall, Harold was off to Alaska, and Mary was going in the other direction, to Maine.

Mary wrote letters to Harold about town life and the anecdotes about her pregnancy, such as feeling that first kick. Harold—or Hal, as Mary called him—described life at Ladd and some of his nights out in Fairbanks. He seemed conflicted, though, about being so far from the front lines. He wanted action. But he also was full of warm and fuzzy thoughts about returning home safely to Mary, the expected baby (still called Dick), and his medical studies at Bates College in Maine. "It looks as though Dick will see his proud papa because there is no combat involved in this job," he wrote on November 6, 1943. "Hal seems to be getting some of the breaks in this war, doesn't he? Will you be ashamed of me, Mary, if I never get to combat?"

The letter, though, takes a darker turn near the end. Hoskin, like everyone assigned at Ladd, knew that the weather can be just as worthy a foe as any Japanese Zero.

"If I don't come back . . . I wouldn't have lived in vain nor wasted my life because I had known you," he wrote. "The two greatest privileges a man can have is fighting for his wife and family in what he believes is a just cause, regardless of the outcome to himself."

It was one of the last letters Mary received from Harold. She wrote one December 19—with her baby bump starting to show— that arrived in Alaska days after the crash. In the months to come, she groped for any explanation of his disappearance. The only one she refused to consider was the scenario in which Harold would never return. Could he be in a hospital somewhere, unable to write? Perhaps he was rescued in the wilderness but couldn't make it back until spring? The image of him suffering haunted her. It was not so different from the anguish felt by Crane, imagining his parents' grief at the news of their missing son and their unfulfilled yearning to know more.

Strolling in town with baby Joann, Mary would sometimes see trucks pass by with German POWs who were shipped to this far-off corner of Maine. It was among the dozens of POW camps on American soil—holding mostly Germans but some Italians and others—after Britain asked for help in handling a swelling number of captured soldiers.

They were the lucky ones, Mary thought. They were safe even if their families didn't know it.

The Maine prisoners were, in fact, better off than many. Conditions were easy and food plentiful, not at all like the bleak POW camps in Europe or some hellhole under the control of the Soviets. A U.S. Army airfield in Houlton began receiving German prisoners the summer after Hoskin's crash. German volunteers had the chance to work picking peas and potatoes or cutting wood for the equivalent of eighty cents a day in chits to be redeemed at the camp canteen. It went a long way. Cigarettes were thirteen cents a pack, beer a nickel.

A German private named Hans Krueger was captured by the D-Day invasion force and eventually sent to Maine. He recalled how the prisoners would wink at the passing young Houlton cuties from the back of an open-back truck with just one guard. Security was so relaxed, Krueger said, that sometimes they would throw pebbles at the guard tower. It could take ten minutes to wake up the sentry. On foggy mornings, "you could have marched out the entire company" before anyone would notice. But why? Nearby Canada was also at war with the Third Reich. And conditions at the camp—with all-you-can-eat meals—were heavenly after the rigors of the front. The whole experience made Krueger, in his words, "pro-American all the way."

"Hal darling. I wish you were here. I miss you and want you so very much," Mary wrote in that undelivered December 19 letter just before the crash. "If you listen real hard, I bet you could hear me say over and over, 'Hal, darling, I love you with all my heart.'"

There were photos of Harold around the house Mary shared with her mother. Harold, however, was generally off-limits in conversation when Mary was around. Her pain was too deep. As Joann grew up, she wanted to talk about her father, hear stories about him before the war. Mary made it clear that it was asking too much, even from her daughter. Mary would just sob and turn away.

"She couldn't talk about him," said Joann. "She would break down. The emotions were that strong, even many, many years after the war. She lost the love of her life."

At the lab in Hawaii, the cataloged items were assessed one by one in late 2006. The older pocketknife could have been World War II vintage, but gave no direct link to the military or Ladd Field. Same for the keys.

The Hack watch was standard Army issue, getting its nickname from the military term *time hack,* meaning to mark the present hour and minute. The button cover was certainly Army as well.

The officer's insignia, however, was the most compelling. Only someone in the cockpit would have had that on their cap: an eagle with olive branches in its right claw and thirteen arrows in its left.

"The material evidence recovered from the B-24D is consistent with military insignia, a style of watch issued by the military . . . and frequently worn by aviators, and personal effects commonly carried by aircrew members during the World War II era," chief anthropologist Fox wrote in his report. "The U.S. Army Officer's Cap Insignia is consistent with the rank structure of one of the unaccounted for individuals and the one individual who survived the crash."

FOURTEEN

MARCH 3, 1944

Charley River

The snow alone should have been enough to make Crane think twice.

It came in windblown slaps that whistled through openings in the tumbledown cabin where he had found the Vienna sausage and decided to rest for several days. The temperature had edged up slightly, but was still cold beyond reason. Crane guessed it just below zero and far lower with the windchill. He was becoming good at judging the weather: the difference between *regular* sub-zero that could kill the unprepared or unlucky in a matter of hours and the blasts of supercold that could claim a life even faster.

If Crane had followed his own rules of no unnecessary chances, he would have spent a fourth day inside the cabin eating cornmeal pancakes and waiting for the snow to let up.

So why, then, was he here, a mile north of the cabin, leaning into a near blizzard and hauling the sledge through fast-piling snow?

Whatever insecurities drove Crane from the cabin that day, he was dangerously close to recklessness. So many tragedies in the Far North have begun this way. Crane pressed on when he should have stayed put. Army field teams researching cold-weather survival during World War II received the same messages over and over from tribal Natives and old-timers: the weather always has the edge. The smart thing is to hunker down. Never push your luck.

Crane was doing just that.

He couldn't see more than a yard ahead. This frightened him most of all. He could walk directly onto a weak point in the ice, and, with the heavy snow, there was little chance of making a fire even if he managed to pull himself free. The last plunge through the ice shook Crane deeply. He began thinking that the longer he stayed on the river, the more opportunities for disaster. Clearly, it made no sense to march off into a snowstorm. It was the other possibilities running through Crane's mind—the parade of *what ifs*—that led him out the cabin door. What if I broke my leg stumbling around the cabin? What if wolves surround it? What if the weather pushes above freezing again and the ice becomes unsteady?

Crane was in acclaimed company. The high latitudes have witnessed extraordinary feats and exemplary bravery—as well as spectacular insolence and irresponsibility. Crane didn't have to look far for examples.

The great tide that began with Canada's Klondike gold rush in the 1890s left a backwash of bodies. Winter trails were dotted with frozen corpses set like tundra gargoyles, their skin plum colored from frostbite and lips peeled back in weird frosty smiles. Stories abound of would-be prospectors, desperate to outrace rivals, setting off into blizzards and never seen again.

It's impossible to calculate how many perished on the way north during the heady gold rush years straddling the turn of the century. Photographs from some of the Klondike jumping-off points—Skagway port in Alaska or the Canadian trailhead at Dawson City—suggest almost comical disregard for the demands of subarctic travel. Some stampeders carried their belongings in tins and coffee cans. The clothing worn by the most ill prepared often seemed more attuned to a Sunday stroll. Some had flimsy leather shoes and derby hats. They look—remarkably and tragically—like Charlie Chaplin's sad-sack character the Tramp in his 1925 silent film, *The Gold Rush*, which lampooned the boreal greed. An 1898 photo shows a group of "actresses" heading to the gold rush boomtowns, hiking their dresses as they forge a stream with luggage in tow.

One route to the goldfields—a difficult passage known as the White Pass Trail from Skagway to the Yukon River on the Canadian side—was so littered with the carcasses of pack animals that it became better known as Dead Horse Trail. Canada's minister of the interior in 1897 lamented, "The inhumanity which this trail has been witness to, the heartbreak and suffering which so many have undergone, cannot be imagined. They certainly cannot be described."

Poet Robert W. Service tried:

There are strange things done in the midnight sun,
by the men who moil for gold.

This is how Service began "The Cremation of Sam McGee" in 1907 about a fictional prospector from Tennessee who freezes to death and whose body is hauled onto a pyre by his friend. The poet is said to have fashioned the work on the tale of a doctor, Leonard Sugden, who Yukon lore says once disposed of a corpse in the firebox of a stern-wheel steamer after receiving permission from the late man's family. The real McGee, named William Samuel McGee, was a Canadian-born erstwhile stampeder whom Service met while working at a bank in Whitehorse. Service received permission to use McGee's name in the poem, whose popularity opened up a cottage industry in the Far North. Souvenir urns were sold containing the "mortal ashes" of the made-up McGee.

The Arctic trails have their secret tales;
That would make your blood run cold.

Two hours out from the cabin, the snow was coming down so hard that it made walking in a straight line difficult. Crane had lost all reference points. As any pilot knows, even the tiniest fraction off course compounds itself with every second. Soon you are hugely misdirected. Crane worried he could stray toward the river-banks, where the water was shallower but the ice thinner.

At first he thought the sledge was snagged. Crane gave another tug. Why was it pulling back?

Crane gasped. The sledge was going under.

He had no time to slip out of the rope. He staggered backward, trying to keep his balance while twisting around in the driving snow to see what had happened. He heard the ice splinter. The back of the sledge was dropping into the water. Its front rose up like a sinking ocean liner. This at least gave Crane some advantage. He had more leverage on the ropes. He pulled back, seeking firmer footing in the snow.

Crane knew he could wriggle out of the harness and let the sledge sink away. He'd be alive, but with absolutely nothing except his clothes. No food. No rifle. Crane dropped to his side, seeking more purchase on the snow and ice. There was some traction, but not enough to counter the weight of the sledge and supplies. He could feel the void. His mukluks slid off the ice and dangled over the hole, dipping into the mix of water and ice shards. The sledge dropped another foot. Crane could hear the river water gurgling. Crane pulled back harder. The sledge tipped and floated in the water.

More ice gave way. His legs dropped into the water. For a third time, Crane was splashing into the frigid Charley. Most of his weight, fortunately, was still on the ice. He spun on his hips and managed to get one soaked leg out of the hole. Crane knew this would be his last chance. If the ice shattered below him, then all was lost. He crawled and pulled. His second leg was out. He was sprawled flat on the ice, grabbing and pulling and thrashing with hands and legs like a creature trying to escape a trap.

The sledge runners bumped up against the edge of the ice hole. Then the sledge rose a bit. Crane was winning. He yanked again, his boots jabbing at the snow even as more fell in the storm.

The front of the sledge angled higher. One more burst, thought Crane. The sledge moved past its center of balance and fell back onto the ice. For a desperate moment, Crane feared it could break through again. The ice held.

There was no time to examine the sledge and how much of his supplies were wet and now crusting over with ice. Crane was shivering badly. Snowflakes stuck to the moisture before it iced up, giving the impression of feathers. Crane leaped up and raced for the riverbank with the sledge in tow. A layer of ice formed over the runners, making it easier to pull.

As Crane fumbled for the matches in his parka, he gave a glance at the sledge. Amazingly, the damage was limited. The rear was encrusted in ice, and some water seeped into his food stocks. But, in the superchill, much of the flour and sugar froze into clumps instead of fully dissolving. He guessed he could thaw them later over a fire. The washbasin container in the middle was high enough to block most of the water. The rifle and ammo, lashed to the top, were fine. So were the rope and canvas.

He fashioned another makeshift tent near his fire. He worried that the snow would have made the driftwood too wet to catch fire, but it took the flame. Once again, Crane stripped off his parka, underwear, mukluks, and socks. His shivering ebbed.

But the river had won. Crane decided to abandon the sledge. He had hauled it close to fifty miles. The rest—however much was left—would be done on foot.

When Crane's clothes were dry enough, he hitched himself to the sledge for one last pull. He headed back to the ramshackle cabin to divvy up his provisions into whatever he could carry on his back. This time, he would wait out the storm.

The return trip to the cabin seemed faster. The wind was at Crane's back, and the snow was no longer spilling into his eyes and collecting in his beard. In the dying light, Crane saw the outline of the shelter.

He spent the evening making a supply triage: what should be saved and what should be left behind. The snowshoes were an easy decision to cast aside. They had been no help. Food was parceled out. It was about enough, Crane figured, for a month if he was careful. The .22 ammo was getting low. No more wild shots. Either he had a good chance for a kill, or he would not pull the trigger. The matches he grabbed for Hoskin back at Ladd were long gone. He still had some he found at Berail's along with a flint, which mustered some decent sparks when struck with his Boy Scout knife.

The storm eased after sunset, but the sky didn't clear. It felt heavy and low and ready to disgorge more snow. Crane made about a half-dozen plate-size pancakes of flour and cornmeal. They would make the trip inside the pockets of his parka.

The next morning, Crane set off. He was now a mix of Alaskan wanderer, huntsman, and traveling kitchen. His rifle was slung across his shoulder. Its muzzle rested against the top of his rucksack, which Crane guessed weighed a staggering fifty pounds. But it still felt light after the sledge harness. His right mitten was wrapped around a heavy staff to probe the ice. Two frying pans were lashed together and hung around his neck.

The snowfall had covered all traces of the spot where the sledge broke through. But Crane could still see the fire ring on the bank.

He gave the ice a solid bash with his stick. It answered with a nice, sturdy vibration that rippled up the pole and through the thick moose-hide mittens.

FIFTEEN

MARCH 9, 1944

Charley River

The hills groaned.

The sound was low and hollow. It seemed almost sad. As if the mountains were struggling to cast off a great burden.

Then Crane would see trees bend and sway. Some would snap. It made no sense to huddle in the groves. Branches and tree trunks sometimes broke like matchsticks and crashed to the ground. The best place to hide was behind large rocks if he could find them. Even they shuddered at the force of the wind.

And, as quickly as it started, it was over.

Crane called them "williwaws," a word learned from flight training about Alaskan weather hazards. He was right about their raw power. A williwaw is sudden and scary. But Crane was a bit off in his geography. For most Alaskans, williwaws are a coastal phenomenon of ground winds riding over a mountain ridge and given a supercharged kick by higher-altitude airstreams, pressure differentials, and gravity. Yet the effect in the interior—where such savage winds have other names—can be the same. In the span of just five minutes, a twenty-mile-per-hour breeze can be whiplashed to nearly four times that speed and then, just as rapidly, fade away.

To Crane, it felt like a beating each time they came. His ribs hurt. His shoulders ached from hunching low for cover. Twigs, pebbles, bits of frozen dirt peppered his face. He asked himself how many more of these he could stand.

If the winds became worse, he wondered whether there may
be a time when he could no longer get up. He would try, but his
legs would resist. He'd drop back into the snow to await the next
storm. And that would be the end.

Such sudden and unruly gales go by other names in other places.
Squamish winds, as they are known, channel through fjords. Chinook winds roar off the Pacific and roll down the leeward slopes
of the Rockies. Mariners from the Aleutians to Patagonia have
described in awestruck tones the ragged and rebellious winds that
pour off seaside mountains. A nineteenth-century sailor off Alaska
said williwaws turned the sea into a frightening "icy froth."

Winds also carry perhaps the most important figure in the mythol-
ogy of the lands where Crane was lost. The Raven is the creator,
savior, and shape-shifting trickster in the Distant Time stories of
the Native Athabascan tribes.

There are multiple variations on the same themes depending on
the storyteller. But in all, the Great Raven, known as Dotson' Sa,
was there at the beginning of everything. One tale carries echoes
of Noah and the biblical flood, perhaps infused by brushes with
Russian Christians centuries ago or possibly just an interesting
coincidence in a land where spring floods are an annual fact of life.

It begins with the waters rising and the Great Raven building a
huge raft to carry pairs of animals of his choice. The Great Raven
then began to remake the world. He asked a muskrat to swim to the
ocean floor to bring back mud. The raft began to transform into an
island that grew bigger and bigger. Dotson' Sa filled the island with
berries and plants, lakes and rivers. Later, it came time to remake
men and women. He first chose rock to make them, but realized
they would live forever. The Great Raven decided clay was better. It
brought mortality. He liked his creation, so much, in fact, that he
desired a human wife, but was driven away by the people who saw
Raven as a nuisance. As revenge, some say Raven unleashed mosquitoes on the earth to pester humankind ever more.

But Raven had his benevolent moods. As always, there are many interpretations of the same story, but one goes like this: A powerful chief once stole the sun and moon and hung them in his home as trophies. The world was dark and cold. Famine set in, as people could not hunt or fish. Animals starved because they could find neither food nor prey. Raven concocted a plan. He knew the chief's daughter went every morning to a small stream to collect water. Raven turned himself into a tiny fish and jumped into her jug. She took a drink and swallowed the fish, making her pregnant. She gave birth to a boy. Years later, when the child was young and precocious, he started crying. His grandfather—the chief who stole the sun and moon—asked what he wanted. The boy gestured to the purloined orbs hanging from the rafters. The chief let the boy play with them. The boy then hurled them back into the sky to return the sun and moon.

In the winters of the past, Athabascan families huddled in shelters, and some burrowed into the ground for added insulation, and they shared these stories and entertained themselves with riddles. Outside, ravens hunted for scraps as one of the few animals that rode out the dark season.

The river valley was wider now. The water flowed slower on the flatlands, making the ice more solid and predictable. But the route was less direct. The Charley meandered as the land leveled.

Without knowing it, Crane had crossed the Tintina Fault, which cuts diagonally south of the Yukon River in eastern Alaska and into western Canada. It marks the northern edge of a geologically complex zone of quartz, granite, feldspar, and other minerals. It's now part of central Alaska's "gold belt." Some of the gold remains deep in the earth around quartz veins and other deposits. But the easier target—and the cause of eureka moments that touched off gold rushes—is the gold that has been washed down into creeks and rivers over the ages. Gold is far heavier than most sediment and sits at the bottom of the waterways.

For Crane, more was changing than the scenery. The days, too, were significantly longer as the earth shifted toward the spring equinox. There were more than eleven hours of daylight now, and it grew by about six minutes each day. Crane started to make considerable distance with the longer days and ever-lighter pack.

Crane had experienced the subarctic nights from their deepest point. He couldn't quite picture the flip side: the near-endless summer days. His friends at Ladd told him about the 1:00 a.m. cookouts and the annual midnight baseball game on June 21. In the 1943 edition, months before Crane's arrival, the Ladd Quartermasters beat Fairbanks 6–2. The winning pitcher was a soldier named Treskovich, whose ethnic roots were enough to bring out a handful of Russians curious to see this peculiar American pastime.

Crane guessed his food would last a few more weeks, probably until early April. He had fewer than two dozen bullets.

The hills moaned again. Crane watched the treetops fold over. He had maybe half a minute until the winds hit. There were times when he regretted giving up the sledge. This was one of them. It would have offered perfect protection. He did the only thing he could: turn his back to the winds and cower low. He covered his face with his mittens. All he could hear was the howl of the wind and the flapping of his fraying parka. From a distance, Crane might not appear like a man at all. He could be another dark outcrop on the river waiting to be covered by the blowing snow.

If the weather turned worse, he wondered how long he could last.

Crane rose. He always checked his rifle first after each wind blast. The fear was that some blowing debris could jam the bolt or clog the trigger. That would be an easy fix in normal circumstances. But Crane had no tools to disassemble the weapon. Even if he could, he dreaded fumbling a rifle piece onto the ground and turning the .22 into nothing more than a fancy club. A few times, bullets slipped from Crane's fingers and were lost in the snow. He now made sure to roll out his sleeping bag as a catch cloth whenever he was handling the ammo. At this point, it might be better to lose a finger than a bullet.

After another bend—and another disappointment of seeing nothing but more wilderness—Crane decided to look for a place to set up camp. His tent needed a rope spine to hold it up. There was no choice but to spend the night among the trees and hope the winds were kind.

There were still a few hours of daylight. Crane took the rifle and scanned the grove. Here was some welcome luck. There was a plump ptarmigan foraging in the open. Crane steadied the rifle and used his training: aim, exhale slowly, pull the trigger. It was a direct hit. He cleaned the bird and then left his pack and started walking up the riverbank with his rifle ready. Where there was one ptarmigan, there were often more.

Around the next bend, Crane stopped dead.

Parallel rows of spruce branches were arranged on the frozen river. Circling them was a path of packed snow. It had to be from a toboggan or something dragged in the snow. Nothing natural could have made this. It wasn't fresh, though. Snowfall and blown drifts had filled some of the tracks. But this was definitely recent and could have only one meaning: the markings for a landing strip used by bush pilots.

It was growing too dark to investigate further. Crane headed back to camp and excitedly plucked and gutted the ptarmigan, running a stick through its center as a cooking skewer. It browned quickly over the fire. Crane feasted, eating everything, including the brittle bird bones. He tallied up the time since the crash. Counting the day they left, that's eleven in December. Plus thirty-one in January. That's forty-two. February was a leap year, so that's twenty-nine. That brings it to seventy-one. He knew it was into March, but was no longer certain of the date. Let's say it's March 9. That's about right. So what's that?

Eighty days.

At first light, Crane left his pack leaning against a tree. He wanted to travel as light as possible. During the previous night, he had moments of insecurity that the spruce-edged landing strip was some kind of hallucination or another source of false hope like Berail's cabin.

Crane went around the river bend. There it was, the same as the day before.

Crane stepped on the trail of packed snow. It was firm and easy walking. The track dipped away from the river. Then, in a long loop, it headed back toward the ice. Crane followed for two hours. The track never seemed to falter or weaken. Oddly, though, he didn't notice other footprints. He guessed it was from a dog-sled, which would cover up most of the paw marks as it dragged over the snow. Fresh snow would do the rest. He thought about his own crude sledge. How long would its traces stay on the river until snow and wind covered over any sign that he had passed that way? They were already gone, most likely.

The track took a sharp turn toward the riverbank, slipping between some large rocks.

On the other side was a cabin. From this distance, it looked not too much different from the others. Don't get your hopes up, Crane told himself. But, if nothing else, he was out of the weather and could stay here for a while. Crane hurried across the frozen river.

He saw animal tracks. Wolves? Be careful, he thought.

Then came barking. Unmistakably, gloriously, a dog's barking.

SIXTEEN

MARCH 10, 1944
Ames's Cabin

Crane couldn't make sense of it at first.

The dog was barking, but he also saw movement in the trees. That definitely was something else. It was too big to be a person. Cautiously, Crane crossed over the riverbank. He stumbled on some rocks under the snow. He took a few steps closer. Then he relaxed. Crane was staring at a clothesline with some cloth diapers and a red-and-white checkered tablecloth waving in the breeze.

"Ho!" he yelled. "Anyone there?"

For the first time in eighty-one days, someone answered.

The cabin door opened. A man looked back at Crane. He was dressed somewhere between trapper and dandy: old-style riding breeches that flared out above the knee and decorated with six stripes around the ankles, a wide leather belt, dark wool shirt, and heavy socks. A hand-rolled cigarette smoldered in his right hand.

Crane was having trouble taking it all in. Finally, he blurted, "I'm Lieutenant Crane of the United States Army Air Forces. I've had a little trouble. . . . I, um, I. Boy, am I glad to see you."

"Air Forces?" said the man. "You crash?"

"Yes. I mean, my ship went down a while ago."

"Near here? I didn't hear anything."

"No, no. I've been walking. You see, I, well, I've been walking for a while. The plane went down December 21. A B-24. What . . . what day is today?"

"December 21! You sure about that? Today is March 10."

"That's what I thought. No mistake. I've been walking. Well, I found a cabin and stayed for a while. I, ah, I, I . . . I apologize. I just haven't spoken with anyone in a long time."

The man slipped on some low-cut boots and walked out onto the packed snow. He draped his arm around Crane's shoulders, leading him back to the cabin.

"Okay. It's all right. We gotta get you inside. What did you say your name was again?"

"Leon Crane, first lieutenant. I'm from Philadelphia. Originally, I mean. I'm out of Ladd Field."

"Well, you're not close to either," he said, extending his hand. "I'm Albert Ames."

They crossed into the cabin. Ames pulled the door shut with its oversized brass knob. The first thing Crane noticed was the smell of coffee. A Native woman, whom Crane correctly figured to be Ames's wife, stood to the side, holding a baby. She was quiet and did not come directly to greet him. The cabin was warmed by a big wood-fed stove that made wheezing sounds when it was going full blast. It was warm enough that the woman wore only a cotton dress and slippers. There were two other children, a girl and a boy, who ducked behind their mother at the sight of Crane and his tattered and stained flight suit.

"This is Nina," Ames said, introducing the woman.

"Nina," Ames continued, looking over at his wife, "we better fix some food for our guest. You hungry, Lieutenant?"

"I ate some pancakes this morning. I shot a ptarmigan last night. But I could definitely eat more. If you don't mind, I'd really love some coffee."

"Sure thing," said Ames, putting the cup down in front of Crane while Nina stoked the fire in the stove. The two kids crept closer. Crane learned the girl's name was Molly. Her brother, whose name was Daniel Lee Ames, was simply called Big Boy. The infant, Albert Norman, was Little Boy.

"December 21 you say," Ames said, holding out his hands as if trying to weigh the distance between then and now. "That's a long time. Now, tell us again. How the hell did you get here?"

"First," Crane said, "I have to find out where I am. What river is this?"

"My friend, you are really lost. This is the Charley," he said. "You're about a mile south of the Yukon River."

"The Charley. I thought that might be right. I wasn't sure, but that's what made most sense. So that means Woodchopper is off to the west, right?" Crane asked, remembering the map from Berail's cabin.

"That's right. Now, tell us, where exactly did your plane go down? And why do you care about Woodchopper?"

Crane began the story, letting it unfold slowly and in full from the beginning: how they reported their last position heading out from Big Delta, bailing from the B-24, burning his father's letter, finding Berail's cabin.

"Phil Berail!" Ames cut in. "Hell, I know Phil. Everyone knows him. He lives over in Woodchopper. I see why you were asking. You're a very, very lucky man, Lieutenant. Phil's was the last cache on the river. If you missed that, I don't think you'd be sitting here with me now."

"What do you mean, 'the last'?"

"I mean, the last one. There are no more. Berail was the last one to keep up a full store of supplies down the Charley. I don't think he's been down there in years, though."

"This is his rifle," said Crane. "These are his mittens. This guy saved my life."

"Well, then, you'll have to thank him in person when we get you to Woodchopper. Here, look at this."

Ames pulled out a large and detailed map of Alaska. It was mounted on plywood. Ames traced his finger along the Charley River, beginning from where he guessed was the crash site. It was more than ninety-five miles as the river flowed.

"That's impressive," said Ames. "You said you were from Philadelphia?"

Over a lunch of moose steaks, they traded stories.

Crane's world of urban buzz and streetcars seemed marvelously exotic to Nina Henry Ames, a member of an Athabascan clan who was born in Fort Yukon. Her older relatives were so bound to traditional ways that they found no need to learn more than broken English. Crane talked about the winters in Boston, which now seemed child's play. Albert Ames joked that now there were two rivers of the same name in his life: the Charles in Boston and the Charley here.

To Crane, the lives of the Ames clan were equally extraordinary. They had been trapping and fishing along the Charley and other rivers since the early 1930s in a lifestyle not that much removed from that of Nina's forebears. But, for Albert, it was a matter of choice. He decided to head into the wilderness after some globe-trotting. Ames, in fact, had seen much more of the world than Crane. Albert left South Dakota as a footloose teenager just after World War I. He bounced around the East Coast for a while, stopping in Atlantic City to see his aunt. He cavorted along the boardwalk and gawked at the extravagances of the seaside hotels such as the Traymore, whose bathroom taps included the option of heated ocean water. Ames later found a place on a freighter bound for China. On the return journey across the Pacific, he stepped off the gangplank onto the Alaskan territory.

Ames outfitted himself with a backpack and some sturdy shoes and, for reasons only he knew, started to walk into the interior. The Alaska Railroad was not yet finished all the way to Fairbanks, but it could have carried him off the coast. Instead, Ames ended up hoofing it to Fairbanks. In those days, traveling by foot did not seem entirely outlandish. Ames often made better time than the automobiles trying to traverse the wilderness on dirt roads and through hinterlands where mechanics were much more familiar with airplanes than cars. Ames liked to tell his real-life tortoise-and-hare stories about how he repeatedly pushed the same rattle-trap car out of ruts and mud holes as he walked north.

In Fairbanks he landed a job as a "horse packer," hauling goods up to Circle on the Yukon River. On one of the runs, he met the young and pretty Nina. They built their magnum opus, the cabin on the Charley, in 1941, using nice spruce logs with square notching that stacked together tightly. The seams were filled with hard-packed moss. The peaked roof was insulated with sod. The flooring was sturdy boards, and a trap door led to a well-stocked root cellar. All in all, it was bigger and more solid than Berail's outpost.

By now, Ames and Nina were experienced trappers, setting lines along the Charley and deeper into the hills for fox and marten and, when luck was shining, mink and ermine. These were reasonably good times in the fur trade. The war had boosted demand for fur to line winter gear for troops. But, at the same time, the government set a price ceiling as part of the wartime economic measures. The maximum price for mink, fox, and other pelts could not exceed the highest paid for comparable goods in March 1942. Nevertheless, a silver fox pelt could fetch up to forty dollars, about 30 percent higher than 1938. Some spin doctors in the fur industry went so far as to claim that furs were a morale booster in the war effort. They lifted "the spirits of our woman-hood to meet the sorrows" of tough times, one furrier claimed. In the summer, the Ames family operated a fish wheel, a floating rig that spins like a Ferris wheel from the current and scoops up spawning salmon.

Crane was right about the branch-lined strip on the frozen Charley. It was a winter runway for the occasional supply plane operated by Wien Alaska, which was the gold standard of bush-plane operations at the time. The airline was an ambitious family-run affair. Its founder, Noel Wien, flew into Fairbanks in 1924 in an open-cockpit biplane. He later had his first cabin aircraft, a single-engine Fokker F.III, shipped in pieces from Europe. Ames's other connection to the outside world was his team of up to twenty sled dogs.

Suddenly, Crane asked, "You have a mirror?"

"Was waiting for you to ask," laughed Ames. "I'm guessing you haven't seen yourself in a while."

"Not a good look since the crash."

Nina pointed the way to a mirror in the back of the cabin. She giggled.

"Well," said Crane. "I see what you mean."

He ran his fingers through his two-inch beard and matted hair, pulling out a few twigs and spruce needles in the process. Crane thought he looked like a Hollywood version of a sourdough, the local term for an Alaskan who has seen it all and decided to stay. The name is believed to come from the bread fixings carried by many of the gold rush prospectors.

"I must say, Lieutenant," said Ames, walking up behind him, "you look pretty good otherwise. I'm not certain I would have fared so well out there with just the supplies you had. And I'm used to this kind of winter."

"Luck," Crane shrugged.

"Damn good luck," said Ames.

Nina got out her scissors after lunch was cleared away. She planned to give Crane a haircut.

"Wait a minute," said Ames. "We need photos."

He dug out the old box camera. "Nina," he said, "we should take a photo outside. Can you do it?"

She nodded. Crane and Ames posed side by side in the snow. Crane squinted a bit. His parka was half zipped over his flight suit, which in places was held together by crude stitches and rope. Ames stood to Crane's left. Ames had a cigarette in his right hand and had the other in the pocket of his Alaskan jodhpurs.

"A few more with just the lieutenant," Ames urged.

Crane took off his parka for several more shots. His smile was somewhere between relief and bewilderment.

Back in the cabin, Nina went to work. Tufts of his heavy, dark hair dropped onto the blue oilcloth covering the table. Nina trimmed the sides closely, but left more of Crane's curls on top. Molly and Big Boy stared at the grimy stranger.

Ames gave Crane a pair of overalls and a razor. Nina carried a basin of warm water over to the mirror. For a half hour, Crane worked on his beard, first with the scissors and then razor. He was about to shave off his mustache when Ames held up his hand.

"Wait. You look too damn healthy," he joked. "No one will believe you. Keep the mustache."

Crane did.

"Say," asked Crane. "You have a radio?"

"Sure do. But just a shortwave receiver. Not one to call out."

"Well, can't ask for too much," Crane smiled. "What's happening with the war? Last I heard, back in December, the Brits were bombing the hell out of Germany."

Ames tuned in the shortwave radio. The war headlines included a report from Anzio and how the Allies were holding up to German shelling. A Coast Guard petty officer third class, J. J. McAndrews, wrote in his diary that day: "Boy, Anzio has really been bombed to hell. We loaded up with troops who have been fighting since the beachhead had been established and are now going back to Naples for a few days rest."

Crane felt a bit down. He had imagined—in the times when he allowed himself to imagine his rescue—the war would have turned even more in the Allies' favor. It was looking good. But Crane liked to fantasize that he would come out of the wilderness and the end would be near.

"Where's the nearest radio to call Ladd Field?" Crane asked. "My parents probably think I'm dead. Guess everyone else probably does, too."

"No doubt. No doubt," said Ames. "The nearest radio . . . Well, that would be on a plane. We can get you over to Woodchopper, but not right away. Best rest up for a couple of days. We got two planes coming into Woodchopper soon. Well, I mean hopefully soon. You really never know."

One was a mail plane, which was already late because of the weather and the thousands of other glitches that can happen in the Alaskan winter. The other plane scheduled was for a pregnant woman who was heading to a hospital in Fairbanks.

All the next day, Crane watched Ames prepare for the trip. It was strange for Crane to be idle. He was a bystander, drinking endless cups of coffee. He tried to hide his impatience, but they all sensed it.

"Soon," Ames repeated, looking up from the dogsled as he made some repairs. "Soon, Lieutenant."

The temperature was close to minus twenty. There was a trace of new snow, which gave everything a fresh sheen. Crane came out to help Ames load the dogsled. He noticed Ames was moving smartly in snowshoes with those same infuriating traditional ties that baffled Crane.

"Easy," Ames chuckled.

In thirty seconds, Ames showed Crane the trick: wedge in your toe around one loop and wrap the longest bind behind your heel and tie it shoelace fashion.

"That's it?" Crane clucked. "If I had figured that out, I could have made the trip in one-third the time."

"Either way," said Ames, "you made it."

SEVENTEEN

MARCH 13, 1944
Woodchopper

Reaching Woodchopper took two days. At times, the dog team couldn't carry both men. Crane followed behind on Ames's snowshoes, amazed at the speed he could make. The night was spent with one of Ames's trapper friends, who broke out some dried fish for the unexpected guests. Crane took some bites and then ducked out for another run to the outdoor privy. His stomach was in knots. No doubt it was from the rich moose steaks and gallons of coffee. In more than eighty days on the Charley River, this was the first time Crane was marginally sick. He imagined how devastating any illness would have been out there.

"You okay to travel, Lieutenant?" Ames asked the next morning.

"Made it this far," said Crane, still unsteady from diarrhea. "I'm not going to stall out now. Let's go."

"Fair enough," said Ames. "Your call."

That afternoon Ames steered his dogs past the empty Woodchopper Roadhouse, where Woodchopper Creek joins the Yukon River. Years earlier, the two-story boardinghouse—a bunk and meal for a couple of bucks—was the biggest and most elegant structure along that stretch of the river. Now, it stood as a silent monument to vanities built upon gold.

The roadhouse was put up around 1910 by a German immigrant known as Valentine "Woodchopper" Smith. It became a port of call for gold miners, wanderers, sourdoughs, and steamboat crews loading up on cords of wood. It didn't take much to impress this hard-bitten crowd. Smith, however, went the extra mile. He added touches such as rocking chairs, toilet seats covered in cold-beating caribou hide, and meals served with a knife, fork, *and* spoon. By roadhouse standards, these were five-star trappings. Smith garnered the reputation as the backcountry's überinn-keeper. The competition was not much.

Many other roadhouses across interior Alaska had a slapdash, take-your-chances quality in their best moments. Judge James Wickersham—the same justice who came up with the idea of naming Fairbanks after his Senate buddy—didn't know whether to laugh or cry at the hangdog state of one roadhouse, where booze boxes and milk crates were repurposed as chairs and the tavern door was a piece of clapboard nailed to wooden poles. The owner of another down-on-its-heels roadhouse was known to fire warning shots from her rifle at passing travelers who had the temerity to pass by in search of better accommodations.

But the success at Smith's establishment eventually brought imitators. Nearby, at the mouth of Coal Creek, a small-time miner named Frank Slaven put up his own place in 1932, investing the serious sum of one thousand dollars. His menu included fresh chicken and vegetables from his garden. He even lugged in leather chairs to give the main room a hotel-lobby feel. When the big dredge operations arrived in the midthirties, Slaven sold his claims along Coal Creek for a small fortune and spent his winters in decidedly milder Seattle.

The Woodchopper Roadhouse story doesn't end so well. By the midthirties, it had passed into the hands of an older couple, Jack and Kate Welch. Jack liked his booze, but held it together enough to keep the roadhouse's doors open. Kate was the postmistress for several years and liked to keep up with local gossip by steaming open letters and taking just a wee peek inside. One miner who had a cabin on the Yukon advised a friend to use sealing wax on letters to avoid prying eyes.

One spring the ice breakup bottlenecked near the roadhouse. The rising waters—fifteen feet or more—threatened to carry away the building. The Welches had just enough time to cut loose their dogs so they could scamper to higher ground. The couple retreated inside the roadhouse to make their stand. Table-size chunks of ice battered the log walls during a frightening night. Jack manned the windows, using poles to push away some of the ice slabs. By morning, the water receded. The first floor was ravaged—including Jack's prized *National Geographic* collection, waterlogged beyond hope—but the place survived. The couple was just never the same after that harrowing night.

Kate remained mostly bedridden with worsening rheumatism. Jack's mental state, meanwhile, appeared increasingly unglued. One night early in World War II, he became convinced German troops where bearing down on the Yukon. He grabbed his rifle. In either a slip or suicide attempt, Jack ended up shooting himself in the side. Their nearest neighbor—the same man who urged for the wax-sealed letters—raced the couple to the nearby Woodchopper mining camp on a dogsled. The winter watchman radioed for a plane to take Jack to a Fairbanks hospital.

It was all too much for Kate. She died while her husband recovered. Jack's already precarious psyche then went off the edge. He simply couldn't accept the news that he was a widower. He became convinced Kate was hiding from him. He returned to the now-idle roadhouse a broken man, wandering around and asking if anyone had seen his missing wife. One day someone noticed that Jack's skiff was missing. Soon, there were reports from villages along the Yukon River of a mysterious, quiet man in a small boat riding the currents. Jack was never found, but local lore says he was last seen at the mouth of the Yukon floating out to the Bering Sea.

By the time Crane and Ames passed by, the Woodchopper Roadhouse was empty. Storms had knocked out windows, and animals were finding places to call home. Remnants of the roadhouse's former glory, such as fabric wallpaper, fluttered in the wind.

Ames pointed his sled upstream. They soon mushed into the mining outpost of Woodchopper. Here, too, was a place with its best days behind it.

The war had effectively halted the two big dredges on Woodchopper and Coal Creeks, cutting off the main flow of cash and steady jobs. Gold was not a priority for Washington, which had wartime sway over what factories and mines produced and where equipment was allocated. Gold production across Alaska dropped more than 85 percent during the war years. At the twin dredges on Coal and Woodchopper, it was a serious blow. Since the midthirties, they had pulled up more than $3 million of gold based on a price at the time, which hovered near $34 an ounce. They were successful, but not wildly so.

Fewer than two dozen people continued to stick it out in Woodchopper during the war. What kept Woodchopper alive—as with many other villages in Alaska's interior—was the airstrip.

After Ames fed his dogs, he learned their timing was good. A Wien plane was scheduled to arrive the next day for the very pregnant Evelyn Berglund, who was due in less than two weeks. She was one half of an interesting backcountry duo with her husband, Willard Grinnell. They later divorced, and Evelyn went on to write a memoir, *Born on Snowshoes,* that recounts her upbringing in a cabin nearly astride the Arctic Circle and her later years trapping and hunting with her two sisters. She was eleven years old when she saw her first bush plane, which seemed to her like it "came from another world." She was fifteen when the family got a radio, which worked fine except when it rained.

Ames led Crane over the frozen mud paths of Woodchopper. Crane asked about a place to eat.

First, there is someone you have to meet, said Ames, knocking on the door of a simple log cabin.

Lieutenant Leon Crane, Ames said with exaggerated formality, let me introduce you to Mr. Phil Berail.

Word had already reached Berail that his cache had saved Crane's life. A story like that, once Ames told the first person in Woodchopper, took only a few minutes to make the rounds. Berail, a big man with a voice to match, was already something of a living Yukon legend at age sixty-five. This just added to his fame.

The Indiana-born Berail first drifted north in 1904. He had big appetites in all things and was ready for anything. He did a bit of logging before building a series of cabins in the Charley River basin. He learned the wilderness talent of getting by with whatever job came along. Berail prospected, but never got more than a pinch of gold dust. He did some mining, but got antsy at being underground. He eventually landed a position as hydraulic foreman at the Coal Creek dredge. In the winter when work shut down, Berail would head to his main cabin—the one that Crane found. Once in a while, he would rig up the dogsled to make a weeklong run to check on how the Coal Creek facilities were weathering the cold.

Berail seemed cut from an earlier age. Modern ways often grated at him like sand in his soup. When Berail learned that the dredge had to deduct Social Security payments, he was appalled.

"What's this Social Security monkeyshine?" he asked the dredge chief, Ernest Patty.

Patty explained the new law. Berail stormed out, grumbling about how America was turning into a nation of "softies."

"He always reminded me of a figure straight out of some northern myth," wrote Patty years later.

But what struck everyone—and was the source of endless story swapping—was Berail's almost scary tolerance for discomfort or pain. Nothing seemed to make him wince. One day he came into the dredge office holding an oil-stained cloth. Inside was part of a finger severed on a machine. He refused to be put on a plane to Fairbanks for treatment. Instead, he said he would wrap the stump in a clean rag he had back at his cabin. His only concession was allowing some antiseptic and a real bandage.

Another time, Berail broke his arm. Again, he refused an airlift to Fairbanks. He went home and made his own sling. The injury, to no one's surprise, never healed properly. Berail had to hold his coffee cup with two hands after that.

Ernest Patty's son Dale once said Berail "must have had all his nerves disconnected."

Another old Yukon hand, Gordon Bertoson, affectionately described Berail as a *skookum,* a multipurpose word in Pacific Northwest jargon that can describe extraordinary toughness. "He could walk for hundreds of miles, that guy, if he wanted to," said Bertoson. "Tough, tough."

"I don't know what to say except thank you," Crane said to Berail. "I wouldn't be here if I didn't come across your cabin. I owe you my life."

"Bah, think nothing of it," said Berail, holding up his hand with the missing finger. "This is why it's there. By the way, how did the place look? Everything holding up?"

"To me it looked like paradise," said Crane. "But, yeah, everything was perfect. I did, however, knock out the skylight frame to use on a sledge."

"You had dogs?"

"Nope. Pulled it myself."

Berail shook his head. And people think I'm tough, he must have thought. The idea of a city-boy pilot walking out of the wild would be talked about for years in Woodchopper. Drinks, meals—whatever Crane wanted—were on the house. He was the hero of the moment. His money was no good. This was convenient, because he had none.

"Glad that old cabin was of use to someone," said Berail. "I'm not sure I'll ever get back that way anyway. Getting on in years a bit, I guess."

Ames cut in. He wanted to get moving to Circle, the next big town downstream on the Yukon River. Crane handed Ames two handwritten notes for the radio transmitter in Circle operated by the Army Signal Corps. The messages were relayed to Canada and then sent as telegrams. They probably wouldn't make it out for days at best, but Crane couldn't pass up the chance. Who knew what could happen between Woodchopper and Ladd Field? One telegram was to his family. *Am safe. Stop. Heading back. Stop. Call soon. Stop. Love, Leon. Stop.* The other went to Colonel Russell Keillor, one of the commanding officers at Ladd. Or at least he was the last time Crane was there.

Crane stayed in Woodchopper as a guest of Berail. They talked into the night. Crane's gut was still out of whack, but it couldn't easily beg out of Berail's hospitality. For such an occasion, Berail broke out his beloved 180-proof rum, which he used to have shipped in by Yukon River steamer. He made sure to order enough for the winter before the first freeze. Nowadays, he put in orders with Wien pilots, who weren't supposed to transport alcohol but made an exception for Berail.

The next morning, a single-prop Stinson V77 outfitted with skis whined out of the clouds and onto the snow-covered airstrip in Woodchopper. At the commands was veteran bush pilot Bob Rice, who had joined up with Wien Alaska after years of freelance flying to any place with a flat patch to put down a plane. Sometimes it was so cold on an overnight stop that Rice resorted to an old bush-pilot trick: drain the plane's oil and take out its battery to keep warm indoors.

You the missing pilot? Rice asked Crane.

"Not anymore."

Ha, right, said Rice. Well, we'll be on our way soon.

Nearly everyone in Woodchopper, including Berail, watched the Stinson leave with Crane sitting alongside Willard Grinnell, the pregnant Evelyn, and their two-year-old son, Dick.

Halfway to Ladd Field, Rice flicked on the radio to the Wien frequency. He asked the operator to call the base.

"They will care about this," said Rice when questioned by the Wien operator. "I've got a passenger I think Ladd Field will be very interested in."

EIGHTEEN

MARCH 14, 1944
Fairbanks

A few minutes later, pilot Bob Rice listened to the radio message relayed from Ladd. Rice turned to Crane and flashed his big smile.

"They want to know if you are dead or alive, Lieutenant."

"What?"

"That's the question from Ladd when Wien told them I had you on board. Are you alive or dead?"

"Hell's bells," said Crane. "Guess I'm still alive."

Rice went back to the radio. "This is Bob on the inbound Wien flight from Woodchopper. Concerning Lieutenant Crane, tell Ladd that he's very much alive."

For about a minute, they heard only static as Rice set a course southwest over low hills covered in snow. Then the airline operator came back: "Roger that, Bob. They say there are a lot of people waiting to see him."

Rice, a wiry man who seemed blessed with a perpetually good mood, gave an exaggerated grin in Crane's direction. This should be interesting, Rice thought. He'd seen a lot flying the bush. But nothing could match bringing back someone pretty much given up for dead.

Rice made friends easily. Within a few minutes, he was swapping stories with Crane about managing the tricky skies in Alaska. Rice would have made a good military aviator. He was meticulous in the cockpit. He never went in for the cowboy style of some other bush pilots. Everything was checked and double-checked and, just to be sure, triple-checked. There was no glory, he would say, in crashing.

Rice's decision to come to Alaska, however, was a rare snap call. He was racking up flying miles in his native Washington state by taking friends around the countryside and on the occasional run to Seattle for some nightlife. He seemed content. Then someone came into his father's grocery store with wide-eyed tales about the bush-pilot life in Alaska. Rice was soon packing.

He literally helped map out Alaska from the air. He arrived in the days before most planes had instruments. Rice compiled "situational awareness" logs. They identified landmarks such as rivers and power lines, giving pilots reference points and an idea of the visibility. As an apparent good-luck charm—and conversation piece—Rice kept the polished bone from a walrus penis. It was as long as his forearm.

As the plane bounced toward Fairbanks, Crane turned to chat with Willard Grinnell. Crane was deeply intrigued by the backcountry life since finding Ames and his family. It was so different—so free-form—from anything he had known. To Crane, Grinnell seemed to be a bred-in-the-bone woodsman after more than a decade trapping to the east of the Charley River near the Canadian border. Grinnell surprised him, though.

I was once a total tenderfoot myself, Grinnell told Crane over the noise of the plane.

What? said Crane. You're serious? You mean you learned how to live off the land?

Well, I learned a lot from Evelyn, of course, said Grinnell, giving a quick nod to his wife. She is the real expert. Let's just say I had some hard on-the-job training in the early days.

It was—like with Crane—a live-or-die proposition in Grinnell's first days in the wilds. In October 1933, Grinnell was wedged into a bush plane with some trapping gear, a few provisions, and a fellow named Ben Moreland, who described himself as an out-of-work schoolteacher in Fairbanks. Grinnell and Moreland planned to make a go of trapping. The plane landed on a gravel spit on a river, dropped them off, and headed almost immediately back to Fairbanks. The two men watched in silence as it disappeared over the hills. That night, it dropped down to minus thirty. They had a woodstove, but no tent. "We built a brush lean-to on the bank and, in kapok sleeping bags, hugged the stove—one on each side," Grinnell wrote in a letter decades later. The next morning, they got to work on a cabin, even though neither had any experience notching logs or making a roof. "It was build or freeze," Grinnell wrote. "So we built."

As soon as the river ice was strong enough, the schoolteacher decided he had had enough. He hiked out and eventually found a seat on a plane back to Fairbanks. Grinnell stayed. The bush was, he would say, in his blood even if he had a lot to learn. His father was among the first prospectors to reach Nome in the winter of 1898–1899 before heading back south with a lot of stories but no riches.

Rice's Stinson banked left over Ladd a little before seven. There was still forty-five minutes of daylight. Crane could see Hangar 1, the metal roofs of his barracks, and the runway where the *Iceberg Inez* took off. At the same time, cars were racing toward Weeks Field, where Rice was instructed to land. It was within sight of Ragle's house.

An ambulance and staff car were waiting. So was a group of airmen looking like a gaggle of reporters gathered for a celebrity arrival. Crane looked the part with his dashing new mustache and still dressed in his ragged flight suit. Crane figured he should return to base in uniform as much as possible. In the crowd were some of the guys from the overtime poker game that got Crane off to a late start eighty-five days before.

"The plane landed and out popped old Crane," Maine airman Arthur Jordan wrote in his diary that night. "What a thrill that was. We grabbed him and rushed out into the field. En route, he told us the beginning of an unbelievable struggle for survival."

Questions were fired from all sides. But he had some of his own first.

Any news of Pompeo? Hoskin? The rest of the crew?

Crane was crushed to learn there had been no word on anyone since the crash. The search missions never even spotted the wreck, he was told. Crane thought about his first days lost, scanning the sky for a plane near his spruce-branch SOS. No one ever came close.

An arm reached across and pulled Crane into the staff car. Crane barreled through the Ladd gates and was led directly to Colonel Keillor's office in Hangar 1. Keillor was waiting at the door.

"Well done, Lieutenant. Well done," said Keillor, who kept his hair parted down the middle in the style more fitting of the twenties. He gave Crane a long handshake, and—in a scene that would be fodder for gossip at Ladd—the colonel started to weep. "We have a lot to ask you. But, first, is there anyone you want to call?"

"My parents, sir. I'd like to call my parents in Philadelphia."

Crane gave Keillor the West Philadelphia exchange, SH for Sherwood, and the rest of the five digits. Keillor contacted the operator. It was past midnight on the East Coast.

Crane's father answered.

"This is Colonel Keillor from Ladd Field in Alaska. I have some good news for you," he said. "Will you please hold the line?"

The heavy black receiver was passed to Crane. "Dad . . . ," he began. "It's Leon."

Crane sidestepped the breathless questions from his parents. It was too soon to tell the whole story. Crane could barely grasp it all. He told his father that he had "a little trouble" and had to walk out of the woods. He was fine, though. Don't worry. I'm back.

Crane had an appointment at the hospital for a full checkup. First, though, he wanted to eat and get a hot shower. He walked the underground passageways. The people he passed slapped his back. Some newcomers at Ladd were told, that's the guy.

"The news was traveling like wildfire," Arthur Jordan continued in his diary. "No one believes he is back until they see him."

At the hospital, word came down that an airman lost in the wilderness for nearly three months was coming in for a full physical. The incredible thing, the story went, is that he looks in remarkably good shape.

On duty that night was a nurse from Iowa, Wilma Koehrsen. She received orders to help with the Crane examinations when he made his way to the hospital.

First, Crane had other business. He passed the base exchange, where he grabbed the matches that morning for Hoskin. He stopped at the mess hall.

What can I get you? the guy behind the counter asked.

Crane ordered a milkshake.

Outside, it was thirteen degrees. The coldest days of winter were behind.

Three days later, on March 17, a Seattle newspaper ran a story under the headlines: "Luck Saved Crane in Arctic Wilds; City Flier, Foodless Nine Days, Found Cabin with Stock of Provisions." Margaret Sibert, a sister of the *Iceberg Inez*'s prop specialist, noticed the article. She dashed off a quick letter to Anna Pompeo, mother of the crew chief. For one last moment, hope was rekindled.

"Dear Mrs. Pompeo," she wrote. "It seems unbelievable that one of the boys got back. I'm keeping my fingers crossed for the others."

NINETEEN

MARCH 7, 2007

Gorham, Maine

Only waiting remained.

It was six months since the JPAC field team left the crash site above the Charley River. So far, few details of the investigation had been shared with the Hoskin family: John and his wife, Mary, in Maine, and Harold's daughter, Joann, in Florida. But clearly there was something of interest in the evidence bags. John had been asked to give a DNA sample. He went to his doctor for a cheek swab, which was sent by overnight courier to the military lab in Hawaii.

March was a busy time for John, who even into his eighties moved with the energy of a much younger man. He took up tax preparation after retiring as a minister at the Free Baptist Church near their home in Gorham, a suburb of Portland, with mills, clapboard storefronts, and stone fences going back nearly 350 years. Mary was eager to get back into the garden after Maine's messy "mud season" bridging winter and spring.

More than five thousand miles away in Hawaii, the scientific director of the Central Identification Laboratory was putting the final touches on his report. At stake was whether the bone fragments found at the B-24 crash site could be linked conclusively to Second Lieutenant Harold Elton Hoskin, serial number 0 736 523.

A match would wrap up another loose end from the crash, leaving only the crew chief, Pompeo, among the missing. Still, other mysteries in the crash may never be fully answered.

Such as, what went wrong? The *Iceberg Inez* appeared to have no more than the normal hiccups coming off the assembly line.

The plane had been grounded at least once because of "bad flying characteristics" on takeoff and landings. Military reports also noted concerns with "general instability of the controls" on the plane. This might seem scary to commercial air travelers. But experts in World War II aviation, including Jeremy Kinney at the Smithsonian Institution, see no significant red flags from such observations. Wartime aircraft were in near-constant repair and retooling from normal wear and tear. The rule of thumb for military aviation at the time was to build it fast, get it flying, and make adjustments along the way. It became even more complicated by the rigors of the Far North winter. One B-24 out of Ladd Field was once christened the "Queen of Whitehorse" because it was stuck for months in the Canadian city with a list of ailments, including malfunctioning hydraulics, clogged gas lines, and out-of-whack tachometers.

The *Inez* had some special challenges as well. It was loaded up with cold-weather testing equipment. "Very heavily instrumented" was how it was described in a military report. This had previously overtaxed the plane's electrical system, leading to at least "one complete electrical failure due to instrumental overload."

But military engineers said they had fixed any electrical circuit problems. The B-24D was in "perfect flying condition" when it took off for the prop-feathering mission, according to a postcrash report filed in February 1944—written before Crane's return to Ladd and his account of the last moments of the *Iceberg Inez*.

Crane told investigators that the instrument panel was "acting strangely" as they climbed through the opening in the clouds, trying to reach twenty-five thousand feet. The first signs of trouble were failures of the gyro and flight indicator. They show, among other things, the plane's horizontal orientation to the ground. To some experts who have studied the crash, losing both instruments suggests some kind of blockage or breakdown in the vacuum selector valve, which sucks in air from the engines on the pilot's side. The system powers the gyro and deicing systems on the leading edges of the wings. Others wonder if electrical overloads started to skew the instruments.

Regardless of the cause, engine number one cut out and could not be restarted, Crane said. By this time, the electrical system was going haywire.

It's possible—but can never be proven—that electrical shorts brought down the radio, leaving the operator, Wenz, unable to contact Ladd Tower as the plane went into a spin.

Moments after Hoskin and Crane managed to stop the first spin, they heard a "cracking noise" in the tail, Crane said. "From then on we had no control of the elevators," he continued. This deprives the pilots their main ability to hold the plane's pitch, basically keeping it from seesawing. The plane was soon in a second spin. All that was left for Crane and Hoskin were the three other engines—which may or may not have been working—as well as the rudders and ailerons, the hinged panels on the wings that control the plane's side-to-side swaying. Even with those few tools, they again managed to halt the spin.

At the time, the B-24's nose was dangerously high, slowing the plane and bringing it close to another stall, Crane told investigators. He said he tried to bring the nose down using the trim tabs, which are small rudder-like panels on the wings and tail. "Not effective," he said.

"The ship came into a stall again and whipped off into another spin," Crane said, according to the military report. "Lieutenant Hoskin gave the order to jump and we both left our seats."

At some point before, another key system failed. Bolts in the vertical stabilizer had been sliced away by the competing forces of the spin and the efforts to regain control, investigators believe.

There was no way to right the plane, which was now bucking and swaying by the forces of the fall.

"Violently mishandled" is how an April 13, 1944, report described the stresses on the aircraft. That is not a reflection on the crew's action. Instead, it means the plane and its systems were simply pushed to the limit of what steel and cable can handle.

"The crash," the report said, "was attributed to structural failure, specifically to the fact that vertical stabilizer attachment bolts in both upper and lower holes of the front fitting failed without distortion of the fitting." A search radius of several hundred yards from the crash did not locate the plane's rudder or vertical stabilizer assemblies, suggesting they broke off as the aircraft was in its doomed plummet.

In one posthumous legacy of the crash, the report recommended that the attachment bolts for the vertical stabilizers be made bigger and undergo heat treatment to strengthen against brittleness. Loss of the vertical stabilizers had been considered a factor in a number of other B-24 crashes, including one uncontrolled spin on a B-24E that went down August 12, 1943, near the California desert town of Indio.

A B-24 combat veteran, Bill Gros believes a stall is the only credible explanation for the first spin. "We flew a number of times with one engine out with no big trouble," said Gros, a former radio operator and the last surviving member from his World War II bomber crew. "One engine out is not going to put you in a spin unless there is something else happening."

That factor could have been trying to keep the plane in a tight circle while it climbed through the pipe of clear air, Gros said. The short-radius climb could have slowed it enough for a stall. Normally, the instruments would have indicated the approach of stall speed. But Gros speculated that the electrical system disruptions reported by Crane could have compromised more than just the flight indicator and gyro. It may have given off-the-mark readings on flight speed as well, he suggested.

"This plane was rigged up with extra electronics for the cold-weather testing," he said. "They said they addressed the problems of overload, but who knows?"

Once the plane fell away in the spin, the force of trying to level the craft was enough to wrench apart the elevator controls and stabilizers. "That's what doomed the aircraft," Gros said. "The stress just tore the systems apart. From then on, you knew it was going down."

After mulling over the Alaska crash site for years, historian Doug Beckstead added his own theory on the cause for the B-24's initial spin. He believes the mechanism that controlled the angle of the propeller blades malfunctioned during the feathering tests. "The blades started changing angles as if they had a mind of their own," he wrote in 2007. "That, in itself, could cause the engine to tear apart. Then the blades locked up perpendicular to the airflow, which is akin to having an anchor dropped at the end of the wing."

Randy Acord, who served with Crane at Ladd Field and became an expert on American aviation history, had still another idea. He placed the blame on the vacuum selector valves. He told interviewers in 1991 that pilots were "uneasy" about feathering because it required shutting down one or both of the engine's vacuum pumps. Acord believed that moisture got into the lines and froze, blocking the airflow into the valves. "When the vacuum ceased, they lost all their flight instruments."

Figuring out whether Hoskin went down with the plane rested with a handful of remains: four tooth fragments and shards of bone—none bigger than three centimeters.

The teeth were compared against Hoskin's military file from November 1942. There was just not enough physical evidence to make a definite connection. The analysis then turned to the pieces of shattered skeleton: bits of skull, vertebrae, femur, and other splinters.

First, it was determined that the remains were from one individual. "No duplication of skeletal remains," wrote the lead anthropologist. This was an important first hurdle.

The lab technicians then went through their checklist:

Gender: *Probable male.* The right distal humerus—the section of arm bone just above the elbow—was shaped in ways characteristic of men in more than 90 percent of cases in some studies. It was the same for the estimated size of the cranial cavity and the size of the third metacarpal, the middle finger.

Age of deceased: *Twenty to thirty years old,* most likely under twenty-four. The conclusion was based on the degree of fusion within the bones. One portion of rib recovered carried the size and appearance common in men in their early twenties. Hoskin was twenty-two years and eight months on that last flight.

Stature: *Indeterminate.* Not enough skeleton was found to make a judgment.

Race: *Indeterminate.*

Trauma: *Fire and blunt-force impact.* Portions of bone displayed apparent fractures and charring consistent with "high-temperature burning."

Length of time remains were at location: *Unclear.* Small plant roots, sediment, and a "green moss-like material" on the bones suggest "some undefined period."

Anthropologist Elias J. Kontanis finished the report with a nod toward Hoskin, but still not enough for a confirmed match. "There is a general biological agreement" between the remains and Hoskin's physical characteristics, he wrote.

All that was left was the magic bullet for modern investigators: DNA matching. Three pieces of bone were chosen in December 2006 for the analysis: the right humerus and two leg fragments, the left fibula and tibia.

With the Hoskin case, experts also had at their disposal one of the powerful tools in DNA forensics: mitochondrial DNA. The mitochondrial sequence is passed by the mother. Generally, off-spring from the same maternal line have a common mitochondrial DNA map with some unique, and naturally occurring, mutations with each generation. It's this mix of shared DNA sequence and the various anomalies that allow geneticists to trace family lines from children to mother to grandmother to great-grandmother and so on. It's theoretically possible that nonrelatives could have the same mitochondrial, or mtDNA, sequence, which means it cannot stand alone as irrefutable evidence. But the chances of an outside-the-family match are extremely remote, and it's a generally accepted marker of a person's ancestral line.

The mtDNA is a sort of battery pack. Among its central roles is either to produce or to synthesize proteins. The military analysts looked at more than 680 strands, or bases, from the mtDNA in the bone fragments. This was compared against 1,124 bases from John Hoskin's sample.

The connection came back consistent and compelling. The bases were the same. So were the mutations.

The findings moved up the chain to the scientific director of the Central Identification Laboratory, Thomas D. Holland, who has been involved in military forensics across Asia and the Middle East. In his spare time, he created a fictional alter ego in a novel, *One Drop of Blood*, whose plot includes seeking to identify forty-year-old remains.

On March 7, 2007, Holland wrote his conclusions. "In my opinion, the results of laboratory analysis and the totality of the circumstantial evidence made available to me establish the remains . . . as those of 2nd Lt. Harold E. Hoskin."

A few days later, a call was placed to Gorham, Maine, from the Army's Service Casualty Office in Kentucky. Mary Hoskin picked up the phone in their kitchen.

"John," she called out, "there's someone here who wants to speak to you about Harold."

TWENTY

SEPTEMBER 7, 2007

Arlington National Cemetery, Section 60, Grave 310

The burial ceremony for Second Lieutenant Harold E. Hoskin took place on a sunny morning in northern Virginia. "Please remember," advise the signs at Arlington National Cemetery, "these are hallowed grounds."

Eight military pallbearers carried the coffin into the Fort Myer Old Post Chapel. The blues and reds of the chapel's towering stained-glass windows were etched sharp and vivid in the late-summer light. Rows of chandeliers cast a softer glow that was reflected on the varnished pews.

The chapel began to fill. Each mourner carried a different piece of the story that began long ago over the Charley River.

Harold's younger brother John, in a charcoal suit with a red tie, held hands with his wife, Mary, wearing a navy blue dress. Hoskin's daughter, Joann, sat nearby in an aquamarine outfit. When she learned of the Arlington ceremony, she took out a plastic box that had remained closed for years. This was her late mother's private treasure, holding some of Hoskin's belongings and fifty-six letters sent by him. For the first time, Joann looked inside the box and opened each letter, carefully preserved and with just a hint of that pleasant musty library smell.

Page by page, she discovered her father, the details of a love affair cut short, and—to her bemusement—their playful exchanges about their predictions of the baby boy "Dick" due in the spring. Some of Harold's first letters from Alaska were written on tourist-style stationery decorated with drawings of Alaskan scenes, including one with a raised storage platform similar to Berail's cache that saved Crane's life. The letters then were dashed off on plain white paper in Hoskin's slanting script. One of the last he wrote to Mary, dated December 7 at 8:00 p.m. Alaska war time, was different from the others. This one was full of remembrance—as if looking back on a life lived—rather than the normal hopeful banter about their plans once he was home. For whatever reason, Harold retold stories that Mary knew by heart, including a reference to the car they nicknamed Elizabeth.

Joann read. It almost seemed like a letter to her.

Ladd Field
12-7-43. 2000 AWT
Mary Darling,

It's just two years ago today that the Japs hit Pearl Harbor. A lot has happened, hasn't it? I can't help but reminisce a bit, presumably because I've been a lot of places and done a lot.

I was sitting in the zoology lab at Bates with some classmates and we were all listening to a radio. We couldn't believe what the announcers said about Pearl Harbor. The next day at dinner we moved a big radio in the mess hall and all of us listened to the president declare war. There were a lot of very serious men afterward. A lot of us soon left school. I left at the end of January and stayed around home until the middle of April. I was sworn in the Army on the 13th of April and arrived in Santa Ana on the 25th. Flying school came and went and on the first of January this year, I got my wings. On the 9th of August in '42 I called you up and asked you to take me as your husband. You agreed and I started to become the happiest man alive. My commission made moving a sure thing. You came out . . . to Tucson and on the 19th of January at 2100 MWT we were married. I carried you across the threshold of 145 N. Main Street into our first apartment ($100 per). We were happy, but not too sure of ourselves. Remember how I left to fly at midnight and didn't fly . . . Boy, was I mad because I didn't call up first so I wouldn't have to leave.

And then when we were sitting in the movies and I sent you home because I had a pain in my stomach. The next morning I had my appendix out and in a couple of weeks we were home [in Maine].

Then the long trip back to Tucson and me finally starting to fly again. We moved to Greenfields to save $50 a month. Soon we went to El Paso and I nearly lost you because I didn't know where you were and you couldn't reach me at the officers' club.

Our honeymoon at Ruidoso, something neither of us will ever forget . . . Buying Elizabeth—finding out about Dick—and then my alert planning ahead for after . . . Gosh, what a lot has happened in two years. I've been in the Army 19 months out of 24.

Well, hon, I've got a hard day ahead, so I guess I'll hit the sack. All my love to my dearest wife.

Your husband,
Hal

Joann cried then. She cried now, sitting in the chapel waiting to hear words of remembrance for a father she never knew.

When Joann was a young girl in Maine, she used to imagine—in that quicksilver time just on the cusp of sleep—that she would hear a knock on the door and her father would be there. Other times, she would think of her father standing on a snowy hill bathed in sunlight and telling her, "I'm happy here."

Farther back in the chapel, one of Richard Pompeo's sisters, Ethel Myers, leaned heavily on a cane and was helped into her seat by son David, a retired Air Force and Pennsylvania Air National Guard airborne electronic systems operator who flew about two hundred combat missions from Vietnam to Afghanistan. Pompeo was now the only unaccounted-for crew member from the B-24.

Doug Beckstead traveled from Alaska and basked in praise from the military brass over his dedication in searching the crash site and refusing to believe that Hoskin was forever lost. He took his seat near the front.

The Bible reading was from 1 Thessalonians 4. "For the Lord himself will come down from heaven, with a loud command, with the voice of the archangel and with the trumpet call of God, and the dead in Christ will rise first," it ends. "After that, we who are still alive and are left will be caught up together with them in the clouds to meet the Lord in the air. And so we will be with the Lord forever. Therefore encourage each other with these words."

Not far from the chapel, a section of the old parade ground at Fort Myer is surrounded by groves of beech and hickory trees that abut Arlington National Cemetery. In September 1908, thousands of spectators gathered at the spot for a spectacle that promised to be more astonishing than anything they had witnessed before, more *wondrous* than their first glimpse of electric lights, more *spell-binding* than moving pictures or gramophones. One of the famous Wright brothers was on hand with an honest-to-God airplane for tests with the military that would stretch for more than a week.

The crowds got to see not only new flight records—set day after day—but also one of the sad firsts in military aviation.

Just after five o'clock on September 17, with winds falling off just enough to try another flight, Orville Wright yelled over to a West Point–educated lieutenant to climb aboard. "You might as well get in," Wright told Thomas Selfridge. "We'll start in a couple minutes."

Wright and his team were at Fort Myer with the latest version of their biplane, *Flyer,* in hopes of persuading skeptical Army brass of the need for greater airpower in combat. Orville had already taken up two Army officers to show the craft could carry two people and exceed forty miles per hour, a requirement for the military deal. On September 12, Orville stayed up for one hour and fifteen minutes, making seventy-one laps around the field in a new endurance mark. Even the many doubters—who considered human flight little more than a carnival stunt—came away impressed.

The next in line for a flight was Selfridge, who was on the Army review board studying the plane. Selfridge was a believer. He had become fascinated by the nascent age of flight. Just nine months earlier, Selfridge went aloft in Alexander Graham Bell's audacious kite known as the *Cygnet,* made of nearly thirty-four hundred tetrahedral cells. He was also one of three officers trained to command *U.S. Army Dirigible Balloon No. 1.*

Selfridge was picked to lead exhibition flights of the blimp in Missouri as soon as Orville wrapped up his tests at Fort Myer. A Navy officer had been scheduled to go up with Wright on September 17, but he gave up his spot so Selfridge could get a jump on his travel to the Midwest.

The *Flyer*'s 39-horsepower engine fired up, and the craft was soon circling over Fort Myer. During three laps it rose as high as 150 feet. The crowd applauded in appreciation. Just before Wright began his descent, the right propeller began to falter. The plane shook. One of the props broke, clipping a guy wire. The craft's nose dipped. Wright could not regain control. The *Flyer* nose-dived into the grass from about 75 feet. It was a tangle of splintered spruce, still-warm engine parts, and torn muslin. Selfridge, who was not wearing headgear, suffered a fractured skull and died that evening. Orville Wright had head protection, but was left with several broken bones and spent seven weeks hospitalized. It's widely considered the first aviation fatality by the American armed forces.

After the Hoskin service in the chapel, the casket was placed on a caisson, drawn by six chestnut horses—two of them without riders as part of the solemn tradition. Joann again burst into tears. "I just totally let go," she said later. "To think they were doing all this for my dad."

The cortege moved slowly toward the grave site in Section 60.

The few direct living emissaries from World War II—John Hoskin leaning on his wife's arm and Pompeo's sister holding tightly to her cane—passed by reminders of those who didn't return from war in this new century. Section 60 is one of the main burial grounds for war dead from Iraq and Afghanistan. Many of the graves were visited frequently by young spouses and small children. They left behind trinkets. Maybe a wind chime. Or a balloon. Sometimes a photograph or letter, now tattered and curled by the weather. Such gestures were against the protocol of the Arlington caretakers. But, this time, they looked the other way. No one could bring themselves to clear away the personal remembrances. They would remain for years.

A group of Patriot Guard Riders—bikers who gather to pay respects to veterans—snapped to attention with crisp salutes as the Hoskin procession neared the grave site. Mary draped her arm around John. The flag was taken from the coffin. It was folded into a ceremonial triangle shape by an honor guard. A military chaplain presented it to Joann.

Beckstead stood off to the side. He would have liked to have shared the moment with one of Crane's children. They were invited by the Hoskin family, but none could carve out the time. Bill, who visited the crash site with Beckstead, especially wanted to attend. He simply couldn't break commitments already made. He called Beckstead in Washington just before the funeral.

You know, Bill said, none of this would be possible without you.

Bill passed along thanks from the entire Crane family. Beckstead promised they would see each other soon. They never did.

A bugler played taps. A B-2 stealth bomber passed overhead. The honor guard raised their rifles and fired. The shells from the twenty-one-gun salute were gathered and distributed. Beckstead received one.

It was carried back to Alaska.

EPILOGUE

Crane stepped onto the scale. The Army doctor, assigned to give Crane a physical after his return, nudged the lead weights along the balance. He jotted down 165. Then he looked at the records from Crane's arrival at Ladd Field. He did a double take and checked the scales again. Remarkably, Crane weighed about the same.

Other tests brought the same results: Crane's health was nearly perfect except for some minor frostbite damage to his fingers and abrasions from the sledge's rope harness.

Ladd Field commanders quizzed Crane for anything that could pinpoint the crash site. Crane gave his best guesses based on the location of Berail's cabin, which he assumed would be visible to spotters in the air. That's good, said the Air Forces brass, but what would be better is having you show us in person. When would you feel ready to head back into the Yukon? Crane said he was ready now.

A few days later, Crane was again over the mountains rising up from the Charley. It took almost no time to spot the B-24 wreckage. There it is, he said quietly. The reconnaissance plane took a few circles over the area to precisely log the location for the later recovery teams, which found the bodies of James Sibert and Ralph Wenz.

On one pass, Crane was able to look north up the Charley one more time. The plane then banked and set a course for Ladd. Crane would never return.

He was given a short leave to return to Philadelphia. Crane was relieved in more than one way. Ladd Field authorities had interviewed Ames, Berail, and others to confirm Crane's account of his passage down the Charley River and close the book on the investigation. "I was more worried about their asking where the devil I'd been," he told the *Philadelphia Record* after arriving home.

His plans in Philadelphia were to rest, eat, and spend "all that back pay" from his time lost. He did pose for one press photo at home at 5464 Baltimore Avenue. He pulled out a map to show his father, dressed in a suit and tie as usual, his route over the Charley.

Less than six months after returning to Ladd Field from leave, Leon Crane was assigned a test flight on a P-63 Kingcobra. Crane's task on September 3, 1944, was to give the plane a test run to check on reported "engine roughness" before it was to be handed over to a Soviet flier. The Red Army star had already been painted on. After about forty-five minutes circling Fairbanks, Crane brought the plane in. The landing looked fine, but a tire blew out seconds after touching the tarmac. The plane swerved sharply to the right. Its nose jammed into the scrubland. One propeller was bent. The crash alarm sounded on base. Crane cut the fuel, unstrapped his harness, and jumped from the cockpit. He was not injured.

An investigation concluded the right brake had locked up. The heat from the friction fused together three of the brake discs, blocking the tire from spinning and causing the blowout. The report urged the manufacturer, the Bell Aircraft Corporation, to redesign its braking systems. "Landing accidents of this nature . . . are entirely too common for this model aircraft." The plane was abandoned by the U.S. military after the war, but lived on as target-practice aircraft for gunners.

At some point, Crane started dating the Army nurse from Iowa, Lieutenant Wilma Koehrsen, who was on duty the night he returned to Ladd Field. She had been reassigned to Ladd from Cold Bay in the Aleutian Islands. They were married in Fairbanks in January 1945. Crane's last moments in Alaska came on July 24, 1945, just two weeks before the first atomic bomb attack on Japan, when he and Wilma boarded a southbound plane. Crane remained in the Army Air Forces until December 1945.

Crane had a career in aeronautical engineering at Boeing Vertol and, later, as a home builder in and around his native Philadelphia. He rarely spoke of his time lost in Alaska. His six children—who mostly called him Leon rather than Dad—grew up knowing only loose threads of the story.

On the times he did share some small recollection of Alaska, it was always diminished further by his own caveats. Other people faced far worse in the war, he'd say. This was a breeze in comparison, he would add. Think of all those who didn't come home, such as the crew of the *Iceberg Inez*. Or those who were horribly maimed. Or were lost in the Holocaust, like those in his ancestral lands in Ukraine. He would shake his hand. What did I do? I just walked.

But in the late 1990s—as he slowed down and, like many, had more time to reflect on the war—Crane sat down with the son of a onetime business partner and former Army Air Forces buddy to give a videotaped oral history. He brushed over his time along the Charley River, still refusing to assume any heroics. He did, however, share a bit more about his last moments inside the B-24.

"Scared shitless," he said.

"I grabbed my chest chute, snapped on the harness . . . opened the bomb-bay doors, and I was gone."

"God-awful place, Alaska," Crane continued. "Ice and snow and cold as hell."

Crane kept a single souvenir: one of the photos snapped outside the Ames family cabin.

Crane died on March 26, 2002. Death notices and the short obituaries made no mention of the Charley River. If Crane shared much about the crash and the Charley with Wilma, she never let on. She gave no more details after Leon was gone. She did, however, live long enough to hear stories from two of their children.

In the summer of 2005, Miriam and Bill Crane—she a pilot, he a builder—joined Doug Beckstead to retrace Leon's journey.

For eight days they traveled the route by plane and raft. At Phil Berail's cabin, now just ruins, they found some of the tools from the cache described by Crane. They later stood outside Ames's cabin on the spot where their father saw the front door open and a trapper with a smoldering cigarette stare back and ask, where did you come from?

By the time Beckstead led the trip, there were few people left from Crane's time on the river.

The unyielding Phil Berail died in 1961, five years after breaking his hip in a fall off a pickup truck at Coal Creek mining camp. "As far as is known," said the funeral notice in the *Fairbanks Daily News-Miner*, "he has no family."

A few years later, pilot Bob Rice finally decided he needed a break from the Alaskan bush and flew his plane south, bound for the Caribbean, making it as far as St. Lucia. It didn't take. He eventually returned to Alaska. Rice died in 1983.

At Ladd Field in 1950, a building was named in honor of Master Sergeant Richard Pompeo.

In 2005 Pompeo's nephew David Myers also visited the crash site with Beckstead. Myers climbed inside the crumpled fuselage to the spot where his uncle would have been onboard. "I tuned the knobs and they worked like new," Myers wrote. "I was sensing an amazing feeling as I did it, realizing that my uncle used that very unit and those knobs would still have his fingerprints on them."

Myers and Beckstead looked over the country where Pompeo may have landed after bailing out. "I am at peace with the idea he will always remain on that beautiful, quiet mountain," Myers wrote, "and I feel I was able to give him a proper goodbye from a family member."

In Pinedale, Wyoming, an airfield carries the name of Staff Sergeant Ralph Wenz. His body was moved from Fairbanks to his hometown of Sutton, Nebraska. His daughter, Carol, died in 2012. She named the first of her two sons after her father.

The remains of First Lieutenant James B. Sibert were interred at Arlington National Cemetery in 1948.

Harold Hoskin's wife, Mary, worked as a bookkeeper and remarried twenty-four years after the B-24 crash. She died in 2005, a year before JPAC opened its investigation that would uncover and identify her husband's remains.

Crane's wife, Wilma, died on May 1, 2007.

John and Mary Hoskin had one encounter with Crane. They were visiting relatives near Philadelphia in 1991. On a lark, they decided to contact Crane. At first, John hesitated. He didn't see the point in revisiting what could not be changed. Let it rest, he urged. Mary, though, wanted to see Crane. Who knew what details he might cough up? She told John to remember his father and how he pestered the military for more information on his son. Mary knew the acclaimed writer and journalist John McPhee was able to pry a little from Crane in the 1970s. It was worth a try to get more, she told her husband.

As usual, Mary's spark-plug personality ruled the day. John agreed.

It wasn't so easy to find Crane. They couldn't locate a phone listing. But there was one for a Dr. Crane. It turned out it was Leon's older brother Morris. Sure, he said after a moment's pause, I can give you Leon's number and address. As it turned out, this was exactly how McPhee tracked down Crane years before.

John and Mary had tea with Leon at his home, which was then in one of Philadelphia's pleasantly pastoral suburbs. Crane was courteous and attentive. But, to their surprise, he was somewhat defensive when the conversation moved toward the crash. Crane repeatedly said it was no one's fault. He couldn't have done anything more. The plane was uncontrollable. It was, he said, just one of those things.

"I would call it something like survivor's guilt," said Mary. "It's as if he seemed troubled by what happened, why Harold couldn't get out and why he was the only one to live."

They asked about his struggles on the Charley. Leon offered nothing they didn't already know. He just didn't want to talk about it. Nothing could budge him.

"Strange," recalled John. "The whole thing was strange. In my mind, the whole affair was closed, even though we didn't have Harold's body. But not for Leon Crane. It still seemed to eat at him."

In Anchorage, Beckstead's boxes and files packed with his research from the crash site were left without an owner. On the first day of July in 2014, Beckstead died suddenly at his home. Among the items, carefully filed and dated, is Beckstead's notes from a phone call in July 1994 with Crane just a few weeks after Beckstead first visited the resting place of the B-24.

"Leon did not want to talk about the crash. He did not want to talk about his survival," Beckstead said nearly a decade later.

"He left some part of himself back in Alaska. It's something he does not want to disturb or share. The wilderness can do that to people who face it alone. It becomes a private thing, an almost sacred thing."

ACKNOWLEDGMENTS

My thanks go out in many directions for guidance, assistance, and support with this project.

I'll start at the top: my wife, Toula Vlahou, and daughter, Zoe. They make me better in every way. Toula's wisdom, research, and deft editing grace every page. Zoe's humor and truly original observations on life make my life so much richer.

My immensely gifted editor Robert Pigeon made this book sharper and smarter every step of the way. My friend and agent, Robert Shepard, once again lifted my work with his vision and insights.

The families of Leon Crane, Harold Hoskin, Richard Pompeo, and Ralph Wenz provided invaluable help. I am in their debt. Special thanks go to William and Joyce Crane, Thomas Crane and Steve Crane, John and Mary Hoskin and Joann Goldstein, David Myers and Michael Slaybaugh, and Dick Wenz, Jana Wenz Bloxham, and Ray Wahl.

Similar appreciation goes to Douglas Beckstead. He wanted to write his own book about his efforts to recover and identify Hoskin's remains. Sadly, he left us before he could realize this dream.

To better understand the B-24, my thanks go to Bill Gros, who flew thirty-one combat missions aboard a B-24D; the Collings Foundation, especially Hunter Chaney; Craig Fuller at AAIR Aviation Archaeological Investigation & Research; Jeremy R. Kinney at the Smithsonian National Air and Space Museum; William Darron; Michael S. Simpson; and Jim Lux.

Others deserve my deep gratitude.

In Alaska: Linda Jackson; Denise Gray; Dee Rice; Charles "Chuck" Gray; Bob Eley; David Wozniczka; Angela Linn at the Museum of the North; Rose Speranza, Charles Hilton, and the staff at Project Jukebox at the University of Alaska's Special Collections in Fairbanks; Nicole Jackelen of the University of Alaska in Anchorage archives; Pete Haggland and Richard Flanders at the Pioneer Air Museum in Fairbanks; Linda Douglass, Lisa Graham, Constance Storch, and Natalie Loukianoff at Fort Wainwright; Timo "Chris" Allan and Chris Houlette at the Yukon–Charley Rivers National Preserve; former Ladd Field researcher and writer Kathy Price; and the late Ladd Field veteran Randy Acord.

In Hawaii: Major Jamie Dobson and Lee Tucker at the Joint POW/MIA Accounting Command.

In Philadelphia: Elizabeth Stegner, Mike Hardy, Joe Minardi, and Joe Shapiro at the University City Historical Society; Bob Lieter at the *Jewish Exponent*; Allen Meyers; Nathaniel Popkin at PlanPhilly; Jessica M. Lydon at Temple University's Special Collections Research Center; and Mary Dean at West Philadelphia High School.

In Massachusetts: John Linn Ragle, Myles Crowley at the Massachusetts Institute of Technology Special Collection Library, Dr. Bruce Bistrian, Jack Murphy, Ellen Foley, and the staff of the Brewster Ladies' Library.

In the New York and Washington, DC, areas: Lieutenant Colonel Melinda Morgan, Susan Gough, military analyst Mike Lyons, and Bruce Guthrie.

And in other points on the map: Amy Fischer at Western Union; Major Russell Vanderlugt at West Point; Peter Hatem in Maine; Terry Leonard at *Stars and Stripes*; Gregory L. Fox at JPAC; Dan Poynter; Paul Ames; Gino Ferri; Pinedale, Wyoming, historian Ann Chambers Noble; Theresa Rice; Robyn Russell; and Jerry Johnson.

SELECTED BIBLIOGRAPHY AND SOURCES

Leon Crane's firsthand accounts are taken from several sources: military records, the unedited transcript of an interview for the *New York Journal-American,* a similar story under Crane's byline published in the *American* (August 1944), and a videotaped oral history conducted in the late 1990s. Descriptions of U.S. military operations in Alaska during World War II, including the search for the missing bomber, were aided significantly by documents from Pentagon archives, oral histories, interviews with veterans and experts, and details from press reports at the time.

Many of the military records concerning the recovery and identification of Harold Hoskin's remains were kindly provided by his brother John.

Other details in the book are derived from archival sources, published material, and more than one hundred interviews by phone or during research trips to Philadelphia, Maine, Alaska, Washington, and elsewhere.

Historical details on the Yukon–Charley Rivers National Preserve and related subjects were found in a variety of National Park Service publications. Background on Ladd Field, including the Lend-Lease period, comes from sources including historical accounts compiled for the U.S. military by researcher Kathy Price.

Temperature data from Fairbanks and surrounding areas were taken from University of Alaska meteorological records.

Other books and sources include the following.

Introduction

Defense Prisoner of War/Missing Personnel Office. http://www.dtic.mil
/dpmo/.
Operations in Snow and Extreme Cold. Field manual. Washington, DC:
Army Air Corps, 1941.

Chapter One

Chandonnet, Fern. *Alaska at War, 1941–1945: The Forgotten War
Remembered*. Fairbanks: University of Alaska Press, 2008.
Forman, Wallace R. *B-24 Nose Art Name Directory*. North Branch, MN:
Specialty Press, 1998.
Memorandum Report on Consolidated B-24D. Washington, DC: Army
Air Corps, Materiel Division, 1942.
Rottman, Gordon L. *U.S. Army Air Force*. Oxford: Osprey, 1993.

Chapter Two

"Fliers, Forced Down in Arctic, Reach Safely Following Epic Trip."
Havre (MT) Daily News, January 31, 1942.
"Poon Lim Awarded Medal for 133 Days on Life Raft." *Chicago Daily
Tribune*, July 17, 1943.

Chapter Three

Bombing at Dutch Harbor: Report, Commander, Northwest Sea Frontier.
Seattle: National Archives and Records Administration, July 17, 1942.
Garfield, David. *The Thousand-Mile War: World War II in Alaska and
the Aleutians*. Garden City, NY: Doubleday, 1969.
Ragle, Richard Charles. *The War in the Aleutians: The First Two Weeks*.
http://jlragle.com/FRAMES2/rcragle.htm.
Rearden, Jim. *Sam O. White, Alaskan*. Missoula, MT: Pictorial Histo-
ries, 2006.
"Russian Flier, Pitched Out of Bomber over Alaska, Lives to Tell Tale."
Lethbridge (AB) Herald, August 31, 1944.
"Statement by Capt. Jack S. Marks." Papers of Admiral Robert A. Theo-
bald, June 9, 1942, Hoover Archives, Stanford University.

Chapter Four

Beckstead, Douglas, and Anita Slomski. *The Long Trip Home*. Washington, DC: Parks, 2007.

Birdsall, Steve. *B-24 Liberator in Action*. Carrollton, TX: Squadron/Signal, 1979.

Journal of San Diego History 24, no. 4 (1978).

Pattillo, Donald M. *Pushing the Envelope: The American Aircraft Industry*. Ann Arbor: University of Michigan Press, 1998.

Simons, Graham M. *Consolidated B-24 Liberator*. South Yorkshire: Pen & Sword Books, 2012.

Chapter Five

Byrd, Admiral Richard E. *Alone: The Classic Polar Adventure*. New York: G. P. Putnam's Sons, 1938.

Payer, Julius J. *New Lands Within the Arctic Circle: Narrative of the Discoveries of the Austrian Ship* Tegetthoft *in the Years 1872–1874*. Vol. 2. London: Macmillan, 1876.

Van Lanen, James M., et al. *Subsistence Land Mammal Harvests and Uses, Yukon Flats, Alaska: 2008–2010 Harvest Report and Ethnographic Update*. Juneau: Alaska Department of Fish and Game and Council of Athabascan Tribal Governments, October 2012.

Chapter Six

Freeman, Moses. *Fifty Years of Jewish Immigrant Life in Philadelphia*. Translated from Yiddish by Julian L. Greifer and Maxwell Scarf. Philadelphia: Temple University Collection.

Grove, Mary Confehr. *History of the West Philadelphia High School*. Philadelphia: Temple University Collection, Faculty of Teacher's College, 1936.

Meyers, Allen. *The Jewish History of West Philadelphia*. Charleston, SC: Arcadia, 2001.

Weaver, Wallace W. *West Philadelphia: A Study of Natural Social Areas*. Philadelphia: University of Pennsylvania, 1938.

Chapter Seven

Flatt, Dr. Adrian E. *Frostbite*. Dallas: Baylor University Medical Center, July 2010.

Jarvenpa, Robert. *Northern Passage: Ethnography and Apprenticeship Among the Subarctic Dene*. Long Grove, IL: Waveland Press, 1998.

Streever, Bill. *Cold: Adventures in the World's Coldest Places*. New York: Little, Brown, 2009.

Chapter Eight

Cole, Terrence. *Crooked Past: The History of a Frontier Mining Camp, Fairbanks, Alaska*. Fairbanks: University of Alaska Press, 1991.

Osgood, Cornelius. *Winter*. Lincoln: University of Nebraska Press, 2006.

Chapter Nine

Smith, Dinitia. "Gerold Frank Is Dead at 91; Author of Celebrity Memoirs." *New York Times,* September 19, 1998.

Chapter Ten

Hays, Otis. *The Alaska-Siberia Connection: The World War II Air Route*. College Station: Texas A&M University Press, 2006.

Jordan, George Racey, with Richard Leroy Stokes. *From Major Jordan's Diaries*. New York: Harcourt, Brace, 1952.

Layman, Richard, and Julie M. Rivett. *Selected Letters of Dashiell Hammett, 1920–1960*. Washington, DC: Counterpoint, 2002.

Stefansson, Vilhjalmur. Papers. Elwyn B. Robinson Department of Special Collections, University of North Dakota, Grand Forks.

Chapter Eleven

Patty, Ernest. *North Country Challenge*. New York: David McKay, 1969.

Chapter Twelve

Cold Weather Survival. United States Search and Rescue Task Force. http://www.ussartf.org/cold_water_survival.htm.

Roberts, David. *Alone on the Ice*. New York: W. W. Norton, 2013.

Chapter Thirteen

Bergquist, David. "My Brother's Keeper: Harold E. Hoskin and His Brother John." *Echoes, the Northern Maine Journal* (Caribou), no. 86 (October–December 2009).

Opium: A Japanese Technique of Occupation. Washington, DC: Office of Strategic Services, 1945.

"Recollections of Pvt. Hans Krueger." Kriegsgefangen Research Forum. http://home.arcor.de/kriegsgefangene/memoirs/hans_krueger.html.

Chapter Fourteen

Mallory, Enid. *Robert Service: Under the Spell of the Yukon*. Custer, WA: Heritage House, 2006.

Service, Robert W. *Collected Poems of Robert Service*. New York: G. P. Putnam's Sons, 1907.

Chapter Fifteen

Dauenhauer, Richard. *Koyukon Riddles*. Anchorage: Alaska Bilingual Education Center, 1975.

de Laguna, Frederica. *Tales from the Dena: Indian Stories from the Tanana, Koyukuk & Yukon Rivers*. Seattle: University of Washington Press, 1995.

Goldfarb, Richard J., et al. *Geology and Origin of Epigenetic Lode Gold Deposits, Tintina Gold Province, Alaska and Yukon*. Washington, DC: U.S. Department of the Interior and U.S. Geological Survey, 2007.

Hoffman, Richard G. *Human Psychological Performance in Cold Environments*. Washington, DC: Textbook of Military Medicine, Department of the Army, Office of the Surgeon General, and Borden Institute, 2001.

Raven's Athabascan Tales. Fairbanks: University of Alaska, Alaska Native Knowledge Network. http://www.ankn.uaf.edu/npe/culturalatlases /yupiaq/marshall/raven/athabaskan.html.

Ruppert, James, and John W. Bernet. *Our Voices: Native Stories of Alaska and the Yukon*. Lincoln: University of Nebraska Press, 2001.

Chapter Sixteen

Isto, Sarah Crawford. *The Fur Farms of Alaska*. Fairbanks: University of Alaska Press, 2012.

World War II Combat Diary of J. J. McAndrews. Cleveland, OH: Coast Guard Great Lakes. http://greatlakes.coastguard.dodlive.mil/2013/11 /world-war-ii-combat-diary-of-j-j-mcandrews-d-day-and-saying-goodbye.

Chapter Seventeen

Beckstead, Douglas. *The World Turned Upside Down: A Mining History of Coal Creek and Woodchopper Creek, Yukon–Charley Rivers National Preserve, Alaska*. Fairbanks: National Park Service, 2000.

Hunt, William R. *Golden Places: The History of Alaska-Yukon Mining*. Anchorage: National Park Service, 1989.

O'Neill, Dan. *A Land Gone Lonesome: An Inland Voyage Along the Yukon River*. New York: Counterpoint, 2006.

Shore, Evelyn Berglund. *Born on Snowshoes*. Cambridge, MA: Riverside Press, 1954.

Chapter Eighteen

McPhee, John. *Coming into the Country*. New York: Farrar, Straus, and Giroux, 1977.

Patty, Stanton H. *Fearless Men and Fabulous Women: A Reporter's Memoir from Alaska & the Yukon*. Seattle: Epicenter Press, 2004.

Chapter Nineteen

Ambrose, Stephen E. *The Wild Blue: The Men and Boys Who Flew the B-24s over Germany*. New York: Simon & Schuster, 2001.

Gunston, Bill. *The Illustrated Encyclopedia of Propeller Airliners*. London: Phoebus, 1980.

Chapter Twenty

Batzli, Samuel A. *Fort Myers, Virginia: Historic Landscape Inventory*. Technical report. Washington, DC: U.S. Army Corps of Engineers, June 1998.

Poole, Robert M. *Section 60: Arlington National Cemetery*. New York: Bloomsbury, 2014.

Proietti, Senior Master Sgt. Matt. "B-24 Pilot Finds Final Resting Place at Arlington." *Arctic Sentry* (Anchorage), September 14, 2007.

INDEX

Acord, Randy, 203

Adakian (newspaper), 126

Adak Island, base newspaper,
126–127

African Americans, northern
migration of, 7–8

Air-ferry business in Alaska,
40–41

Alaska
adventurers and, 126
aviation in, 14, 39–42
gold mining/gold rush, 100–102,
133–135, 166–167, 173, 188
Japanese attacks on, 11–12
plane wrecks in, 59–60
understanding of nature in,
68–71
winter weather, 6, 14, 139–140
World War II and, 11–13

Alaska Agricultural College and
School of Mines, 133

Alaska Army National Guard, 154

Alexander II, 78

Alford, Thomas Carl, 76

American magazine, 112

Ames, Albert, 177–184, 214
trip to Woodchopper with
Crane, 185, 188–189, 191

Ames, Albert Norman (son),
178

Ames, Daniel Lee, 178

Ames, Molly, 178

Ames, Nina, 178, 180, 181,
182–183

Ames's cabin, 216
Crane's discovery of, 175–176
Crane's stay at, 177–184

Antarctica, Mawson in, 145–148

Anzio, 136, 183

Arctic air corridor, 119

Arctic ptarmigan, 131–132, 175

Arctic Village (Marshall), 41

Arlington National Cemetery,
111
Hoskin burial rites, 207–210,
211–212
Silbert interment, 216

Athabascan people, 68–69
Chief Charley, 102
Great Raven and, 172–173
Nina Ames and, 180

Attu (Alaska), Japanese attack and
control of, 49–50

A-20 Havoc fighter-bomber, 43

Aurora borealis, 104

Aurora (ship), 147

Ballaine Lake (Alaska), 124
Banzai suicide charges, 50
Barnette, Elbridge Truman,
    100–102, 133
Bauer, Eddie, 8
"Beautiful Dreamer" (Foster), 121
Beckstead, Douglas, 3, 154
    on cause of crash, 203
    death of, 218
    exploration of crash site, 53–54,
        59–60, 109, 110, 112
    at Hoskin burial, 210, 212
    retracing Crane's journey,
        215–216
Bell, Alexander Graham, 211
Bell Aircraft Corporation, 214
Berail, Phil, 135, 179
    cabin, 99, 106, 129–131, 216
    death of, 216
    early career in Alaska, 99–100,
        102, 189
    military interview with, 214
    pain tolerance of, 189–190
    visit with Crane, 188–189,
        190–191
Berglund, Evelyn, 188, 191, 194
Bergman, Ingrid, 104
Bertoson, Gordon, 190
Big Delta (Alaska), 17, 18, 25, 27
    Crane's decision to head toward,
        88
    as focus of Iceberg Inez search,
        37–38, 50
Bismarck (battleship), 57
Blackjack, Ada, 126
Blizzards, perils of, 165–166
Bloom, Jessie, 64
Bloom, Robert, 64
Blotto-botto conditions, 37

Boeing, 57
Boeing Vertol, 215
Born on Snowshoes (Berglund),
    188
Bradley, Omar, 54
Brooklyn Botanic Garden, 49
B-17B bomber, Ragle and, 45, 46,
    47
B-17 bombers, 59
B-17 Flying Fortress, 18, 47
B-24 Liberator, 13–14
    in combat, 52
    crashes, 15, 34
    development of, 57–59
    problems with, 18, 200
    production of, 56–57, 59
    size of, 51
    use in World War II, 55–56
    See also Iceberg Inez
B-24D Liberator, 11
B-26 Marauders, 45
Bush pilots, 39, 40–41, 193–194
Byrd, Richard E., 72

Camp Barkeley, 157
Caribou fog, 16
Casualties, civilian war, 54–55
Catalina Flying Boat, 110
Central Identification Laboratory
    (Oahu, Hawaii), 154, 199, 205
C-47 transport, 119
Chaplin, Charlie, 166
Charley River (Alaska)
    Chief Charley and, 102
    Crane in relation to, 33, 50, 64,
        65, 95–96, 103, 131, 173, 179
    military forensic investigation of
        crash sites near, 110
    mining and, 133–135

Charley River valley, 25
Chena River (Alaska), 100
Chief Charley, 102
Chinook winds, 172
Churchill, Winston, 119
Circle (Alaska), 190
Civilians in war, 54–55
Clear-air turbulence, 17
CL-4S biplane, 57
Coal Creek (Alaska), 133, 134, 186, 189
Cobrastochkkas (P-39 Airacobra fighter), 120
Cold, extreme
  clothing for, 92
  physical effects of, 34–35, 89–90
Cold Nose Boys, 12, 13–14, 45, 92–93, 121
Cold Weather Test Detachment, 12–13, 14
Colony Glacier, 154
C-124 cargo plane crash, 113, 154
Consolidated Aircraft Corporation, 57, 58, 85
Copper Creek (Alaska), 33
Corvette escort ships, 55
Crane, Bill, 212, 215–216
Crane, Leon, 2
  at Ames's cabin, 177–184
  at Berail's cabin, 96, 97–107, 129–131, 139–141
  care of hands, 129–130
  childhood, 7, 8, 80–83
  college career, 7, 83–84
  crash of *Iceberg Inez*, 20–23
  death of, 215
  decision to head downstream after crash, 32–33

desire to set parents' mind to rest, 135–136
discovery of Ames's cabin, 175–176
dream of Hoskin, 87–88
early interest in aviation, 81, 83
encounter with John Hoskin, 217–218
envisioning own death, 92–93
falling through ice, 144–145, 148–150, 168–169
father's letter, 9, 25–26
fire building, 35–36, 149
first camp while waiting for rescue, 36
first days hiking out, 88, 90–92, 93–96
food and supplies at Berail's cabin, 97–99, 106–107
frostbite dangers and, 88
in "hibernation," 71–72
hiking out after leaving Berail's cabin, 141–145, 148–152
hope for Hoskin's survival, 32
hunger and, 33–34, 61–62, 63, 64, 89–90, 106
hunting, 65–68, 131–132, 151, 175
ice-break and, 139–140
immediate aftermath of crash and, 23–26
job as copilot, 15
last leg of hike, 165–166, 167–170, 171–172, 173–176
leave home, 213–214
making fire the first night, 25–26
marriage, 214–215
matches and, 11, 24

Crane, Leon (*continued*)
  media coverage of survival, 3, 197
  military flight training, 84–85
  odds of rescue, 27–30
  oral history, 215
  orienting self after crash, 64–65
  parachuting out of plane, 21–23
  planning for survival, 64–65
  planning to hike out from
    Berail's cabin, 130–131, 132–133, 135–136, 137, 141
  as poker player, 5–6, 7
  postmilitary career, 215
  preparation for flight, 8–16
  P-63 test flight, 214
  religious upbringing, 63
  report on crash, 200–201
  return to Ladd Field, 191, 193–197, 213
  routine flight of *Iceberg Inez* and, 17–19
  second cabin stay, 151–152, 169–170
  sense of time and, 63
  Soviets at Ladd Field and, 121–122
  stay in Woodchopper, 185–191
  supply sledge and, 137, 141, 142, 145, 148, 168–169
  survivor's guilt and, 217–218
  takeoff, 16–17
  visit with Berail, 188–189, 190–191
  wilderness education of, 71–72
  winds and, 144, 171, 174
Crane, Louis, 9, 135
  auction company, 74–75, 82
  immigration of, 77, 79, 80
  life in West Philadelphia, 82–83
  notification of Leon's crash, 74
  notification that son still missing, 152
Crane, Miriam, 215–216
Crane, Morris, 75, 82, 83, 217
Crane, Nathan, 75, 80, 83
Crane, Sonia
  belief Leon still alive, 93
  immigration of, 77, 79, 80
  Leon and image of mother mourning, 135
  life in West Philadelphia, 82
  notification of Leon's crash, 74–75
Crane, Wilma (Koehrsen), 214–215, 217
"The Cremation of Sam McGee" (Service), 167
Cygnet (kite), 211

da Vinci, Leonardo, 94
Davis, David R., 58–59
Dawson City (Alaska), 133
Dead Horse Trail, 167
de Havilland, Olivia, 127
Demianenko, Constanta P., 43
Denali (Alaska), 91
DNA matching, to identify Hoskin remains, 204–205
Dotson' Sa, 172–173
Dredging, for gold, 134
Dutch Harbor Naval Operating Base, Japanese assault on, 43–47

Earhart, Amelia, 83
East India Company, 159
Edison, Thomas, 78

Eielson, Carl Ben ("Arctic Lindbergh"), 39–40
Elevator controls, 20–21
Emerson, Ralph Waldo, 69–71
English, Norman, 76

Fairbanks, Charles W., 101
Fairbanks (Alaska)
  as air hub, 41
  establishment of, 100–102
  Soviet airmen and, 122–124
  as transit point during World War II, 12
Fairbanks Daily News-Miner (newspaper), 41, 216
Feathering tests, 14, 19
Ferri, Gino, 90
Feynman, Richard, 83–84
Fire extinguisher, on board plane, 16
Fitzgerald, T. A., 152
Fleet, Reuben, 58
Flyer (biplane), 210–211
Fokker F.III, 181
Ford Motor Company, 56
Fort Mears (Alaska), 44
Fort Myers (Virginia), 210
45th Infantry Division, 136
Fort Yukon (Alaska), 31, 51, 180
Foster, Stephen, 121
Fox, Gregory L., 109, 110, 113
Frank, Gerold, 112
Franklin, John, 146
Frostbite, 34–35, 88–89

Gable, Clark, 55–56
Gabor, Zsa Zsa, 112
Gaffney, Dale, 42
Garland, Judy, 112

General Motors, 122
George VI, 31
German POWs in Maine, 161–162
G-forces, crash of Iceberg Inez and, 20, 21
Gilmore, Tom, 100–101
Gold belt, 173
Gold mining, Alaskan, 100–102, 133–135, 173
  deaths incurred during, 166–167
  decline of, 188
The Gold Rush (film), 166
Great Raven, 172–173
Grinnell, Dick, 191
Grinnell, Willard, 188, 191, 194–195
Gros, Bill, 59, 202–203
Grumman Duck, 113
Guadalcanal, 52

Haggland, Pete, 41
Hammett, Dashiell, 126–127
Hangar I (Ladd Field), 11, 13
  Soviet side of, 117, 121
Hanukkah, 63, 64
Harding, Warren G., 42
Harland and Wolff shipyards, 55
Harper, Arthur, 91
Harper, Walter, 91
Hellman, Lillian, 126, 127
Herodotus, 111
Hibernation, 71–72
Hickam Air Force Base (Hawaii), 153–155, 162–163
Hiebert, Augie, 42
Hiroshima, 158
Holland, Thomas D., 205
Horan, James D., 112

Horse packer, 181
Hoskin, Harold, 152
  burial ceremony, 207–210,
    211–212
  Crane dream of, 87–88
  crash of *Iceberg Inez* and, 20–23
  description of B-24 Liberator,
    157
  forensic investigation, 153,
    154–155, 163, 199–200,
    203–205
  Iceberg Inez takeoff and, 16–17
  identification of remains,
    199–200, 203–205
  letters to wife, 160–161,
    208–209
  parents' reaction to crash news,
    156
  as pilot of B-24D Liberator, 11
  preparation for flight, 13–16
  routine flight of *Iceberg Inez*
    and, 17–19
  search for remains, 110,
    112–113
Hoskin, Joann, 160, 161, 162, 199
  father's burial and, 207–209,
    211–212
Hoskin, John, 155, 157–160
  brother's burial and, 207, 211
  encounter with Crane, 217–218
  identification of brother's
    remains, 199, 205
Hoskin, Mary (Harold's wife)
  German POWs in Maine and,
    161–162
  letters to and from husband,
    160–161, 208–209
  life after husband's death, 217
  notification husband missing, 76

refusal to accept idea husband
    would not return, 155–156,
    161, 162
Hoskin, Mary (John's wife), 199,
    205, 207, 211, 217–218
Hunger
  Crane and, 33–34, 61–62, 63,
    64, 89–90, 106
  physical effects of, 33–34,
    62–63
Hypothermia, eating snow and,
    61

Ice, perils of, 144–145, 147,
    148–150
Iceberg Inez (B-24D no.
    42–40910), 11
  contemporary investigation of
    crash site, 53–54, 59–60,
    109–110, 112–114
  crash of, 20–23
  discovery of crash site, 213
  initial report on crash/search
    results, 115–117
  letter to families regarding
    crash, 152
  production of, 85
  reasons for crash, 200–203
  routine flight of, 17–19
  search for crash site, 37–39,
    50–51
  takeoff, 16–17
Ice-break, 139–140
Iditarod Trail, 133
Italy, Allied progress in, 136, 183

Jacobs Radial L-4 engine, 41
Japan
  assault on Dutch Harbor, 43–47

attacks on Alaska, 11–12, 43–47, 49–50
attacks on Attu and Kiska, 49–50
surrender, 158
US occupation of, 159
Jefford, Jack, 122
Jewish anarchists, 79
JLB (cold-weather survivor), 34
Joint POW/MIA Accounting Command (JPAC), 110–112
Hoskin investigation, 199–200
investigation of B-24 wreckage, 153–155, 163
Jones, Etta, 49
Jones, Stuart "Slim," 82
Jordan, Arthur, 51, 93, 121, 195, 197
Jordan, George Racey, 119–120, 121
JPAC. *See* Joint POW/MIA Accounting Command (JPAC)

Kalb, Bernard, 127
Kandik River (Alaska), 102
Karagodskys, 77, 79. *See also* Crane, Louis; Crane, Sonia
Kawasaki, 55
Keillor, Russell, 191, 196
KFAR (radio station), 124
Kinney, Jeremy, 200
The Kiri Leaf Falls (play), 49
Kiska (Alaska), Japanese attack and control of, 49–50
Knights of Liberty, 79
Kodiak Island, 48
Koehrsen, Wilma, 197, 214–215, 217
Kontanis, Elias J., 204

Korean War, 111
Koyukuk (Alaska), 41
Krueger, Hans, 162
Krupp, 55

Ladd Field (Alaska)
celebration of holidays at, 64
Cold Weather Test Detachment, 12–13, 14
Crane's return to, 191, 193–197
defense of Dutch Harbor and, 45
Ragle at, 42–43
Soviet presence at, 117–118, 120–122
Thanksgiving menu, 64
underground tunnels, 5, 11
Laddon, Isaac Machlin (I. M.), 57–59, 84
Larrey, Dominique Jean, 89
Lavelle Young (stern-wheeler), 100
Lend-Lease program, 117–122
Soviets in Fairbanks and, 122–124
tradecraft conspiracies and, 123–124
Lindbergh, Charles "Lucky," 81
The Line (red-light district), 122
Lockheed, 12
London, Jack, 71
Lubin, Siegmund, 78
"Luck Saved Crane in Arctic Fields; City Flier, Foodless Nine Days, Found Cabin with Stock of Provisions" (newspaper article), 197
"Lung frosting," 9
Lupo, Francis, 111

Manhattan Project, 123
Marks, Jack, 45, 46–47, 48
Marshall Islands, 136
Martin, James, 39
Martin, Lily, 39
Massachusetts Institute of Technology (MIT), Crane at, 7, 83–84
Mawson, Douglas, 145–148
McAndrews, J. J., 183
McGee, William Samuel, 167
McGill University, 57
McGovern, Joseph, 76
McIntosh, Mary Roberta, 160. *See also* Hoskin, Mary (Harold's wife)
McPhee, John, 217
McRae, Alexander, 133–134
Medical Journal of Australia, 146
Mein Kampf (Hitler), 56
Mental acuity, starvation and loss of, 89–90
Mertz, Xavier, 146
Metro-Goldwyn-Mayer, 40
MIA. *See* Missing in action (MIA)
Midnight Sun (newspaper), 120
Military aviation, 40
  advances in, 55, 57–59
  cold weather testing in Alaska, 12–13, 14
  Flyer test flight, 210–211
Military forensics. *See* Joint POW/MIA Accounting Command (JPAC)
"Million Dollar Valley," 119
Mind, effect of starvation on, 62–63
Missing in action (MIA)
  identification of remains, 154

JPAC and, 111–112
  telegrams notifying families, 75–76
  in World War II, 2, 112
MIT. *See* Massachusetts Institute of Technology (MIT)
Mitochondrial DNA, 204–205
Mitsubishi, 55
Monroe, Rose Will, 56–57
Monsen, "Big Money," 41
Moreland, Ben, 194–195
Mount Athos (Greece), 1, 3
Mount Gannett (Alaska), 154
Mount Harper (Alaska), 91
Mount McKinley (Alaska), 91
Myers, David, 209, 216
Myers, Ethel, 209, 212
Myrtle Creek (Alaska), 41

Nakajima reconnaissance aircraft, 46
Nanuk (schooner), 40
Nash, Charlotte, 81
Nature
  Native tribes' understanding of, 68–69
  transcendentalists' understanding of, 69–71
Nautilus (submarine), 126
Neuberger, Richard L., 123
Nigro, Frank, 120
Ninnis, Belgrave, 146
Nixon-Nirdlinger, Frederick G., 80–81
Noonan, Fred, 83
Northern migration of southern blacks, 7–8
Northwest Passage, 70
Noyes, Irene, 123

One Drop of Blood (Holland), 205
Osgood, Cornelius, 130, 145

Pacific theater, Allied success in, 136
Patriot Guard Riders, 212
Patty, Dale, 190
Patty, Ernest Newton, 133–134, 189
Pavlova, Anna, 146
PBY Catalina, 57, 58
Pearl Harbor, attack on, 42, 84, 118
P-40 Warhawk fighters, 46
Phi Beta Delta, 83
Philadelphia
    Crane's childhood in, 7, 8, 80–83
    migration of southern blacks to, 7–8
    Russian Jewish immigrants in, 76–80
Philadelphia Record (newspaper), 214
Pickrell's Solution, 35
Pinchuk, Iurii, 85
Pioneer Air Museum (Fairbanks, Alaska), 41
Pompeo, Anna, 197
Pompeo, Richard, 152
    building at Ladd Field in honor of, 216
    crash and, 21, 22, 23
    flight preparation and, 16
    previous rescue of, 31, 117
    still missing in action, 113, 200, 209
Poon Lim, 31
Pratt & Whitney, 12

Prinz Adalbert (steamship), 76, 77
Propaganda
    B-24 and, 55–56
    dropped on Attu, 49
P-63 Kingcobra, 214
Psychological Warfare Teams (US Army), 49
Psychology of survival, 145–148
P-39 Airacobra fighter, 15, 120, 122
P-36 fighter, 34

Rabies, wolves and, 143
Ragle, Jane, 42, 125
Ragle, John, 125
Ragle, R. C. (Richard Charles)
    call to active duty, 42–43
    defense of Dutch Harbor and, 45–48
    family life, 124–125
    Iceberg Inez search and, 38–39, 50–51
    premilitary career, 39–42
    report on crash/search results, 115–117
    search for Demianenko and, 43
Rauscher, Manfred, 84, 94
The Raven, 172–173
Red squirrels, 65–68, 131
Rice, Bob, 191, 193–195, 216
Roadhouses, Alaskan, 185–188
Rockwell, Norman, 56
Rolvaag, Ole, 144
Roosevelt, Franklin D., 51, 52
Roosevelt, Theodore, 101
Rosie the Riveter, 56–57
Russian Jewish immigrants in Philadelphia, 76–80

Russian Officers' Club, 120

Saturday Evening Post (magazine), 56, 132
Scud (clouds), 18
Search for *Iceberg Inez*, 37–39, 50–51
 odds of rescue, 27–30
Selfridge, Thomas, 210–211
Service, Robert W., 145, 167
Shackleton, Ernest, 146
Shpola (Ukraine), 82, 85
Sibert, James B., 152
 discovery of body, 213
 fate of, 23, 54, 113
 flight preparation and, 15–16, 17, 18
 interment of remains, 216
Sibert, Margaret, 197
Situational awareness logs, 194
6th Depot Repair Squadron, 13
Skookum, 190
Slaven, Frank, 186
Sledges, 137, 141, 142, 145, 147, 148, 168–169
Smith, "Mudhole," 41
Smith, Valentine "Woodchopper," 185–186
Smoke signaling, 72
Snow, thirst and, 61
Snowshoes, 141, 184
Soviets
 in Fairbanks, 122–124
 spy rumors regarding, 123–124
Soviet Union, Lend-Lease program with United States, 12, 117–122
Spirit of St. Louis (airplane), 81
Squamish winds, 172

SS *Ben Lomond*, 31
SS *Illinois*, 77–78
Starvation, loss of mental acuity and, 90. *See also* Hunger
Stefansson, Vilhjalmur, 126
Stevens Village (Alaska), 41
Stevinson, Harry, 29
Stewart, Jimmy, 55
Stinson V77 plane, 191, 195
Sugden, Leonard, 167
Survival, psychology of, 145–148
Survival stories, 30–31
Survivor's guilt, Crane and, 217–218

Tanana River (Alaska), 37, 64, 100, 101, 139
Test crews, for military flights, 12
Thanksgiving menu, at Ladd Field, 64
Thirst, snow and, 61
Tintina Fault, 173
Titanic (ship), 77
"To Build a Fire" (London), 71
Trans Alaska Corporation, 40–41
Transcendentalists, 69–71
Trappers, 181
Treasure Island (film), 40
20,000 Leagues Under the Sea (Verne), 126
Twin Mountain (Alaska), 143

U-boat attacks, 51–52, 55
Umnak (Alaska), 47
United States
 Lend-Lease program with Soviet Union, 12, 117–124

Manhattan Project, 123
U.S. Army Dirigible Balloon No. 1, 211
US military
  aviation program (*see* Military aviation)
  B-24 Liberator and, 58
  counteroffensive for Attu, 49–50
  letters to families regarding crash, 152
  propaganda efforts, 49
  study of Far North survival techniques, 90
University of Alaska, 39
University of Pennsylvania, 83
USS *Monitor*, 112

Vacuum selector valves, 203
Vertical stabilizers, 202
Vietnam, search for MIAs, 111
Vitamin A poisoning, 146–147

Wada, Jujiro, 133
Washington-Alaska Bank, 101
Weeks Field (Alaska), 42
Welch, Jack, 186–187
Welch, Kate, 186–187
Wenz, Carol, 216
Wenz, Ralph, 152
  airfield named after, 216
  crash and, 21, 23
  discovery of body, 213
  failure to make last radio call, 28–29, 201
  fate of, 113
  flight preparation and, 16

  radio contact with Ladd Field, 18
  Western Union telegrams, 73–76
Wheeler, Burton, 118
White, John, 123–124
White, Sam O., 40
White Pass Trail, 167
Wickersham, James, 101, 186
Wien, Noel, 181
Wien, Ralph, 40
Wien Alaska, 181, 188, 191
Wilderness survival, enemies of, 89–90
Wilkins, Hubert, 126
Williwaws, 171–172
Willow Run Aircraft Factory, 56–57, 59
Windmilling, 14
Winds, 144, 174
  williwaws, 171–172
Wiseman (Alaska), 41
Wolf packs, 143
Women's Army Corps, 121
Woodchopper (Alaska), 106, 131, 134, 185–191
Woodchopper Creek, 131, 185
  dredge mining on, 134–135
Woodchopper Roadhouse, 185–188
World War I, end of immigration wave, 79–80
World War II
  Alaska and, 11–13
  Allied progress in, 136
  cold weather gear, 8
  development of new technologies for war, 55
  JPAC and, 111–112

World War II *(continued)*
  Lend-Lease program, 12,
    117–124
  missing in action, 2, 112
WP (cold-weather survivor), 34–35
Wright, Orville, 210–211
Wright Field (Ohio), 84

Yega, 68

Yukon-Charley Rivers National
    Preserve, exploration of *Iceberg Inez* crash site, 53–54,
    59–60
Yukon River, as reference point,
    26
Yukon Sun (newspaper), 133

Zero fighters, 55